The First
State University

THE FIRST
STATE UNIVERSITY

A Pictorial History of
THE UNIVERSITY
OF NORTH CAROLINA

Third Edition, Revised and Enlarged

by *William S. Powell*

The University of North Carolina Press
Chapel Hill and London

96   95   94   93   92   5   4   3   2   1

Library of Congress Cataloging-in-Publication Data

Powell, William Stevens, 1919–
    The first state university: a pictorial history of the University of
North Carolina / by William S. Powell.—3rd ed., rev. and enl.
        p.   cm.
    Includes index.
    ISBN 0-8078-2049-0 (alk. paper)
    1. University of North Carolina at Chapel Hill—Pictorial works.
2. University of North Carolina at Chapel Hill—History.   I. Title.
LD3944.5.P6   1992
378.756'565—dc20   91-47718
                                                                        CIP

This book is one of a series of works commissioned by the Bicentennial Observance Policy Committee of the University of
North Carolina at Chapel Hill. The University of North Carolina
Press gratefully acknowledges the assistance of the Committee in
publishing these volumes.

CONTENTS

ACKNOWLEDGMENTS

The first edition of this book appeared in 1972. For reading the rough drafts of text and captions and offering many valuable suggestions for that edition I am deeply indebted to Dr. Carolyn A. Wallace. Her knowledge of the University Papers in the Southern Historical Collection contributed in many ways to the improvement of what I submitted for her suggestions. Wayne Mixon was my right-hand man from first to last, making reconnaissance expeditions to various campus offices, urging speedy and careful work from the photographers, running errands to verify obscure points, and, with a sharp eye for misspelled words and missing commas, reading what I wrote before it reached its final form. His good memory for faces enabled him to identify many people in group pictures from their individual pictures in the *Yackety Yack* and elsewhere. The late Dr. L. R. Wilson, class of 1899, whose keen mind at the age of ninety-five and beyond was the envy of many a younger man, proved to be an invaluable source of information in many ways, but especially in his ability to identify people and recall events depicted in old photographs. Alvin Woody aided in the initial search for pictures and prepared an index of useful material in printed sources. Michael G. Martin, University archivist, was always alert for pictorial material and for obscure facts. For special topics I called from time to time upon Miss Alice Noble, Miss Mary Cobb, Albert Coates, Mrs. Lucile Kelling Henderson, C. Hugh Holman, Mrs. Laura MacMillan, A. G. Ivey, L. C. Scarborough, and Ross Scroggs, all now, alas, deceased. John Sanders, Roger Foushee, Miss Porter Cowles, J. Isaac Copeland, Roland Giduz, J. Maryon Saunders, Jerry C. Cashion, Samuel M. Boone, and Quenton Sawyer also responded to my calls for advice and facts. Former Chancellor Robert B. House and Professor Hugh T. Lefler, both also deceased, read the manuscript and examined many of the photographs. Chancellor J. Carlyle Sitterson and Charles M. Shaffer answered my questions and made recommendations as the work on the book progressed.

Numerous persons responded to my requests for photographs, and those whose contributions appear in the book are noted in the Credits section. To each of them I am indebted; I am also appreciative of the offers made by others even though their photographs were not used. In all cases, copies have been made of these privately owned pictures, and they are now filed in the North Carolina Collection.

This is primarily a picture book, of course, and design and layout are as important as the text. Mrs. Joyce Kachergis, then at the University of North Carolina Press, is truly an artist in the field of book design, and she took more interest in this book and devoted more time to it than her position demanded. The beauty of the original edition, the attractive layout, and the appropriateness of many of the pictures are evidence of her talent. Matthew Hodgson, director of the Press, and Mrs. Gwen Duffey, then the managing editor, were consulted almost daily at many stages, and their good advice had much to do with the reception this work received.

Perhaps my friends on campus, in Raleigh and elsewhere, and my family were pleased to examine this book for themselves and to realize that they would no longer be obliged to listen to me talk about it. Whatever faults might be found here, however, must not be charged to any of them, as I made many arbitrary decisions from day to day and on occasion even stubbornly resisted their advice.

Many of those who assisted me so generously in both the first (1972) and second (1979) editions of this book performed the same service still again. In the preparation of this third or Bicentennial edition I once again called on many people for advice and suggestions. To them I now express my deepest thanks. Former chancellors Christopher C. Fordham, Ferebee Taylor, and J. Carlyle Sitterson shared their recollections of some memorable events of their administrations. John L. Sanders made recommendations concerning the earlier editions of this book and suggested some new material for this one. Assistant to the Chancellor Douglass Hunt helped me to recall the names of some people whose faces were visible in photographs of groups. Photographers Will Owens and Fred Stipe offered their usual superior professional service. And for advice and help of various kinds I again turned to the staff of the North Carolina Collection and the Southern Historical Collection in Wilson Library—especially to Alice Cotten, Jerry Cotten, Jeffrey Hicks, H. G. Jones, Michael Martin, and Richard Shrader. University students Ben Jolly, John Lomax, and Patrick Wooten voluntarily came to my assistance a number of times by running errands and making special searches for photographs. At the University of North Carolina Press, Matthew Hodgson, Sandra Eisdorfer, David Perry, and Johanna Grimes spurred me on with assurances of continuing interest and with their good advice. Richard Hendel, book designer at the Press, clearly has established new standards of excellence in his field. My wife, Virginia, in her accustomed eagerness to help, offered useful suggestions that perfected the text and improved the index.

Finally, I cannot resist expressing appreciation to the person or persons who developed the personal computer. Neither this book nor several others that I have recently been associated with could have been done so expeditiously without it. Jane A. Lindley of the Department of History gave me introductory lessons and set me on the path to a new and exciting skill at the keyboard.

Chapel Hill, North Carolina
1 October 1991

I
THE ESTABLISHMENT
OF THE UNIVERSITY

INTRODUCTION

Before the eventful year of 1776, young men of North Carolina who sought formal education beyond that available in small local academies or from tutors employed by their parents found limited opportunities in the colony. In 1767 on the western frontier of Orange County, within the limits of what is now the city of Greensboro, the Reverend David Caldwell opened a school that soon came to be known as the Log College. Caldwell, a graduate of the College of New Jersey, now Princeton University, became a Presbyterian missionary in the colony about 1765, and his excellent school served as theological seminary, academy, and college. He erected a two-story log school building that had a library. Throughout the remaining years of the eighteenth century this institution had an average annual attendance of about fifty, many of whom entered the junior class at Princeton, or after 1795, at the University of North Carolina. John Motley Morehead, later governor of the state, studied under Caldwell, and he recalled that the "course of studies in the languages—Latin, Greek, and Hebrew, as well as in the sciences, was extensive for his day." Morehead remarked that Caldwell "often . . . made me recite from four to six hours a day. Indeed you could not get along with him, with any comfort, without knowing accurately and thoroughly everything you passed over."

David Caldwell retired from the classroom at the age of ninety-five but he lived on until his hundredth year. His school closed for a short period in 1781 when the British plundered his home and his library. He operated his school, however, except for brief intervals, from the time it opened until 1822. His services were recognized in 1810 when the University of North Carolina awarded him the honorary degree of Doctor of Divinity.

One serious attempt was made before the American Revolution to establish an institution of higher education in North Carolina. Queens College was opened in Charlotte in 1771 under the supervision of the Reverend James Alexander, a graduate of the College of New Jersey. The General Assembly chartered the college and directed the trustees to appoint "some learned, pious, exemplary, and discreet person to be president." The Board of Trustees was given the right of perpetual succession, and the president had authority to confer the degrees of bachelor and master of arts and to grant the appropriate diplomas. The regulations of the college were to "correspond and be as near as may be agreeable to the laws and customs of the Universities of Oxford and Cambridge or those of the Colleges of America." A tax was levied to support the college.

The charter of Queens College was sent to London for approval, and Governor William Tryon assured authorities there that "it is but an outline of a foundation for the education of youth." In large measure because this college would serve Presbyterians, dissenters from the established Anglican Church, the charter was not ap-

In this house, which is still standing in Halifax, a committee to draft a constitution for North Carolina met in November and December 1776. Four members of the committee, Waightstill Avery, Hezekiah Alexander, and Robert Irwin, all of Charlotte, and Abner Nash of New Bern, had been trustees of Queen's College. Article XLI of the constitution directed that "all useful learning shall be duly encouraged and promoted in one or more universities."

The Constitution of 1776 was printed and circulated so that the people of North Carolina could familiarize themselves with it. Article XLI appeared on page 15.

proved, but the college continued to operate anyway. Its name was changed to Queen's Museum in 1773 and to Liberty Hall, a more appropriate name for the times, in 1777 when it moved to Salisbury. The young college fell victim to the Revolutionary times and, losing its higher aspirations, became merely an academy.

Student records of neither of these young colleges survive to provide an alumni directory. Only the occasional reminiscences of old men suggest the esteem in which the colleges were held. It is evident, however, that a number of men of importance in the new state of North Carolina received good training in them.

For those who could afford to attend them, colleges outside North Carolina offered the opportunities denied at home. Alumni records of American universities of the seventeenth and eighteenth centuries are far from complete, but from the surviving records it is clear that at least two North Carolinians attended Yale before 1795 when the University of North Carolina opened its doors. One went to William and Mary and one to Brown, five to Harvard, two to Hampden-Sydney, and about twenty-five to Princeton. Several also prepared for a career in law by study at the Inns of Court in London, and one was graduated from the University of Glasgow.

The men who attended the Fourth Provincial Congress at Halifax in April and May 1776 drew up resolutions calling on the other colonies to join in declaring independence. These were men of vision and ambition for North Carolina. Their recommendation had its effect and the American Declaration of Independence was the immediate result. In December the Fifth Provincial Congress assembled, again in Halifax, and one of its primary accomplishments was a constitution under which a new state government for North Carolina was to evolve.

The University of North Carolina was an eventual product of that congress and its constitution. The delegates recognized the importance of an educated citizenry that would support the government and provide trained officeholders. Article XLI of the Constitution of 1776, traditionally said to have been proposed by Waightstill Avery, a Princeton graduate and a former trustee of Queen's College, looked to the establishment of schools and one or more universities in the state. This article was almost word-for-word the same as that in the Pennsylvania Constitution. Among those attending this very important congress were men whose surnames are reminiscent of others of the same name—descendants and relatives—who contributed much to the University of North Carolina through the succeeding years. Indeed, some of these men themselves aided the young institution —Elisha Battle, Benjamin Blount, the Reverend David Caldwell (who left his Log College long enough for this important public service), William Hooper (a name represented during several generations in University affairs), William Graham, Egbert Haywood, James Kenan, Alexander Mebane, Thomas Person (whose munificence provided the University's second building), and Lemuel Sawyer (whose son of the same name was the first University alumnus to serve in the United States Congress).

At the beginning of the Revolutionary War there were only nine colleges in the thirteen states and of them only the College of Philadelphia (later the University of Pennsylvania) was nonsectarian. The idea of the state university was a new concept of the period, and while the University of Georgia was the first to secure its charter, the University of North Carolina was the first to open its classrooms for students. Thirteen difficult years passed between the adoption of the Constitution and the chartering of the University of North Carolina. During that time the Revolutionary War was concluded and the weak state government was somewhat strengthened through the experience of its leaders. Anti-Federalist forces succeeded in securing the rejection of the United States Constitution by North Carolina in a convention in 1788, but at a second convention, meeting in Fayetteville in 1789, the Constitution was approved. The General Assembly was meeting in the same town at the same time, and a few days after the adoption of the Constitution a bill was introduced in the General Assembly to charter a University. A similar bill in 1784 had been defeated, but William Richardson Davie, a Federalist who had helped write the Constitution and who had advocated its adoption by North Carolina, introduced a new bill in 1789. Davie had been a student at Queen's Museum in Charlotte; the chairman of the committee out of which the bill came was Matthew Locke, who had been a trustee of Liberty Hall Academy. Davie's bill was approved on December 11; it bore a preamble pointing out that "in all well regulated governments it is the indispensable duty of every Legislature to consult the happiness of a rising generation, and endeavour to fit them for an honourable discharge of the social duties of life, by paying the strictest attention to their education." Forty prominent men were named trustees and instructed to meet in Fayetteville at the time of the next session of the assembly to select a president and secretary and to begin their duties. A second bill, passed ten days later, provided for the erection of buildings and for modest financial support.

The trustees held their first meeting, an informal and unofficial one, in Fayetteville on 18 December 1789. Plans were made to seek contributions and it was announced that Benjamin Smith had given the University twenty thousand acres of land. On 15 November 1790, again in Fayetteville, the trustees held their first regular meeting and elected William Lenoir to act as president pro-tem. Before the conclusion of the meeting the recently elected governor, Alexander Martin, a graduate of the College of New Jersey, was chosen president of the board.

With the proper legal authorization, the hope of financial support, and an enthusiastic Board of Trustees, the University of North Carolina was launched.

The General Assembly, meeting in the Cumberland County Court House from 2 November until 22 December 1789, passed an act on 11 December to charter the University of North Carolina.

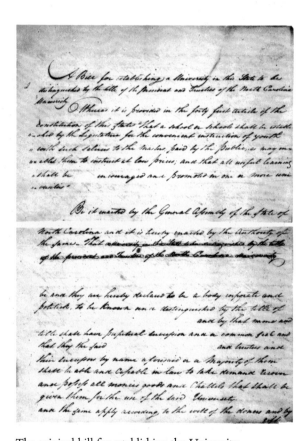

The original bill for establishing the University, which was introduced in 1784 by William Sharpe of Rowan County (later Iredell), is in the Legislative Papers, House of Commons, for November 1784. Largely because it was supported by men of Federalist sympathies it was defeated.

William Richardson Davie (1756–1820), member of the House of Commons from Halifax was the author and introducer of the University bill in 1789 which was passed.

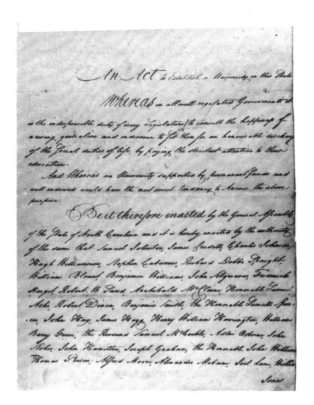

The original engrossed act to establish the University is in the manuscript laws for 1789.

William Lenoir (1751–1839) was chosen to act as president pro-tem of the Board of Trustees at its first meeting in 1790. When he died at the age of eighty-eight he was the last surviving member of the original board.

Benjamin Smith (1756–1826) was a member of the first Board of Trustees. His generous gift of twenty thousand acres of land in Tennessee for the benefit of the University was made on 18 December 1789, the same day that the General Assembly passed an act to raise a building fund for the University. Smith served as a member of the Board of Trustees from 1789 until 1824 and was president in 1810.

Alexander Martin (1740–1807), first president of the Board of Trustees and a member of that body from 1790 until his death, was governor in 1784 and strongly urged the passage of the bill of that year to establish the University. He was also governor from 1789 until 1792 when he urged the policy of public support for the University.

At a meeting on 24 November 1790, the trustees appointed a seven-man committee "to form a device for the common seal of the University." The committee apparently was not diligent in carrying out its duties, so on July 20 of the next year it was abolished and James Hogg, Alfred Moore, and John Haywood were ordered to "cause a Seal to be made, with such device thereon as to them may appear proper." By early September it was ready. "They chose the face of Apollo, the God of Eloquence, and his emblem, the rising sun," Dr. Kemp P. Battle wrote, "as expressive of the dawn of higher education in our State."

The Reverend Samuel McCorkle prepared a sermon advocating support for the new University, which he preached in 1793 at a number of places across the state.

Both the bill to establish the University and the charter directed that, when funds were available to purchase land and to erect buildings, a meeting of the trustees should be held "for the purpose of fixing on and purchasing a healthy and convenient situation, which shall not be situate within five miles of the permanent seat of government, or any of the places of holding the courts of law or equity." Governor Martin recommended to the General Assembly on 2 November 1790 that a loan be made to the trustees to begin their building program. With hopes high, this call was issued to begin the selection of a site, but the legislators finally declined to make the recommended loan and the location of the campus was postponed.

A

CHARITY SERMON.

FIRST DELIVERED IN

SALISBURY, JULY 28;

And afterwards in other Places in ROWAN, and the counties adjoining;

Particularly at SUGAR's CREEK, in MECKLENBURG County, at the Opening of the SYNOD of the CAROLINAS, October 2:

And laſt, at the Meeting of the Hon. the GENERAL ASSEMBLY of NORTH-CAROLINA in FAYETTE-VILLE, December, 1793.

By the Rev. SAMUEL E. M'CORKLE, D.D.

PASTOR OF THE CHURCH AT THYATIRA AND SALISBURY IN ROWAN COUNTY, NORTH-CAROLINA.

HALIFAX:

PRINTED BY ABRAHAM HODGE.

M,DCC,XCV.

SIR,

AT a Meeting of the Truſtees of the Univerſity of North Carolina the 25th of November; 1790, It was Reſolved, That this Board do meet on the third Monday in July next, at the Town of Hillſborough, in order to fix on the place where the Buildings of the Univerſity ſhall be erected, and to do and perform ſuch other acts and things as appertain to, and may tend to forward and promote that Inſtitution.

Which Reſolution I was directed to inform you of and requeſt your attendance accordingly.

I have the honor to be,

With great reſpect,

SIR,

Rockingham County, April 1, 1791.

Your moſt humble Servant,

James Taylor jun.

Of the nearly seventy men who served on the Board of Trustees before the end of the eighteenth century there were many who gave frequently and generously of their time. These four were typical. HOGG, a Cross Creek (Fayetteville) merchant who later moved to Hillsborough, served as a trustee from 1789 until 1802. He was a member of the committee that selected the site for the University and of the visiting committee whose duty it was to examine students at commencement. He was in large measure responsible for the choice of Chapel Hill as the site of the University through his success in persuading his Orange County friends to contribute land and money. HAYWOOD of Raleigh was state treasurer from 1787 until his death and a member of the Board of Trustees from 1789. As a member of the building committee he bore a large share of the responsibility for the construction on campus. He was a successful fund raiser and rendered good service on the committees on curriculum and on University lands. POLK, originally from Mecklenburg County and educated at Queen's College, moved to Raleigh in 1800. He served as a colonel during the Revolution and was the last survivor among North Carolina's field officers in that war. He was a land surveyor and held a number of public offices. As a member of the Board of Trustees from 1790 until 1834, he served as president from 1802 to 1805. Throughout his term of service he was one of the leading fund raisers for the University. He also negotiated many University land sales, particularly when he worked as a surveyor in Tennessee. BLOUNT, a Tarboro merchant and member of Congress (1793–99, 1805–9), was a trustee from 1792 until his death. He was one of the commissioners who located the state capital and was also in the group to locate the University. He was a member of the building committee and the library committee of the trustees and was responsible for the purchase of a number of books for the University.

James Hogg (1729–1805)

John Haywood (1755–1827)

William Polk (1758–1834)

Thomas Blount (1759–1812)

Early in January 1792 the trustees appointed a committee to visit likely locations for the University in Wake, Franklin, Warren, Orange, Granville, Chatham, and Johnston counties. If this committee reported to the August meeting no record of it survives. At that time, however, William R. Davie, Alfred Moore, Willie Jones, Hugh Williamson, and John Sitgreaves were appointed to settle on a specific site within fifteen miles of Pittsboro, Williamsboro, Hillsborough, Charlotte, Goshen (in Granville County), or Cypretts Bridge on New Hope in Chatham County. A few days later the trustees agreed with the recommendation that the University be located within fifteen miles of Cypretts Bridge. During the first week in November, Frederick Hargett, Alexander Mebane, James Hogg, William Hill, David Stone, and Willie Jones visited a number of sites in that region, and on November 5 they "proceeded to View New Hope Chapel hill in Orange County." An old chapel of the Anglican Church stood at the crossroads here on an elevated wooded site. There were a number of clear springs in the vicinity. Accessible roads and the fact that it was near the center of the state were all factors in this site's favor, but most important of all, local citizens offered to donate 1,290 acres of land and £768 to the University. The committee lingered at the site and two days after the land and money had been offered they concluded that "having now maturely deliberated on the Subject of the appointment Unanimously determined on New hope Chapel Hill for the Seat of the University." The "Old Poplar," first mentioned in a report of 1818, has been the traditional focal point that attracted another committee whose duty it was to decide exactly where, on this vast tract of land, the buildings would be erected. Shown here, in the background to the left of the tree is the second oldest building on the campus, Person Hall, begun in 1796, and long used as the chapel.

Twelve residents of Chapel Hill and vicinity offered the trustees tracts of land ranging in size from 5 to 221 acres. The largest tract was offered by Christopher Barbee who lived about three miles from New Hope Chapel hill. One of his great-granddaughters married William R. Kenan of Wilmington.

Alfred Moore (1755–1810) was a member of the first Board of Trustees and one of the most active. He served on the committees to locate the site of the University, to prepare the ordinance fixing the seat, to superintend the erection of buildings, to select a seal, and to plan the course of study. He was also one of the most generous contributors to the subscription for funds collected in 1793. Present at the laying of the cornerstone on 12 October 1793, he also bought one of the Chapel Hill town lots sold that day.

Benjamin Hawkins (1754–1816) was a member of the first Board of Trustees, and as a member of the committee to report plans for the campus buildings, he made the report to the trustees on 4 August 1792. An alumnus of Princeton, he was a member of the three-man committee composed of two Princeton men and one graduate of the University of Pennsylvania charged with securing for the trustees information on laws, regulations, and buildings of other American universities and colleges. In 1796 he was also made a member of the committee to examine students at the end of the school year.

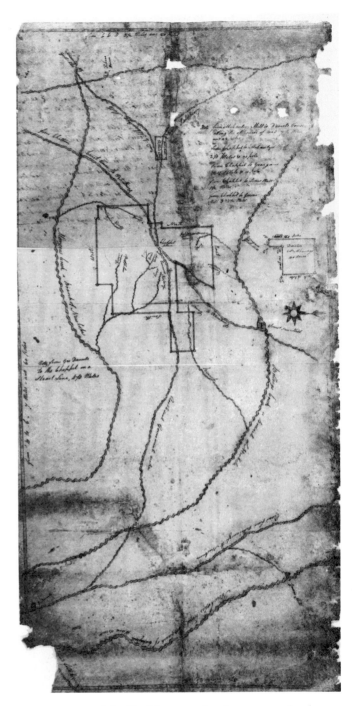

John Daniel was employed as surveyor by the trustees, and late in 1792 he prepared a map of the site of the University. In addition to marking out the tracts of land, Daniel also indicated the springs and creeks, the mills nearby, and the roads leading to Salisbury, Chatham Court House, Petersburg, and to the new seat of state government in Wake County, not yet named.

Anticipating a successful conclusion to their fond hopes of creating a university, the trustees appointed a committee to form a faculty. The committee advertised in the 12 December 1792 issue of the *North Carolina Journal* published in Halifax.

The trustees could also expect an income from the sale of lots to the public in the budding town of Chapel Hill. They advertised in the 21 August 1793 issue of the *North Carolina Journal* published in Halifax and announced a public sale for October 12.

Passed in the closing days of December 1791, this ordinance was printed and circulated in 1792. Its purpose was to take advantage of the recent act of the General Assembly giving escheats to the University, a welcome source of desperately needed money to apply toward buildings on the campus.

On 19 July 1793 a contract was signed with James Patterson for the erection of the first building on the new campus, East Building, now known as Old East. Plans and elevations were a part of the contract.

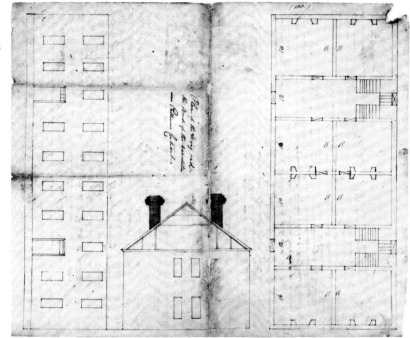

The two sides of the bronze plate commemorating the laying of the cornerstone on 12 October 1793. It was engraved by Roswell Huntington, a Connecticut silversmith who had opened a shop in Hillsborough in 1786.

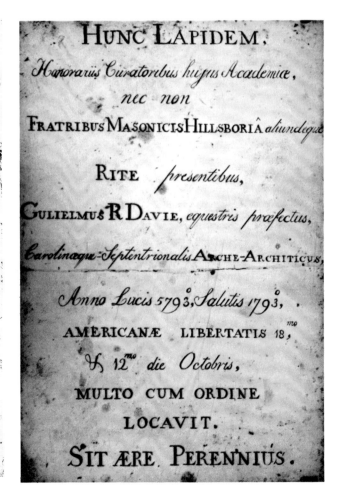

This drawing of the first University building was made in 1797 by John Pettigrew, a student in the University from 1795 until 1797. It was known as East Building until "New East" was constructed in 1859, at which time the name "Old East" came into use.

As plans for University buildings were being laid and the first building actually beginning to rise, the town of Chapel Hill also began to develop. On 8 December 1793 Christopher Barbee, already a generous donor to the University, purchased lot number two in the town as recorded in this deed. It consisted of four acres adjacent to the campus and before long Barbee established a blacksmith shop in Chapel Hill. He rode in to work every day from his home about three miles east.

The Reverend Samuel Eusebius McCorkle, who spoke at the cornerstone laying, foresaw that before long the University of North Carolina would be ready to receive students. In Rowan County, in January 1794, he opened a grammar school "intended as a nursery for the University." He placed this advertisement in the *North Carolina Journal* of 27 November 1793, published in Halifax, perhaps with the hope of luring some young easterners to his western academy near Salisbury.

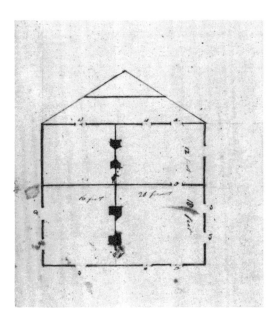

Builder James Patterson entered into negotiations with the trustees for two more essential buildings for the campus. One was Steward's Hall, a wooden building thirty-six by thirty feet, with two brick chimneys, a kitchen with a brick floor, and three other rooms. Two of these might be occupied by students, but the third obviously was to be the dining room. He agreed to complete the building by the first of January 1795 as the trustees had already agreed that the University should open for the reception of students on January 15. Steward's Hall appears to have been just south of Old East, but it ceased to be used as the University Commons at the end of 1816. The building was dismantled in 1847 after having been operated as a private boarding house for a number of years.

This silhouette, cut from white paper by Mrs. William Hooper (*née* Frances Jones) soon after her arrival in Chapel Hill in 1814 as a bride of sixteen, shows Steward's Hall on the left, a small bell tower, and Main, now South Building.

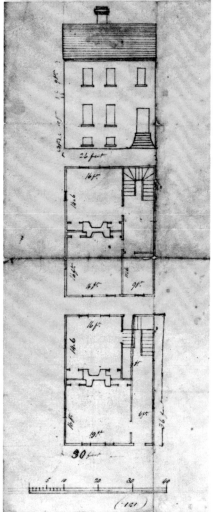

As early as July 1793 the trustees began to consider the construction of a house for the president of the University. Plans shown here are for a house slightly larger than originally proposed, but both included two closets in each of the bedrooms—an unusual feature in those days when movable wardrobes were standard furniture in bedrooms. Samuel Hopkins signed a bond for the construction of the house late in January 1794, and his bill was submitted in November 1795. The bill was for a greater sum than the trustees had agreed upon because they had forgotten to include in their plans the stairs to the cellar; Hopkins also erected a smokehouse and two "necessary Houses," including a private one for the president.

The first President's House was removed in 1913 when the site was cleared for the construction of Swain Hall.

On 15 January 1795 the buildings were sufficiently finished that the University was officially opened by Governor Richard Dobbs Spaight and several members of the Board of Trustees. This is the account published in the *North Carolina Journal*, Halifax, 23 February 1795. Hinton James from New Hanover County was the first student to reach the campus. He arrived on February 12, but two weeks passed before other students joined him.

HALIFAX, February 23.

Pursuant to a request of the Board of Trustees of the University of North-Carolina, his Excellency Richard Dobbs Spaight, Esq. Governor of the state, and President of the Board, accompanied by several Members of the Corporation, and many other gentlemen, Members of the General Assembly, made a visit on the 15th day of January last, to the seat of the University of this state, in order to be present at the beginning of the exercises in that institution:—The unfavourable state of the weather disappointed many of our fellow-citizens who wished to be present on that much desired occasion:—The Governor, however, with the Trustees who accompanied him, viewed the buildings, and made report to the Board, by which they are enabled to inform the public that the buildings prepared for the reception and accommodation of Students, are in part finished:—That the exercises of the institution have begun, and that youth disposed to enter at the University may come forward with an assurance of being received

Students are to pay fifteen pounds per annum, North-Carolina currency, for their board:—Five dollars per annum for room rent, to be paid half yearly in advance:—They are to be furnished with tables and bed-steads, but they are to provide their own beds, &c. They are also to provide wood and candles for their chambers, and pay for their washing.

Richard Dobbs Spaight (1758–1802), the first native governor of North Carolina, presided at the opening ceremonies of the University. An alumnus of the University of Glasgow, he was a member of the Board of Trustees from 1789 until his death. In 1792 he was appointed to the committee to report on a plan for the buildings, and the next year he contributed generously to the subscription collected for the support of the University. As a member of the group of commissioners on buildings appointed by the trustees in December 1796, he was instrumental in designing South Building. In 1801 Spaight helped to draft a bill to permit the University to hold a lottery to raise money to be applied toward the annual expense.

Richard Dobbs Spaight

David Ker

The Reverend David Ker (1758–1805), a native of Northern Ireland who had come to North Carolina in or just before 1790 and settled in Iredell County before removing to Fayetteville, was a graduate of Trinity College, Dublin. The trustees of the University of North Carolina elected him in January 1794 to be professor of humanity and professor of languages, and it was he who received the first students. Professor Ker was acting president, but the trustees made it quite clear that he was not president. As Ker lost his Christian faith, he also grew more outspoken in his condemnation of those who held Federalist political views. He submitted his resignation to the trustees on 11 July 1796, but Charles Harris, his fellow faculty member, wrote that "he went away much against his own will." On 27 September 1796, at his own request, the Orange Presbytery removed Ker's name from "the Presbyterial Book." This was done in response to his stated "intentions of relinquishing the character of a Presbyterian Clergyman." Mrs. Ker was highly educated and remained a devout Christian during her lifetime; she taught school after the family had moved to Mississippi where her husband became an attorney and a judge. Professor and Mrs. Ker were the first to live in the new President's House.

Mrs. David Ker

Charles Wilson Harris (1771–1804), of Cabarrus County and a recent graduate of Princeton, was elected tutor in mathematics in 1795 and the next year was made professor of mathematics and natural philosophy. In July 1796, following the resignation of Professor Ker, he became presiding professor and resigned in December 1796.

This plan of the University and the town lots was enclosed in a letter from Tutor Charles Harris to his uncle, dated 1 June 1795. Old East, Steward's Hall, the President's House, South Building, and Old West are shown, although the last two had not been constructed. An avenue to the east to Point Prospect and another to the north, crossing what later came to be called Franklin and Rosemary Streets, were planned. Nearly a hundred acres of "Ornament-ground" would surround the buildings and on the south side there were two "Springs which ye commissioners intend to improve for ye University."

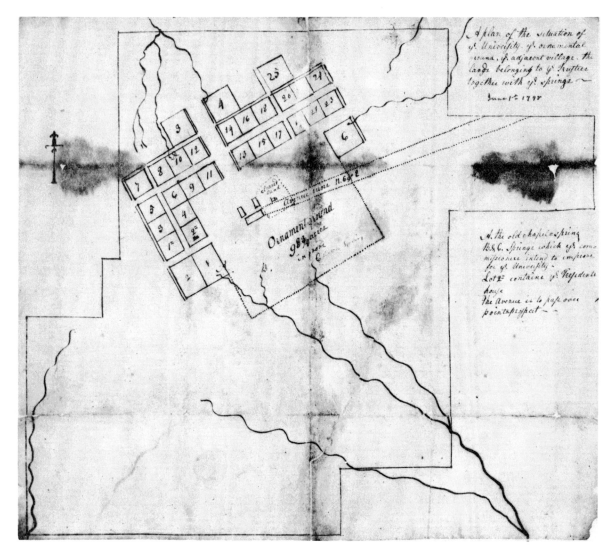

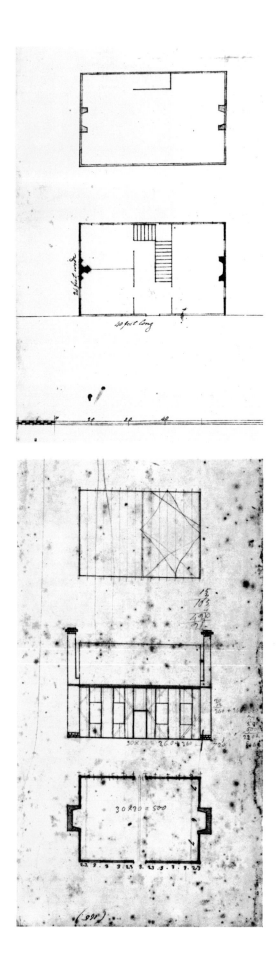

At the close of the first term on 22 June 1795 the state press described in glowing phrases the success enjoyed by those at the University who were "engaged in the noble work of cultivating the human mind." Advantage was taken of the opportunity to commend several schools that were engaged in preparing young men for the University. Mentioned especially were the academy at Thyatira in Rowan County conducted by the Reverend Samuel E. McCorkle, the one in Warrenton under the management of the Reverend Marcus George, and those in Chatham County and in New Bern. The trustees, however, recognized the need for still further opportunity to prepare the youth of the state for the University, and in July 1795 they directed the "building commissioners" of their body to enter into a contract for the construction of a "grammar school" on University property. It soon came to be called the Preparatory School and was first headed by Richard Sims from Warrenton, an outstanding student in the University. Students who successfully mastered the program here were admitted to the University without examination. On 15 October 1795 Samuel Hopkins submitted proposals for building the Preparatory School, and soon plans were being submitted and studied, but it was not until 1802 that a building resulted. In the meantime classes met in the same rooms as the University classes, but the crowding must have been inconvenient as there were over sixty boys in the Preparatory School in 1797. The Preparatory School stood on the northwest corner of the lot later occupied by the Presbyterian Church, but the need for such a special school declined and in 1819 it was closed. The building was sold in 1832 and the money realized applied to the "New Chapel," as Gerrard Hall was first known.

Richard Bennehan (1747–1825), a noted merchant of Orange County, was a member of the Board of Trustees from 1799 until 1804 and served on the committee of visitation during a part of that period. In 1796 he gave thirty-two volumes to the library and also contributed "apparatus" for instructional use. Bennehan was one of two trustees signing a contract with John M. Goodloe in August 1801 to build the Preparatory School. This photograph is from an original daguerreotype made from an oil portrait of Bennehan.

The seat of the University held such promise for patronage that William Nunn and his wife Elizabeth opened an inn in Chapel Hill in October 1795. They inserted this advertisement in the November 9 issue of the *North Carolina Journal*. Theirs was the first of many popular hotels at which students took their meals and often, also, had rooms. After her husband's death Mrs. Nunn, affectionately called Betsy, continued to serve wave after wave of students for half a century. When she died in 1851 at the age of ninety-two, President Battle commented that "many hearts were moved" by her loss to the community.

ENTERTAINMENT.

THE subscriber wishes to inform his friends and the public in general, that he is now living at the University of North Carolina, and keeps a house of Entertainment, where James Patterson lately lived. He assures those who may think proper to call on him, that every attention which may be in his power to give, shall be used to make their time easy and agreeable while with him.

Wm. NUNN.

Orange county, October 23,

73

Joseph Caldwell (1773–1835), a native of New Jersey and a 1791 graduate of Princeton, was made professor of mathematics and presiding professor at the departure of Charles Harris in 1796. In 1804 Caldwell was made president of the University, the first to hold the title. In 1812 he resigned as president but continued as professor of mathematics; with the departure of President Chapman, Caldwell again became president in 1816 and continued until his death. After 1816 he was also professor of moral philosophy, and he held the chair of astronomy in 1834. In addition to his other posts with the University, Caldwell was a member of the Board of Trustees from 1804 until his death.

President Caldwell's gold-rimmed spectacles and some of his books, including this autographed presentation copy of *The American Preacher* published in 1793, are among the University keepsakes now in the North Carolina Collection.

When Governor Spaight was on the campus in January 1795 for the opening of the University he saw "a pile of yellowish red clay, dug out for the foundation of the Chapel." Nearly two years later when Joseph Caldwell arrived he wrote to a friend that "the foundation is laid for a chapel but when it will be completed is entirely uncertain, as the mason and his negroes have spent the favorable fall they have had in raising the foundation to the surface of the ground." When the first graduation exercises were held from July 4 to 10, 1798, the building was probably far enough along to be used. It certainly was in use by the opening of the nineteenth century. This building, now known as Person Hall for General Thomas Person, an early benefactor of the University, originally consisted of just the east wing, which is thirty-six by fifty-four feet. In 1886 the central section was added, and in 1892 the west wing, matching the original east, was completed. After Old East, this is the second oldest state university building in America.

The early and rapid increase in the student body forced the trustees to consider the construction of another building. This advertisement in the *North Carolina Journal* for 21 March 1796 was the initial step in that direction. South Building, however, was a long time in materializing. At Masonic ceremonies conducted by the Raleigh Grand Lodge, the cornerstone was laid on 14 April 1798, but lack of funds prevented the completion of the building until 1814. Incomplete, bare walls stood during most of this time and students built crude wooden shelters inside the brick hull of the building, so scarce were rooms.

THE BUILDING COMMISSIONERS of the UNIVERSITY of North-Carolina, will attend at the town of Hillsborough, from the 6th until the 16th of April next, for the purpose of receiving proposals from any person disposed to undertake the building of a House at the seat of the University, of the following dimensions and description, viz.

It is to be of Brick, one hundred and twelve feet six inches in length—forty-six feet three inches in width, clear of the outside walls, and three stories high. A Plan of the Building, with a particular description of the manner in which it is to be executed, may be seen by applying to the Commissioners at the time and place above-mentioned.

Reasonable advances will be made from time to time, and satisfactory security will be required from the undertaker for the performance of the contract.

JOHN HAYWOOD, Chairman.

Hillsborough, North-Carolina,
January 12, 1796.

In the same year that the University opened, two literary societies were formed. The first, called the Debating Society, was organized in the spring of 1795 when thirty-one students signed the document shown here. Membership increased so rapidly that a second society, called the Concord Society, was soon formed. The next year these common names were dropped and the first became the Dialectic Society and the second the Philanthropic Society. The minutes of the 17 June 1795 meeting of the Dialectic Society indicate that a bit of society business was conducted with a debate being the central feature.

James Mebane (1774–1857), who entered the University when it opened in 1795, was the first president of the Dialectic Society. He served as a member of the Board of Trustees from 1811 until his death and was a member of both the House of Commons and the Senate. In 1850, when the societies moved out of South Building and into separate quarters in Old East and Old West, Mebane made "a neat and appropriate address, giving reminiscences of the past and sound advice to the students." The Dialectic Society afterwards asked the privilege of having his portrait painted by William Garl Browne to grace the Society walls.

Hutchins Gordon Burton (*ca.* 1774–1836) was a member of the first class to enter the University in 1795 although he did not remain to complete his course of study. He became attorney general of North Carolina, 1810–16, served in Congress, 1819–24, and was governor of North Carolina, 1824–27. He was also grand master of the Freemasons in the state from 1825 until 1826.

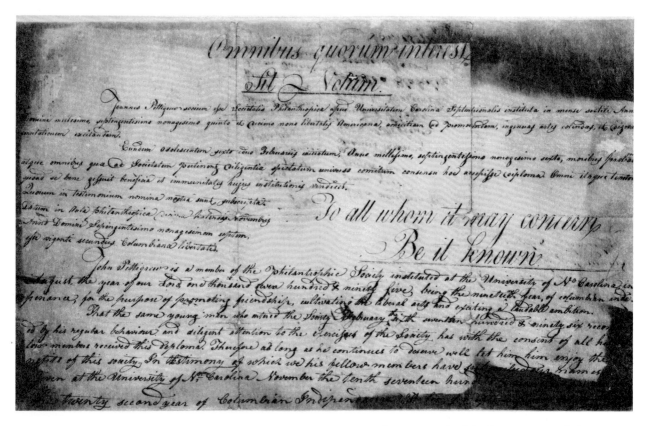

John Pettigrew's Philanthropic Society diploma
dated 10 November 1797 is in Latin and English.

The Widow Puckett House on East Franklin Street
was built about 1796, and Mrs. Elizabeth Puckett
provided rooms and meals for students. The student
body quite soon became too large for Old East, and
many young men had to find places for themselves
in town. Mrs. Puckett also washed clothes for some
of them. For many years this was the home of the
Reverend Dr. James Phillips, mathematics professor
and father of Cornelia Phillips Spencer. Dean and
later Chancellor R. B. House lived here from 1934
until his death in 1987.

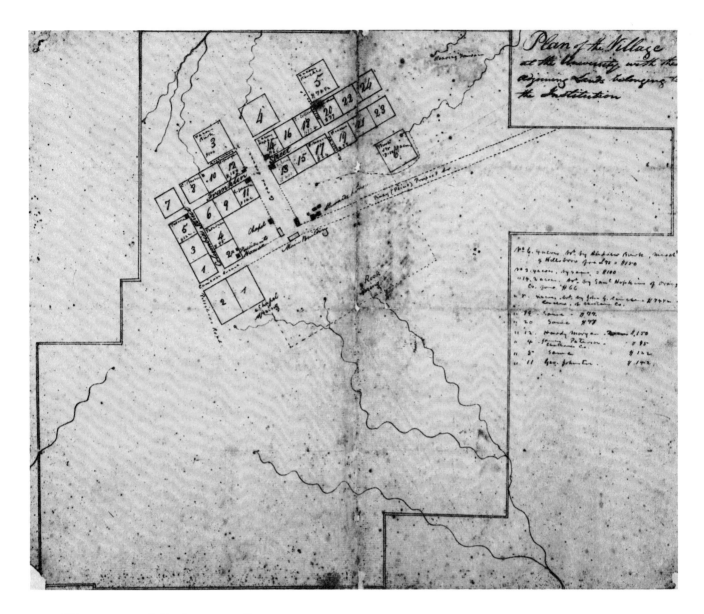

This map was probably drawn soon after 1797. Grand Avenue, a name entered on this map at a later date, led north from the new buildings across Franklin and Rosemary Streets. Four buildings were completed and two projected. They are all shown, in addition to two small unnamed structures just north of Steward's House and convenient to Old East. South Building was projected as a companion to East.

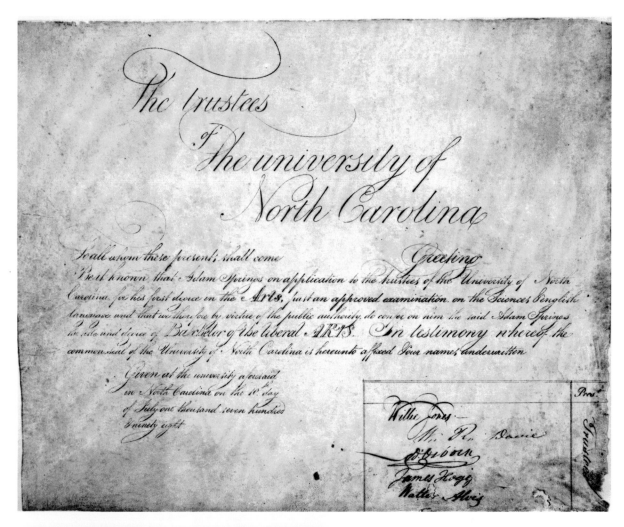

The first commencement got underway on 4 July 1798 with an examination of the students at the University. The degree of Bachelor of Arts was awarded on 10 July to seven graduates: three from Rowan County and one each from Iredell, Mecklenburg, New Hanover, and Wake counties. Adam Springs, to whom this diploma was awarded, was from Mecklenburg County, where he became a planter.

Johnston Blakeley (1781–1814) was a student in the University in 1797, but because of financial reverses suffered by his family he withdrew and entered the Navy. He was a captain in the United States Navy during the War of 1812 and won fame for his valor at sea. He was lost at sea on the *Wasp* in 1814.

At commencement Adam Springs also received a certificate from the Dialectic Society of which he was a member. By this document he received membership in the society for life "so long as he continues to act with propriety and to merit the esteem of the wise and good."

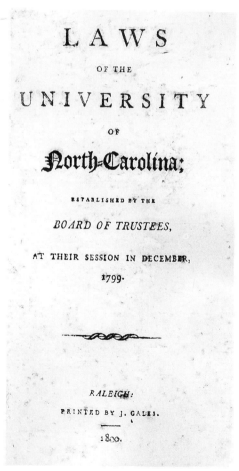

LAWS

OF THE

UNIVERSITY

OF

North-Carolina;

ESTABLISHED BY THE

BOARD OF TRUSTEES,

AT THEIR SESSION IN DECEMBER,

1799.

RALEIGH:

PRINTED BY J. GALES.

1800.

As the eighteenth century drew to a close the trustees consolidated the rules and regulations that they had adopted from time to time since their first meeting in 1790. Copies were printed by Joseph Gales who had just opened his printing establishment in the young town of Raleigh.

Archibald Debow Murphey (1777–1832), distinguished graduate of the class of 1799, served as an instructor in the University during his last two years as a student and as professor of ancient languages, 1800–1801. As a trustee of the University from 1802 until his death he urged the construction of three new buildings, the establishment of a library, the purchase of scientific equipment, the endowment of two professorships, and the addition of six new teachers to the faculty. One of his greatest contributions, however, was in negotiations in Tennessee which enabled the University to establish its claim to lands there. The money from the sale of the lands constituted the antebellum endowment. His active support of public schools, improved means of transportation, the revision of the state constitution, and other good causes were responsible for great changes in North Carolina during the years before the Civil War.

John Branch (1782–1863), a graduate of the University in 1801, was one of the most distinguished alumni of the nineteenth century. He served as governor of North Carolina, 1817–20; in the United States Senate, 1823–29; as secretary of the navy, 1831–33; and as governor of the Florida Territory, 1843–45. He also was a trustee of the University from 1817 until 1844.

The General Assembly in 1800, reacting against the attempts of the trustees to sell certain lands to which they were entitled in Mecklenburg County, repealed both an act of 1789 giving to the University the escheats of the state and an act of 1799 granting unsold confiscated Tory property to the University. This deprived the trustees of their most dependable sources of income and seriously threatened the life of the University. The trustees brought suit to recover some land escheated before the act had been passed in 1800, and an adverse decision in the lower court was appealed to the court of conference, predecessor of the state supreme court. In the case *University* v. *Foy and Bishop* the court held that the University had been created by the will of the people of North Carolina expressed in a constitutional convention and that the General Assembly could not deprive the University of its means of support nor "deprive the institution of funds already vested and refuse to make any additional appropriations."

An address on George Washington by Professor
Caldwell, who was then presiding professor, was
so well received that the students called upon
Professor Caldwell to provide a copy that they
could have printed. President Washington had died
the previous December.

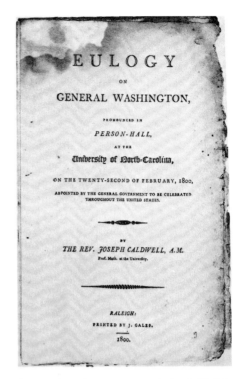

William Gaston (1778–1844) served the University
faithfully as a trustee for more than forty years—
from 1802 until his death. He was a graduate of
Princeton in the class of 1796, the year after the
University of North Carolina opened. He was one
of fifteen men who contributed $200 each toward
the completion of South Building, and he was
genuinely interested in the financial well-being of
the University. A well-trained attorney, he rendered legal opinions for the trustees and was instrumental in the sale of lands in Tennessee for the
benefit of the University. His faithful attendance at
meetings of the trustees and his pattern of voting
show his interest in student welfare, the course of
study, and qualifications of the faculty. His commencement address in 1832 on the abolition of
slavery was an eloquent plea that met a popular
reception. It was reprinted a number of times in
various places in the South as well as in North
Carolina and more than five thousand copies were
distributed.

William Miller (1784–1826) was a student at the
University in 1802 and later held a number of
political positions. He was governor of North
Carolina, 1814–16, and chargé d'affaires to Guatemala in 1825. He served as a trustee of the University from 1817 until his death.

John Henry Eaton (1790–1856) was a student in the University in 1803 and was awarded the M.A. degree in 1825. He served in the United States Senate, 1818–29, and was secretary of war, 1829–31. From 1834 until 1836 he was governor of the Florida Territory and served as minister to Spain, 1836–40.

William Rufus King (1786–1853), a student at the University from 1801 until 1803, served in the United States Senate from 1819 until 1844 when he became minister to France. Upon his return from that post in 1846 he again ran for the Senate and served from 1848 until 1853 when he was elected vice president of the United States. He died shortly after taking the oath of office.

John Owen (1787–1841) was a student at the University in 1804 and served several terms in both houses of the General Assembly before he was elected governor in 1828, a post that he held until 1830. He was also a trustee of the University from 1820 until his death. In 1839 he was the presiding officer at the national Whig Convention at which he was offered the nomination as vice president. He declined, considering it improper to accept nomination from a body over which he presided. William Henry Harrison was nominated for president and John Tyler for vice president. At the death of Harrison in April 1841 Tyler succeeded to the presidency, a post that Owen might have filled. Owen, however, died in October 1841.

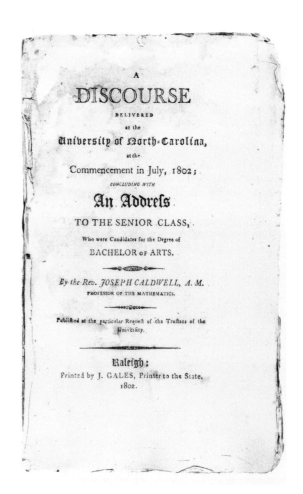

Scheme of a Lottery

AUTHORISED by Act of Assembly, for raising two thousand dollars, to complete the main building of the University of North-Carolina, and for other purposes, to the use and benefit of that Institution.

		DOLLARS.
1 Prize	1500 dollars,	1500
1 ditto	500	500
1 ditto	250, to be last drawn,	250
1 ditto	200	200
2 ditto	100	200
5 ditto	50	250
10 ditto	20	200
10 ditto	10	100
500 ditto	5	2500

531 Prizes, Amount of Prizes, 5700
969 Banks,

1500 Tickets at 5 dollars each.

The Drawing of this Lottery will commence in the City of Raleigh, on the first Saturday in June, being within the session of the Federal Court, and will be closed as soon thereafter as practicable.

The Prizes shall be paid by the Treasurer of the University, at any time after the drawing is closed, with punctuality; subject to a deduction of ten per cent.

The numbers of the fortunate Tickets will be published in the several Newspapers in the state; and all Prizes which shall not be demanded within ninety days after the drawing is finished, will be considered as relinquished and held as a donation to the use of the Institution.

TICKETS to be had at Five Dollars, of the Trustees, of one or more Gentlemen in almost every county in the state, and of the Commissioners at Raleigh.

BENJ. WILLIAMS,
JOHN HAYWOOD,
WILLIAM POLK,   COMMISSIONERS
HENRY POTTER,   appointed by the
HENRY SEAWELL,   Board of
February 2.   Trustees.
                    501

As a means of raising funds to complete South Building the trustees secured legislative approval to conduct two lotteries. The first, drawn in 1802, netted $2,215.45. This notice appeared in the *North Carolina Journal* for 22 February 1802 published at Halifax.

Professor Caldwell's address to the senior class at the commencement of 1802 was published "at the particular Request of the Trustees of the University."

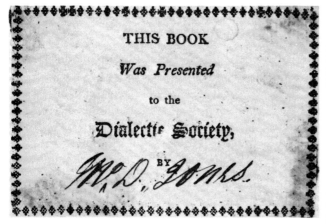

Soon after the organization of the Dialectic and Philanthropic Societies they established libraries and by 1812 they owned between eight hundred and one thousand volumes each.

John D. Jones (1790–1854) of Wilmington, whose gift was acknowledged by the bookplate on the left, was a student in 1804 and later served as a member and speaker of the House of Commons and of the Constitutional Convention of 1835. Harwood Jones of Northampton County, a wealthy planter and Virginia native, was not a graduate of the University but was one of a long line of North Carolina citizens who, through the years, have supported the University.

Bartlett Yancey (1785–1828) studied at the University from 1804 until 1806 when he was forced to leave for financial reasons. He read law with Archibald D. Murphey and was licensed to practice in 1807. He served in Congress from 1813 until 1817 when he entered the state senate, serving as speaker there for ten years. Yancey followed his mentor, Murphey, in rendering active legislative aid to the cause of education, constitutional reform, and internal improvements. He also supported the establishment of the supreme court in North Carolina and reforms in the state treasurer's office. President Adams offered him an appointment as minister to Peru but he declined. As a presiding officer in the senate he was decisive, fair, and impartial. He held promise of a brilliant career in government, but he died at the age of forty-three after a brief illness.

John Robert Donnell (1789–1864) was graduated from the University in 1807, the best scholar in his class. As a lawyer he had a large practice. He married a daughter of Governor Richard Dobbs Spaight and became one of the wealthiest men in the state. He was a generous contributor to the fund to complete South Building. Donnell served as a superior court judge from 1819 until 1836 and as a trustee of the University from 1828 until his death.

Just as the University of North Carolina was aided by the generosity of graduates of older institutions, so graduates of the University assisted in the establishment and development of newer institutions. Robert Hall Morrison (1798–1889), first president of Davidson College, was graduated with honors from the University in 1818. Licensed by the Concord Presbytery, he accepted a call from Providence Church in Mecklenburg County in 1822 and after two years there relocated in Fayetteville where he served the local Presbyterian church and also established the *North Carolina Telegram*, the first religious gazette in the South. Returning to the Charlotte area in 1827, he became pastor of Sugar Creek Church and in 1825 proposed that the Presbytery establish a school to enable young men to begin preparation for the ministry. He prepared a feasibility study, drew up a tentative curriculum, and joined in raising the money for such a school. In April 1836 the chapel cornerstone was laid and at the invitation of the trustees Morrison became the first president of Davidson in February of the next year.

Thomas Gilchrist Polk (1791–1869), who received the A.B. degree in 1809 and the M.A. in 1816, represents something of a second generation University man. He was the son of William Polk, trustee from 1790 until 1834. The younger Polk, a lawyer, served a number of terms in the General Assembly and was a member of the Board of Trustees from 1831 until 1839. He later moved to Mississippi, and during the Civil War he served the Confederacy as a brigadier general.

William Hooper (1792–1876), native of Hillsborough, who received the A.B. degree in 1809 and the M.A. degree in 1812, became a tutor in the University in 1810 and professor of ancient languages in 1818. The University conferred upon him the honorary degree of Doctor of Laws in 1833. He was a member of the faculty during the years 1818–22 and 1828–37. In 1837 he left to join the faculty of Furman Institute in South Carolina. He later held positions at other institutions and was president of Wake Forest College from 1846 to 1848. Dr. Hooper died in Chapel Hill and was buried on the campus beside his stepfather, Dr. Joseph Caldwell, and his mother, who had married Caldwell in 1809.

John Steele (1764–1815) was a member of the General Assembly of 1812 which elected him a trustee of the University. He served from then until his sudden death in 1815 on the day he was elected to another term in the assembly. Steele had been a member of Congress and comptroller of the United States treasury. He had also served with President Caldwell as a member of the commission charged with establishing the boundary line between North Carolina and Georgia.

STATE OF NORTH-CAROLINA.

THIS is to Certify, That *Genl John Steele* was by joint ballot of both Houses of the General Assembly of North-Carolina, at their Sessions A. D. *1812* duly elected a Trustee of the University of North-Carolina; with all and singular the powers and authorities, as fully and amply as are by law vested in any of the Trustees of said Corporation by their Charter.

In testimony whereof, the Seal of said Corporation is hereunto affixed at Raleigh, this *19th* day of *December* . D. *1812*

Robt Williams
Secretary &c

President Joseph Caldwell, anxious to return to teaching and research, asked the trustees to relieve him of administrative duties. This request was granted in 1812 and he was made professor of mathematics. In 1816, at the resignation of President Chapman, his successor, Professor Caldwell tried diligently to find a suitable candidate for the position to recommend to the trustees, but none could be found willing to accept the appointment. With reluctance, Dr. Caldwell again resumed the office, writing, "If I shall ever be found to have gone wrong in discharge of the duties, I hope that the members of the Committee and of the Board in general will be ready to make allowances for defects, which may easily in me proceed from frailty and error without the intention of evil."

Robert Hett Chapman (1771–1833), a Presbyterian minister, native of New Jersey and graduate of Princeton, was chosen president of the University in 1813 in the midst of the War of 1812 with Great Britain. Chapman was a pacifist, "a Peace Federalist" he was called, while the students at the University favored the war. Groups of students committed several outrages on campus; buildings and trees were damaged and many of the large trees died, apparently from injury caused by the students. Some of them cut the hair from the tail of President Chapman's horse, took away a cart, took a gate off the hinges, and turned over a house, undoubtedly one of the "necessary houses" constructed for the President's House. A threat of tar and feathers for the "Tory" president frightened him still further. At the meeting of the trustees on 23 November 1816 it was reported that President Chapman had "in solemn form resigned his office."

Main Building, as South Building was first known, was completed in 1814, sixteen years after the laying of the cornerstone. The event was marked by the firing of a cannon, and soon afterwards the halls of the two literary societies were opened in the new building. It provided both dormitory rooms and badly needed classrooms. The completion of Davie's "Temple of Folly" convinced the skeptics that the University was permanently established.

Aaron Venable Brown (1795–1859), a member of the class of 1814, moved to Nashville, Tennessee, the year after he was graduated from the University and represented his adopted state in the United States Congress. He was also governor of Tennessee, 1845–47, and postmaster general from 1857 until his death.

Charles Manly (1795–1871), native of Pittsboro and graduate of the University with the class of 1814, was secretary and treasurer of the Board of Trustees from 1821 until 1849 and from 1850 until 1868. He was also a member of the board in his own right from 1826 until 1868, during a part of which time he was a member of the executive committee. He was governor of North Carolina from 1849 until 1851. Throughout the whole period of his association with the University he was interested in improving the appearance of the campus and buildings, and in 1857 he introduced the motion that the trustees provide for the erection of a building in which sick students might receive care.

Willie Person Mangum (1792–1861) was graduated from the University in 1815, granted the M.A. degree in 1818, and awarded the LL.D. degree in 1845. He was a member of congress from 1823 until 1826, and of the United States Senate during the years 1831–37 and 1841–53. Following the death of President Harrison, when Vice President John Tyler was elevated to the post of chief executive, Mangum became president of the Senate. He also served the University as a trustee from 1818 until 1859.

Francis Lister Hawks (1798–1866) was graduated from the University in 1815 and received the M.A. degree in 1824 and the LL.D. in 1847. He was a priest in the Episcopal Church, serving congregations in New York City during most of his ministry, but he never forgot his North Carolina origins. He was the author of many books, including a two-volume history of North Carolina published in 1857 and 1858, and a number of books for children. He was vice president of the American Ethnological Society, 1855–59, and president of the American Geographical and Statistical Society, 1855–61.

Denison Olmsted (1791–1859), a graduate of Yale in the same class with Elisha Mitchell, served as professor of chemistry and mineralogy in Chapel Hill from 1817 until 1824 when he also became professor of geology, holding all three appointments until he returned to Yale in 1825. In 1823 the General Assembly established a geological survey of which Professor Olmsted was appointed director. His reports, published in 1825 and 1827, have been described as the first state geological reports in the United States.

John Young Mason (1799–1859), native of Virginia, was graduated from the University in 1816 and was a member of Congress and a judge in Virginia before becoming secretary of the navy under Presidents Tyler and Polk. President Polk and Mason may have had a passing acquaintance in Chapel Hill. Mason was also United States attorney general and United States minister to France. This portrait of him by Thomas Sully was painted in the White House at the same time the portrait of President Polk was painted.

Hugh Waddell (1799–1879) was graduated from the University in 1818. This miniature was made some years before he entered the University and is, for this reason, unusual at this early date. Waddell, a lawyer, served in both houses of the General Assembly and was a trustee of the University from 1828 until 1864. He was among those who organized the Alumni Association and served as vice president. He also contributed towards the construction of New East and New West.

John Motley Morehead (1796–1866) was a member of the class of 1817 who also received the M.A. degree in 1837. He served in the General Assembly for a number of years and was governor from 1841 until 1845. From 1861 until 1864 he was a member of the Confederate Congress. Governor Morehead is best known for his support of railroads in North Carolina. He served the University as a trustee from 1828 until his death. This portrait was painted about 1835.

James Knox Polk (1795–1849), native of Mecklenburg County, was graduated from the University in 1818. During his senior year he was president of the Dialectic Society, and from 1845 until 1849 he was president of the United States. Long underrated, Polk has come to be recognized as a hardworking, decisive leader. As president he had a progressive program that he largely succeeded in implementing. His presidential leadership set the style for the future. He sat for this portrait by Thomas Sully in the White House, 20–25 May 1847.

Robert Donaldson (1800–1872) of Fayetteville was graduated from the University in 1818 and became a lawyer and banker in New York. He was an early model of the ideal alumnus, devoted to Alma Mater and solicitous for her well-being. Donaldson corresponded with the University president most particularly about gardening and landscaping on the campus, about architects for buildings, and about furnishings for the society halls. He sought the support of the trustees in establishing a professorship of agriculture and a "pattern farm" on which the latest developments in agriculture would be demonstrated. At his death, Donaldson left a considerable sum to the University, but his will was declared invalid and the University did not benefit from his last gesture of generosity.

CATALOGUE
OF THE
FACULTY AND STUDENTS
OF THE
University of North-Carolina.
OCTOBER, 1819.

Rev. Joseph Caldwell, D. D. President, and Professor of Moral Philosophy.

Elisha Mitchell, A. M. Professor of Mathematics and Natural Philosophy.
Denison Olmsted, A. M. Professor of Chemistry and Mineralogy.
William Hooper, A. M. Professor of Languages.
Rev. Shepard K. Kollock, A. M. Professor of Rhetoric and Logic.

ROBERT R. KING, A. M. }
SIMON JORDAN, A. B. } TUTORS.

SENIOR CLASS.

Names.	Residence.	Rooms.	Names.	Residence.	Rooms.	Names.	Residence.	Rooms.
Cyrus A. Alexander	Mecklenburg	Maj. Henderson's	Ireson Lea	Caswell	Mrs. Craig's	William Royall	Halifax, Va.	19 S. B.
Richard Allison	Iredell	Maj. Henderson's	Rucker Lea	Caswell	4 S. B.	Thomas B. Slade	Martin	Mrs. Mitchell's
William H. Battle	Edgecombe	12 E. B.	William Lea	Caswell	9 S. B.	Richard I. Smith	Caswell	4 S. B.
Archibald G. Carter	Caswell	16 S. B.	James F. Martin	Stokes	Maj. Henderson's	Charles G. Spaight	Newbern	13 S. B.
Robert T. Coles	Pittsylvania Va.	14 S. B.	Barth'l F. Moore	Halifax	4 S. B.	John M. Starke	Fairfield, dis. S. C.	Maj. Henderson's
Charles D. Donaho	Caswell	21 S. B.	James H. Otey	Bedford, Va.	20 S. B.	David W. Stone	Wake	Mrs. Mitchell's
Thomas J. Green	Warren	6 E. B.	Mat. B. D. Palmer	Windsor	26 S. B.	John Taylor	Granville	Mrs. Burton's
Poulus A. Haralson	Haywood	6 E. B.	Malcolm G. Purcell	Robeson	23 S. B.	Philip L. Thomas	Caswell	14 E. B.
William H. Harden	Rockingham	Mrs. Pannell's	Thomas E. Read	Charlotte, Va.	30 S. B.	Henry C. Williams	Warren	3 E. B.
John Haywood	Raleigh	15 E. B.	Charles G. Rose	Person	3 E. B.	Thomas H. Wright	Wilmington	13 S. B.

JUNIOR CLASS.

Names.	Residence.	Rooms.	Names.	Residence.	Rooms.	Names.	Residence.	Rooms.
Nathl W. Alexander	Salisbury	25 E B	Wash. Haywood	Raleigh	15 E B	William D Morphey	Orange	16 S B
Johnson Alves	Henderson Kent.	Prof. Hooper's	Calvin G. Hatch	Newbern	14 E B	Edward G. Pasteur	Newbern	8 S B
Joseph Caldwell	Ontario, N. Y.	President's	Samuel Headen	Bedford, Va.	3 E B	Etheldred Philips	Nash	12 S B
Robert Cowan	Wilmington	7 S. B.	Pleasant Henderson	Chapel Hill	Maj. Henderson's	Abraham Rencher	Wake	25 S B
Bryan Croom	Kingston	17 S. B.	Thompson Johnston	Bertie	Mr. Moring's	Joseph H. Sanders	Chowan	13 S B
Frederick F. Cutlar	Wilmington	20 E. B.	Moses H. Kirby	Highland, O.	9 E B	William Shaw	Raleigh	10 E B
John R. J. Daniel	Halifax	22 S. B.	Thomas J. Lacy	Nelson, Ken.	18 S B	Samuel H. Smith	Granville	11 E B
Nicholas J. Drake	Nash	18 S. B.	Willis M. Lea	Caswell	3 E B	James Stafford	Mecklenburg	9 E B
Henry T. Garnett	King & Queen, Va.	24 S. B.	Wm. K. Mebane	Orange	21 S B	James Taylor	Granville	10 S B
Nathaniel H. Harris	Orange	11 E. B.	Anderson Mitchell	Caswell	19 S B	Charles L. Torrence	Salisbury	Maj. Henderson's
Rufus Haywood	Raleigh	16 E. B.						

SOPHOMORE CLASS.

Names.	Residence.	Rooms.	Names.	Residence.	Rooms.	Names.	Residence.	Rooms.
James Bowman	Stokes	13 E B	Benjamin Haywood	Raleigh	7 E B	Wash. Morrison	Cabarrus	20 S B
Charles L. Boyd	Chester dis. S. C.	4 E B	Fabius Haywood	Raleigh	15 E B	Jonathan Nixon	Bertie	8 E B
Robert M. Burton	Chapel Hill	Mrs. Burton's	Thomas Haywood	Raleigh	9 S B	Samuel I. Person	Moore	13 E B.
William M. Currie	Caswell	Mrs. Craig's	Thomas Hill	Wilmington	7 S B	William D Pickett	Aytoga, Alabama	33 S B
Thomas P. Davis	Wilmington	12 E B	John Hogan	Randolph	22 S B	Lucius J. Polk	Raleigh	6 E B
John L. Davies	Chester dis. S. C.	14 S B	William D. Jones	Granville	5 S B	Marion Sanders	Sempter, S. C.	5 E B
William Davies	Chester dis. S. C.	14 S B	Samuel Kerr	Rowan	18 S B	James B. Slade	Martin	7 S B
William Gillespie	Crostofield dis. S C	25 S B	Pleasant Kittrell	Orange	Mr. Kittrell's	Benjamin Sumner	Gates	11 E B
Robert Haile	Union dis. S. C.	Maj. Henderson's	Henry Martin	Stokes	Maj. Henderson's	William Travis	Rowan	1 E B
James G. Hall	Camden	President's	Robert G. Martin	Granville	5 E B	George Terry	Mecklenburg, Va.	Mrs. Pannill's
William Hardeman	Franklin, Ten.	36 S B	Robert H. Mason	Greenville, Va.	5 S B	Jas. A. Washington	Kingston	24 S B
John Harvey	Newbern	17 S B	Freeman Mebane	Orange	Mr. Barbee's	Alexander E. Wilson	Mecklenburg	29 S B
Benjamin B. Hawks	Newbern	6 S B	John Monroe	Rowan	24 S B			

FRESHMAN CLASS.

Names.	Residence.	Rooms.	Names.	Residence.	Rooms.	Names.	Residence.	Rooms.
Samuel S. Bell	Newbern	5 S B	Samuel Martin	Stokes	Mr Pitt's	Samuel M. Stewart	Chatham	Mrs. Nun's
Alexander Boylan	Raleigh	10 E B	Benjamin T. Moore	Stokes	6 S B	Robert Williamson	Person	10 S B
John S. Eaton	Granville	3 S B	Victor M. Murphey	Orange	15 S B	George Whitfield	Lenoir	Mrs Mitchell's
Thomas Hunt	Granville	Mrs. Pannill's	Richard Rhodes	Robeson	Mrs Mitchell's			
William M. Inge	Granville	5 S B	Cornelius Robinson	Alabama	2 S B			
George W. McGehee	Person	Mr. Thompson's	Alfred Scales	Rockingham	Mr Thompson's			
Hugh Martin	Stokes	Maj. Henderson's	Alexander Sims	Brunswick Va	2 S B			
Edmund Martin	Stokes	do	James Strain	Orange	Mr Strain's			

Seniors	30
Juniors	31
Sophomores	38
Freshmen	19
Total,	118

N. B.—E. B. *East Building*—S. B. *South Building.*

J. HARVEY—Printer, Raleigh, N. C.

(*On facing page*) This is the earliest known student directory and it contains the names of a number of young men who later became distinguished in North Carolina as well as in other southern states. There were 118 students enrolled, including a single student from Alabama, New York, Ohio, and Tennessee, 2 from Kentucky, 7 from South Carolina, and 9 from Virginia. The name "Main Building" had now given way to "South Building," and by the students' addresses it appears that this new building contained at least nine rooms on each of the first two floors, and at least one student had a room on the third floor. Before South was completed many students occupied make-shift accommodations, but from this directory we see that many of them now enjoyed the luxury of a single room.

The University catalogue of 1819 was printed on one side of a single sheet of paper, but it listed the faculty, the courses offered in the Preparatory School, and those offered in the University.

UNIVERSITY OF NORTH-CAROLINA.

MEMBERS OF THE FACULTY.

PROFESORS.

Rev. Joseph Caldwell, D. D. Prs. and Prof. Mor. Phil.
Elisha Mitchell, Prof. Math.
Denison Olmsted, Prof. Chem. Min. and Geology.
William Hooper, Prof. Lang.
Rev. Shepard K. Kollock, Prof Rhet. and Log.
TUTORS.—Robert King, and Simon Jordan.

System of studies preparatory to admission into the University of North Carolina.

1. Latin Grammar.
2. Corderius.
3. Æsop's Fables, 25.
4. Selectæ e Veteri, or else Sacra Historia.
5. Cornelius Nepos, or Viri Romæ.
6. Mair's Introduction.
7. Cæsar's Commentaries, 7 books.

8. Greek Grammar.
9. Prosody.
10. Ovidii Editio Expurgata.
11. St. John's Gospel, and the Acts of the Aostles in Greek.
12. Virgil. Bucolics, & 6 books of the Æneid.
13. Græca Minora to Lucian's Dialogues.

PLAN OF EDUCATION IN THE UNIVERSITY,

FRESHMAN CLASS.

1st. Session commencing six weeks after the Thursday next succeeding the first Monday in June.

1. Sallust, the whole.
2. Antiquities Roman.
3. Græca Minora, continued.
4. Elements of Ancient and Modern Geography.
5. Arithmetic.
6. Algebra.
7. English Grammar, Composition, Declamation.
8. Theses.

2nd. Session commencing four weeks, reckoned from the Thursday next succeeding the first Monday in December.

9. Virgil. Georgics.
10. Cicero's Orations.
11. Græca Majora. First Volume.
12. Algebra continued.
13. Antiquities.
14. English Grammar, Composition, Declamation, Theses.

SOPHOMORE CLASS.

1st. Session as before. July.

15. Græca Majora, continued. First volume.
16. Horace.
17. Algebra, concluded.
18. Geometry.
19. Theses, Composition, Declamation.

2nd. Session as before. January.

20. Horace completed.
21. Homer's Iliad. 4 books.
22. Geometry completed.
23. Geography
24. Composition, Declamation.

JUNIOR SOPHISTERS.

1st. Session as before. July.

25. Plane Trigonometry.
26. Logarithms.
27. Mensuration of Heights and Distances.
28. Surveying.
29. Spherical Trigonometry.
30. Classicks, Composition, Declamation.

2nd. Session as before. January.

31. Navigation.
32. Conick Sections.
33. Fluxions.
34. Natural Philosophy.
35. Classicks, Composition, Declamation.

SENIOR SOPHISTERS.

1st. Session. July.

36. Chemistry.
37. Mineralogy.
38. Geology.
39. Philosophy of Natural History.
40. Moral Philosophy.
41. Progress of Metaphysical, Ethical and Political Philosophy.
42. Logick.
43. Natural Philosophy.
44. Progress of the Mathematical and Physical Sciences.
45. Astronomy.
46. Classicks, English Grammar, Composition, Declamation.

2nd. Session. January.

47. Chemistry, Mineralogy, Geology concluded.
48. Rhetorick.
49. Chronology.
50. Metaphysicks.
51. Classicks, Composition, Declamation.

CHAPEL-HILL, JUNE 28, 1819.

The cornerstone of Old West was laid on 24 July 1822, and the building was occupied in July of the next year. It was planned to match Old East. This picture shows how the structure appeared later, after it was enlarged in 1848.

New Chapel, later named Gerrard Hall, was begun in 1822, but like South Building, it was slow in completion. The old Preparatory School was sold and the proceeds applied toward the completion of this building. To provide further funds to finish the building, some land in Tennessee which had been given to the University by

Major Charles Gerrard of Edgecombe County was also sold. The building, completed in time for the commencement exercises of 1837 to be held there, was described by the *Raleigh Register* as a "commodious building, with large galleries, just completed with becoming taste and good style."

James Hervey Otey (1800–1863), holder of three degrees from the University—A.B., 1820; A.M., 1823; and LL.D., 1859—was the Episcopal bishop of Tennessee, 1834–63. After his graduation he remained in Chapel Hill as a tutor for a year. It was Bishop Otey who preached the sermon at the funeral of Dr. Elisha Mitchell, his former teacher and colleague, on the summit of Mount Mitchell.

Abraham Rencher (1798–1883), a member of the class of 1822, received the M.A. degree in 1831. He was a member of Congress from 1829 until 1839 and again during the years 1841–43. From 1843 until 1847 he was chargé d'affaires in Portugal and from 1857 until 1861 was governor of the Territory of New Mexico. He served as a member of the General Assembly from 1872 until 1878 and was speaker during the last year.

William A. Graham (1804–75), a member of the class of 1824, was governor of North Carolina, 1845–49, United States secretary of the navy, 1850–53, and a Confederate senator in 1864. He also served as a trustee of the University during the years 1834–68 and 1874–75. He worked diligently to secure the reopening of the University in 1875.

Professor Caldwell went to Europe in 1824 to secure scientific equipment for the University. The astronomical instruments purchased in London were installed in the observatory that was completed in 1827, and they are now in the Morehead Planetarium as a part of an exhibition of historical instruments.

The sidereal clock marked a day of 23 hours, 56 minutes, 4 seconds, based on the exact 360° rotation of the earth.

The refracting telescope was used to study the surface of the moon and to map gross features of the planets. It has a 150-power maximum magnification under normal conditions.

The armillary sphere was used in teaching the system of reference lines used in astronomy.

The altitude azimuth refracting telescope was used for plotting a planet as it moves in its course, permitting orbits to be computed.

The first observatory was located near the Chapel Hill cemetery atop a hill that has since been levelled. It was the first actual observatory structure erected for any college in America. Stone and locally fired brick were used in its construction, but the bricks were improperly fired and soon began to decay. Soon after the death of President Caldwell in 1835 the building had to be abandoned and in 1838 it was partially burned. This sketch made in the late nineteenth century was based on information furnished by John H. Watson, a resident of Chapel Hill while the observatory was in use.

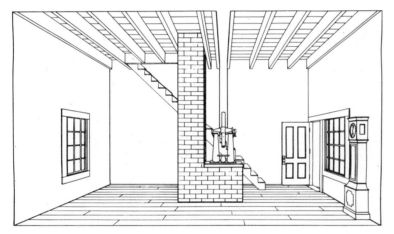

A drawing by Professor Ralph M. Trimble of the interior of the astronomical observatory.

Old East, built in 1793, had a third story added in 1822. Between 1845 and 1848 both Old East and Old West were lengthened. This etching, made at a much later date, shows the south end of the old building with the third floor addition.

Nicholas Marcellus Hentz (1797–1856), a native of Versailles, France, who came to the United States in 1816, was professor of modern languages at the University, 1826–34. He was a versatile man, publishing works on the French language and French literature, painting miniatures, and engaging in the serious study of spiders, a subject on which he wrote several scholarly monographs.

Caroline Lee Hentz (1800–1856), a native of Lancaster, Massachusetts, and wife of Professor Hentz, whom she married in 1824, was a novelist whose domestic, sentimental stories often had a proslavery sentiment. Chapel Hill citizens appeared as characters in some of her novels. In Chapel Hill she was also the patron of George Moses Horton, the noted slave poet.

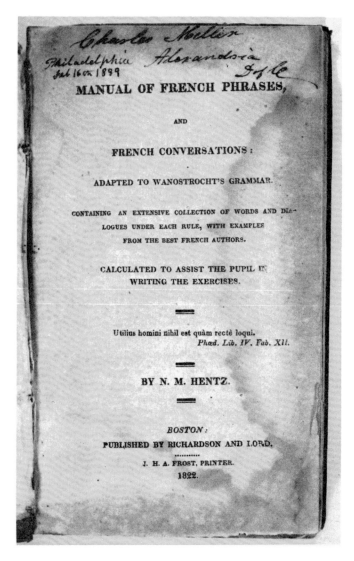

MANUAL OF FRENCH PHRASES,

AND

FRENCH CONVERSATIONS:

ADAPTED TO WANOSTROCHT'S GRAMMAR.

CONTAINING AN EXTENSIVE COLLECTION OF WORDS AND DIA-
LOGUES UNDER EACH RULE, WITH EXAMPLES
FROM THE BEST FRENCH AUTHORS.

CALCULATED TO ASSIST THE PUPIL IN
WRITING THE EXERCISES.

Utilius homini nihil est quàm rectè loqui.
Phæd. Lib. IV. Fab. XII.

BY N. M. HENTZ.

BOSTON:
PUBLISHED BY RICHARDSON AND LORD.
J. H. A. FROST, PRINTER.
1822.

Professor Hentz used a book in his classes which he had written a short while before joining the faculty in Chapel Hill.

Student behavior has been a problem in the University almost from the day the second student reached Chapel Hill. These two entries in the faculty minutes of 10 April and 10 May 1828 tell an interesting story. William Lee Kennedy (1810–70), who was graduated in 1830, was a sophomore in 1828 when a professor observed young Kennedy "very intently and conspicuously engaged in cutting the bench on which he was seated." The professor asked him to stop but he replied "with abruptness . . . that as he assisted in paying for them he should cut them as much as he pleased." Appearing before the faculty, which tried to "convince him of the impropriety of his conduct," Kennedy refused to admit any improper acts, and "through the whole of the interview he continued to express himself with rudeness, and in a spirit of captiousness and altercation." Failing to make Kennedy see the error of his ways, the faculty suspended him for six months.

Where the faculty had failed, Kennedy's father succeeded. The minutes of the faculty meeting a month later contain a letter from young Kennedy to President Caldwell apologizing for cutting the bench and for acting disrespectfully toward the professor. Having informed his father of the reasons for his return home, Kennedy wrote, "the arguments he [the father] used have satisfied my mind as to the correctness of his opinion." The student acknowledged his error and asked to be reinstated, pledging "to conform to the laws of the University and to avoid in future all such acts of imprudence." The forgiving faculty readmitted Kennedy, and he not only was graduated with his class but in 1844 was granted the M.A. degree as well.

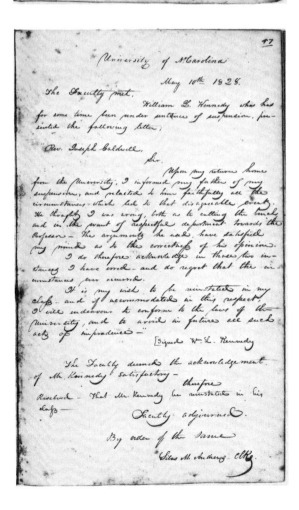

Burton Craige (1811–75) of Salisbury was a member of the class of 1829. He was a member of Congress from 1853 until 1861, and as a member of the North Carolina Secession Convention he offered the Ordinance of Secession that was adopted by North Carolina. During the war he served as a member of the Confederate Congress from 1861 until 1864.

Thomas Ruffin (1787–1870), an active and deeply interested member of the Board of Trustees, was awarded the honorary LL.D. degree in 1834. He was a member of the board during the years 1813–31 and 1842–68 when he took an active interest in the welfare of both faculty and students. On one occasion in 1830 when the financial condition of the University was critical, he made an eloquent plea to the General Assembly for aid.

The desperate financial condition of the University in 1830 prompted this very frank call for an adjourned meeting of the trustees at which steps to save the University might be taken.

Duncan Cameron (1777–1853), a native of Virginia but later a resident of Hillsborough and Raleigh, was a member of the Board of Trustees, 1802–38. An attorney, he was also president of the State Bank of North Carolina, 1829–49. At the time of the financial crisis in 1830, Cameron was a member of the committee of trustees charged with drawing up a memorial to the General Assembly. President Kemp P. Battle later credited the financial advice of Cameron with giving the University an endowment and filling her halls with students. The first executive committee of the Board of Trustees was elected 2 January 1835, and on 10 January, Cameron was elected as the first chairman.

Jacob Thompson (1810–85) was awarded the A.B. degree in 1831 and remained as a tutor until 1833. He studied law and removed to Mississippi where he was elected to Congress in 1839 and served until 1853. He was secretary of the interior in President Buchanan's cabinet from 1857 until 1861, when he resigned. During the Civil War he was inspector general in the Confederate Army and confidential agent for the Confederate government in Canada. He also served as governor of Mississippi, 1862–64.

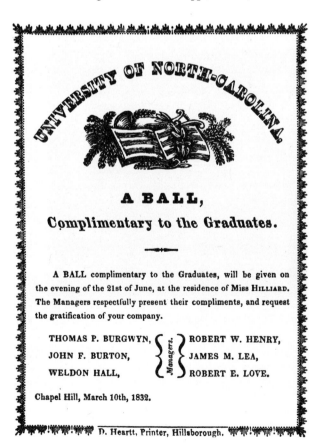

This ball, managed by members of the junior class, was held at Miss Nancy Segur Hilliard's. Born in 1798, she had come to Chapel Hill with her parents in 1817 and in the early 1830s began operating the Eagle Hotel, a popular rooming and boarding house for students and visitors.

The Chapel Hill cemetery contains burial plots acquired in the names of the Dialectic and Philanthropic Societies. The earliest burial in the Dialectic plot was in 1824, and the earliest in the Philanthropic plot was in 1832. Each is enclosed with a sturdy iron fence. This view of a corner of the Philanthropic plot shows the monument, with a dove at its peak, to Joshua P. Perry, a student from Mar-shall, Texas, who died in 1856. The smaller monument to the right marks the grave of John W. Burton, who died in 1845 during his first year as a student. His father, Hutchins G. Burton, was a member of the first class to enter the University in 1795 and became a congressman and governor.

Thomas Samuel Ashe (1812–87), a graduate of the University in the class of 1832, who also received the M.A. degree in 1838 and an LL.D. in 1879, was elected a tutor in the University in 1835 but declined. He studied law; served in the General Assembly; was a member of the Confederate Congress, 1861–64, and elected to the Confederate Senate but did not serve; and sat in the United States Congress from 1873 until 1877. The following year he became an associate justice of the North Carolina Supreme Court. He was a member of the Board of Trustees of the University, 1842–68, and 1877–83.

Thomas Lanier Clingman (1812–97) was graduated from the University in 1832 and afterwards studied law. He served in Congress, 1843–45 and 1857–58, and was elected to the Senate in 1858, where he remained until the beginning of the Civil War. During the war he served as a brigadier general.

James Cochran Dobbin (1814–57) was a member of the class of 1832. He studied law and was a member of the General Assembly for a number of terms. His support in 1848 of a bill to establish a hospital for the insane was crucial to its adoption. He also served in Congress and was secretary of the navy, 1853–57. From 1848 until 1857 he was also a member of the Board of Trustees.

THE HARBINGER.

Erumpere e tenebris et lucem obluctari.

VOL. I. UNIVERSITY OF NORTH-CAROLINA, [CHAPEL-HILL,] TUESDAY, SEPTEMBER 10, 1833. NO. 3.

PUBLISHED WEEKLY
BY ISAAC C. PATRIDGE,
[Under the supervision of the Professors of the University.]

TERMS—Three Dollars per annum, payable *yearly* in advance, or *Four* Dollars if payment be delayed six months after the commencement of each subscription year.—*Advertisements* (which are limited to four columns,) inserted at the customary rates.

☞ *All* letters should be directed to the publisher, at Chapel Hill, Orange County, North-Carolina.

Botany.

FOR THE HARBINGER.

Natural science has been slow to take root in America, and in truth it appears to be the last to be cultivated in all countries. But we think that *Botany* has been even less attended to in this country, than we would, *a priori*, have been led to expect. During the last 60 or 70 years, since Kalm first gathered a portion of our botanical treasures, and laid them at the feet of the delighted Linnæus, a number of Europeans have engaged with ardour, and acquired distinction, in the investigation of North American botany.—Among these are pre-eminent the two Michaux, Clayton, Bartram, Catesby, Walter, Pursh, and Nuttall. At present however there are symptoms that this delightful science is about to awaken a due share of interest in the Eastern and Northern portions of our country. Nuttall lectures at Cambridge, Torrey at New York, Ives at Yale, Eaton at Troy, Dewey at William's College? Barton at Philadelphia, and a number of other gentlemen are known to devote a share of their attention to this subject. In the South however, the prospect is by no means so promising. I do not know that Botany is any where publicly taught in the Southern States. Elliott, and his zealous coadjutor McBride, are dead; Schweinitz and Leconte have abandoned the South. There are however still a few gentlemen dispersed through the Southern country that give some attention to the botanical treasures that surround them, which are even richer than those within the reach of their more northern brethren.* Perhaps there is no country in the temperate zone that can boast of more varied vegetable products than North Carolina. From the mountains to the sea coast, you have those of the alpine, subalpine, alluvial, aquatic, and maritime habitations.—What harvests have not Michaux and Nuttall gathered on our eastern savannahs, and on the summits of the Catawba ridge!

In the following article I have two objects in view, one to mark a few localities of interesting plants, and the other, to shew the familiar uses to which this science may be applied by those who cultivate it; how, in the words of Cicero, it "travels with us," cheering many a dreary ride, and amusing many a solitary walk. H. B. C.

MEMORANDA OF A JOURNEY FROM NEWBERN TO RALEIGH.

BY AN AMATEUR BOTANIST.

Hæc studia peregrinantur nobiscum.—Cicero.

The point from which I set out is one of great botanical riches, but these we cannot stop to survey in their almost boundless variety. A glance is all that we can afford.—The curious Sarracenia and the wonderful Dionæa (Venus' fly trap) have ceased to bloom, (June 30th) while the flower buds of Nelumbium luteum are peeping above the waters, soon to display their splendid forms, and sit, like yellow-haired Nymphs, above their native element. Of the genus Sarracenia we have three species, S. purpurea, S. flava, and S. Catesbœi, El.

Leaving Newbern on the last of June, the season is one of the least propitious for the botanist. The thousand species of vernal flowers have faded away; and the autumnal plants, as the Aster, Liatris, Solidago, and Helianthus have not begun to shed their gorgeous hues o'er Nature's great parterre. The Rhexias, however, with their fugacious flowers, are now in bloom, among which is pre-eminent the R. glabella, (Deer grass) accompanied by R. mariana, R. ciliosa, and the rarer R. lutea, or yellow-flowered Rhexia. The *Diadelphous* plants too are now very generally in bloom, and among these in different portions of the journey were observed Zornia tetraphylla, Hedysarum nudiflorum, Lespedeza (sessiliflora?) and Tephrosia paucifolia. The delicate Lobelia gracilis is blooming plentifully, while none of its showy congeners have appeared. It is singular, considering its abundance, that no botanist before Nuttall, has described this plant. Calamintha Caroliniana? abundant 17 to 24 miles from town, and beginning to flower. Kalmia angustifolia is in fruit.—That elegant tree, with its pyramidal summit, the Gordona lasianthus, (Loblolly Boy,) displays its beautiful white flowers, and the humble Clethra alnifolia begins to shed its honied fragrance on the air. Here I note, in dry and sandy soils, the Stipa avenacea. In the low grounds of the Neuse the Clematis reticulata (or C. crispa?) presents its delicious pale blue flowers, and the Convolvulus tenellus spreads a profusion of white flowers on the surface of the sandy soil.—Here too I found, two years ago, the Macbridea pulchra of Elliott, the first probably that had been seen in North Carolina. Hopea tinctoria (Yellow leaf or Dye leaf,) here attains the height of a small tree; Rhus radicans, Cissus hederacea, Zizyphus volubilis and Decumaria sarmentosa climb the lofty trees, while the Tillandsia usneoides (Long moss) festoons their branches.

In the streets of Kinston, Martynia proboscidea and Sida abutilon are abundant.—Here are also some fine trees of the American Sycamore (Platanus occidentalis,) and also of Ulmus alata and U. americana, transplanted from the river swamp. Rhus radicans, Zizyphus volubilis, Cissus hederacea, and Decumaria sarmentosa climb the lofty trees, while the Tillandsia usneoides (Long moss) festoons their branches. In a ditch six miles above Kinston I observed that singular grass Schœnus effusus very appropriately called "Saw grass," from the remarkable serrature of its rigid leaves. At Falling Creek noted Cupressus disticha (Bald cypress,) Betula nigra (Birch,) Cephalanthus occidentalis (Button wood,) Nyssa aquatica (Tupelo gum) and some of the finest willow oaks (Quercus phellos,) I have ever seen.

A little farther on we reach that sandy and barren tract which extends to the neighborhood of Waynesborough, and which no traveller probably, save the botanist, can enter with satisfaction. To him it has its peculiar interest, for here he finds plants which he would in vain search for in more fertile districts. This is the native region of Quercus catisbœi, Quercus nigra, and Aristida stricta, (Black Jack and Wire-grass,) but among these I descried with interest Stillingia sylvatica, Onosmodium hispidum, and Baptisia lanceolata. Yucca filamentosa, [Bear grass,] and Asclepias tuberosa [Pleurisy root,] are also inhabitants of this region. At Bear Creek Hibiscus moscheutos is plentiful, and it was again observed in bloom, in the low grounds of the Neuse at Smithfield. From this point to Raleigh, in dry, sandy soils, occurs Rhus pumilum [Dwarf sumach] a very poisonous plant. In a mill-pond, five miles above, is a fine locality of that elegant plant the white water-lilly [Nymphæa odorata.] At this place also is an abundance of the showy Cacalia atriplicifolia, whose flower buds are almost ready to expand [July 2nd.] At a mill nine miles below Smithfield, the *stratified rocks* first make their appearance at a low angle, on the bank of the creek over which the road passes. They appear to be, as Professor Olmstead has remarked, ill defined granitic rocks. The alluvial character of the country however continues for several miles west of Smithfield, the rocks being covered, to a great depth, by sand and water-worn pebbles.

In the flat pine woods, near Smithfield, the Saracennia flava, called "Trumpets," is plentiful, and I observed it, in wet places, [illegible] see it. I think it probable [illegible] very base of the [illegible] which I did not limit. Here too the beautiful [illegible] lum variegatum is blooming abundantly, and accompanied us for several miles west of Smithfield. At this place there are some very large and beautiful trees of the Celtis occidentalis (Hack-berry.) They extend along the Neuse as low as Waynesborough, and perhaps lower. The pines occupying the lands east of Smithfield have recently been 'boxed' for *turpentine*. They are the Pinus palustris, the species which, in the eastern part of the State, yields, to such a vast amount, the turpentine, tar, and pitch of commerce.

West of this point the Silphiums are common; and are beginning to flower, [July 3.] Comptonia asplenifolia occurs in dry gravelly soil. Rubus accidentalis [American Raspberry,] and Schrankia uncinata have been occasionally observed throughout the journey. Crotalaria sagittalis gathered in fruit. Cacalia atriplicifolia again becomes abundant. In a fertile valley seven miles east of Raleigh, Smilacina racemosa [in fruit] and Dioscorea quaternata. Between this and Raleigh gathered in flower Clematis viorna.

One mile east of Raleigh, we reach the quarry, from which is obtained the fine *granite* with which the State is about to rebuild its Capitol. Should the work be faithfully executed of this noble material, the Capitol of North Carolina may vie in durability with the Parthenon of Athens, and the Pantheon of Rome. Could Thorvaldsen be engaged to restore the *statue*, we shall have still less cause to deplore the loss of the late building. When we speak of *restoring* the statue, we do not mean the patch work proposed by Mr. Hughes, but that a new statue be made on the model of the former.—July 4th, witnessed the ceremonies of laying of the corner stone of the Capitol, and in the evening attended the meeting of the Internal Improvement Convention.

Circumstances did not permit me to examine the botany of the immediate vicinity of Raleigh, but in the mineralogical cabinet of Dr. B. I have, more than once, had the pleasure of viewing an elegant collection of minerals from the rich resources of our own State. C.

Newbern, August 26th, 1833.

* Prof. Eaton has just published at Albany the *sixth* edition of his 'Manual of Botany.' It is probable that not 50 copies of the six editions have been sold South of the Potomac.

Biography.

JOHN RANDOLPH, OF ROANOKE.

[We give, as our leading article for this evening, the auto-biographical letter of the late John Randolph, of Roanoke—omitting some few expressions of harshness which might, perhaps, wound the feelings of surviving relations in Virginia. It was written in 1813, to his nephew, who afterwards died—we believe, in England. It never was intended for the public eye by the writer, but with the very few omissions we have made, we cannot perceive the least objection to its publication. The fling at Dr. Witherspoon, will in no wise affect that great and good man's memory. It was obviously the malignant petulance of a dissolute school boy, thwarted in his purposes by being restrained in his pocket money; it is a flaunt daily repeated in the case of every similar guardian. Probably the charges against Mr. Tucker and Edmund Randolph are no better founded.]—*N. York Com. Adv.*

DECEMBER 13, 1813.

You *shall* "know something of my life," nay, every thing, my dear son, that can be desirable or profitable for you to know. It is a tale not devoid of interest or events, and might be wrought up into a more engageing narrative, than ninety-nine out of a hundred of the hasty volumes which minister to the mental green-sickness of our misses and masters. Like yourself, I was left by my father an orphan, when too young to be sensible of my loss. The first thing that I can remember, is, finding myself in my mother's family, the *pin basket* of the whole house. I think that I can recollect some circumstances that must have happened in 1776; but I distinctly remember events that took place in the year following. I shared my mother's widowed bed; and was the nestling of her bosom. Every night after I was undressed, and in the morning before I rose, I kneeled down in my bed, and putting up my little hands, repeated after my mother the Lord's prayer and the "belief;" and to this circumstance I attribute some of my present opinions. I say *present*, because they lay long dormant, and as if extinguished within me.*

In the autumn of the year 1783, my mother married St. George Tucker. From that day there was a change in my situation. The first blow that I ever received, was from the hand of this man and not a week after his union with my mother. At *his* instance, I was sent at the age of *nine* to the school of Walker Murray, (who had been his fellow student at College,) in the county of Orange; *then*, and perhaps yet, a wild and savage country, inhabited by the coarsest, the most ignorant, and vicious of the human race! A new world was opened to me. Our school fellows, (your father and uncle Theodorick were at the same school,) were, with the exception of one or two *gentlemen's* sons, adepts in every species of profligacy,—vulgar, brutal, savage. Our schoolmaster was the most petulant and malignant wretch in creation. We had scarcely the necessaries of life; without an opportunity to acquire [illegible] ordinary school books. Indignant at his treatment, your father, hardly thirteen years old, determined to desert and go home. From our step father, we looked for nothing like sympathy or tenderness. My brother was deterred by his expostulations from executing his purpose. Murray transferred his school to Williamsburgh, and we were transferred along with it. In 1784, the state of my health induced my mother to send me to Bermuda, where I arrived in the month of July; and just twelve months afterwards, she came over with her whole family, and remained till Nov. 1785; when she encountered a long and boisterous passage, in a wretched sloop, to Virginia. This laid the foundation of that disease, which deprived me, two years afterwards, of the best mother that every man had.

My sojourn in Bermuda was of essential service to me in many respects. It was a respite from the austere rule of my step-father, and the tyranny, hardly tolerable, of Murray; and I acquired a temper not to brook tamely their unreasonable exactions. There was a good country-gentleman's library in old Mr. Tucker's house, where I staid; and here I read many sterling English authors. Your father and myself were always bookworms. It was a sort of bond to the affection that united us. Our first question at meeting was, generally, "What have you read? Have you seen this or that work?" By going to Bermuda, however, I lost my Greek; I had just mastered the grammar *perfectly*, when I left Williamsburgh. Walking round the base, (it was a circular iron railing that protected it,) of Lord Botetourt's statue, I had committed the Westminister grammar to memory, so as to be able to repeat every word of it. The pendulum of the great clock which vibrated over my head, seemed to concentrate my attention on my book. My Bermudian tutor, Ewing, had no Greek class, and would not take the trouble of teaching a single boy.

After our return, we went back to Williamsburgh; your father continuing to board with Murray, but attending Mr. Wythe, in Greek, mathematics, and I think Latin, also. Soon afterwards he entered college. We were at the grammar school kept in the old capital, which has been since pulled down, to save the expense of repairing the hall, where Henry spoke and Independence was declared.—The shocking barbarity of Murray towards my brother Theodorick, drove him from the school, (our mother was then in New York for her health,) and soon after, I left it. Having spent some months at home, we (Theodorick and myself,) were sent, in March, 1787, to Princeton, where we were joined in the summer by your father. Dr. Witherspoon, in order to make the most out of us, put Theodorick and myself into the grammar school, although we were further advanced than any of the freshmen or most of the sophomores. In this subterranean abode of noise and misrule, I was pent for five long months; and in September was transferred to the college, with habits acquired in that school by no means propitious to study. At Christmas, Theodorick and I went to New York, to spend what little money we had hoarded for that purpose; little it was, since Witherspoon's necessities drove him to embezzle our funds;) and were recalled in a few days by a letter from your father, enclosing one from our mother, which summoned us to her dying bed side. We hastened home, and saw her for the last time. In January, 1788, she died. The sun rose and set; the rivers flowed; the order of Nature went on. This seemed to me at first unnatural and shocking. My mother had been a faithful executrix of my father's will, a faithful steward of the effects committed to her charge, in trust for her children. She left clear accounts and money (not a small sum) in hand. In May, 1788, Theodorick and I were sent to college in New York; and your father came on here to attend the debates of the Convention, on the question of adopting or rejecting the Federal Constitution of 1787. This visit gave rise to the attachment between himself and your mother, which terminated in their marriage, about eighteen months afterwards.

Your father joined us in New York. He was in his nineteenth year, and the most manly youth, and most elegant gentleman that I ever saw. Mrs. Bingham, of Philadelphia, used to send him invitations to her parties, and he often went from New York to that city to them!—Yet he was neither debauched, nor dissipated. He was regular, studious, above low company of any sort, "the great vulgar or the small;" his apparel," according to Lord Burleigh's advice, was "costly, not fine;" and you might see in his old attendant, Syphax, whom he carried with him to New York, that his master was [illegible] yet recovered from the shock of the Revolution, it was just emerging out of chaos.—The Professor of Humanity, (Cochrane, now in the college of [illegible]) Irishman, educated at Trinity College, Dublin, and a most accomplished scholar. With him I entered as a private pupil, paying eight dollars a month, (out of my own allowance for clothes,) for the privilege. I had devoted the fall vacation at Princeton, (1787) to an attempt at regaining my Greek; and now (July, 1788,) burning with the thirst of knowledge, (which I was not permitted to slake at the fountain of Nassau,) and emulous of literary distinction, I sat seriously to work, and was greatly encouraged by my tutor, who was, or affected to be, amazed, at the rapidity of my progress. To my irreparable loss, he left college about two or three months after I had entered myself as his private pupil. Your father's return to Virginia left me without a friend. "Where," you will ask, "was my uncle Theodorick?" Alas! my poor brother differed in every respect from your noble father. Of all things in the world, he detested most a book. Devoted to pleasure and "fun," as he termed it, he not only set me a bad example, but, with his dissolute companions, absolutely prevented me from reading. Often have they forced the door of my study, and tossed the books over the floor, sometimes out of the window. In two years, he undermined his constitution, and destroyed his health forever; and after lingering a long time, a mere skeleton of himself, he died at Bizarre, just before the birth of your brother St. George. My guardian—for under the impulse of the ascendancy he had acquired over me, I had chosen Mr. Tucker as such—was so scanty in his supplies, that I became necessitous; of course, unhappy; and [why should I conceal it?] gradually fell into the habits and way of life of my unfortunate brother,—with this difference, that I continued to read, but books of amusement only, enervating and almost destroying my intellectual powers, and vitiating my taste. Your father was married on the last day of the year 1789: and in the summer following Theodorick and I left New York for Virginia.

In consequence of my mother's death, her husband left Matoax, to reside in Williamsburg; where Edmund Randolph, just appointed Attorney General of the United States, at that time lived. He proposed to Mr. Tucker, that I should study law under him; accordingly I went to Philadelphia in the month of September, 1790, the year of the removal of Congress from New York. I had seen the old Congress expire, and the new one rise like a Phenix from its ashes. I saw the coronation [such in fact it was] of General Washington, in 1789, and heard Ames and Madison, when they first took their seats on the floor of the House of Representatives. Congress met at Philadelphia and Mr. Randolph was too much engrossed by politics and his own necessities, to think of me. He too, embezzled the funds which

* This letter was written, it will be perceived, before Mr. Randolph's supposed conversion. As illustrative of the general facts above stated, we quote the following anecdote from the S. S. Journal—"The late John Randolph, some years since, addressed himself to an intimate friend in terms something like the following: 'I used to be called a Frenchman, because I took the French side in politics; and though this was unjust, yet the truth is, I should have been a French atheist, if it had not been for one recollection, and that was the memory of the time when my departed mother used to take my little hands in hers, and cause me on my knees to say, Our Father which art in heaven.'"

(*See facing page*) *The Harbinger*, a weekly newspaper published by Isaac C. Patridge, "under the supervision of the Professors of the University," first appeared on 27 August 1833. During the little more than a year of its existence it published a wide variety of reports on topics ranging from a storm at sea off the North Carolina coast to the rotation of crops. An account of marl beds appeared in one issue while another contained poetry. Perhaps the lack of subscribers spelled the fate of this paper. At any rate, before the end of December 1834 publisher Patridge announced the opening of a hotel in Chapel Hill. Another paper, the *Columbian Repository*, began publication in June 1836, but it seems to have ceased publication before the beginning of winter.

William Hawkins Polk (1815–62), younger brother of President Polk, was a student at the University, 1832–33. He was United States chargé d'affaires in Naples, 1845–47, and served as a major in the United States Army during the war with Mexico. Later he was a member of Congress.

The much respected and loved President Caldwell died on 27 January 1835 and was buried in the middle of the cemetery adjacent to the campus. At the behest of the members of the Philanthropic Society a short while earlier Alfred S. Waugh, a sculptor, made a plaster cast of Caldwell and this bust was the result of Waugh's work.

Minutes of the meeting of the Board of Trustees on 5 December 1835 when David L. Swain was elected president of the University.

David Lowry Swain (1801–68) of Buncombe County, recently retired governor of North Carolina who had been a student at the University briefly in 1822, was elected president of the University in 1835. He had been a member of the Board of Trustees since 1831 and continued a member until shortly before his death. During the third of a century in which Swain presided over the affairs of the University many important events occurred on campus, the student body and the faculty grew in numbers, and many new buildings were erected.

John Berry (1798–1870) and his wife Elizabeth
Vincent, from an original daguerreotype. Berry
was a native of Hillsborough who received training
as a brickmason but became a builder and architect. He was employed by the University at various
times from 1836 until 1863 as a contractor and
builder. Smith Building, first a library and ballroom but later the Playmakers Theatre, erected in
1851, is his most noted work on the campus. Berry
was a member of the General Assembly and of the
Secession Convention of 1861 in which he first
supported a declaration of independence from the
United States before signing the ordinance of
secession.

Jesse D. Graves (1819–84) was a student at the
University, 1837–38, but gave up his pursuits in
Chapel Hill to study art in Paris. He was an artist
of recognized ability and this is a self portrait that
he painted in 1845. Many of his paintings were lost
at sea in a storm on his return voyage, and his own
life was almost lost. He turned from art to medicine
and became an outstanding physician.

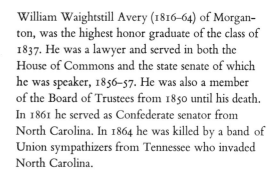

William Waightstill Avery (1816–64) of Morganton, was the highest honor graduate of the class of 1837. He was a lawyer and served in both the House of Commons and the state senate of which he was speaker, 1856–57. He was also a member of the Board of Trustees from 1850 until his death. In 1861 he served as Confederate senator from North Carolina. In 1864 he was killed by a band of Union sympathizers from Tennessee who invaded North Carolina.

Manuel Fetter (1809–88), a native of Lancaster, Pennsylvania, who was educated by the Reverend William Augustus Muhlenberg, was appointed professor of Greek in 1838 and served until the University was reorganized in 1868. He was very popular in spite of his strictness, and he particularly enjoyed a good pun. When the former faculty members were replaced during the Reconstruction period, he left to conduct classical schools at various places in North Carolina but was residing with his son in Virginia at the time of his death. He was buried by the side of his wife in the Chapel Hill cemetery.

George R. Davis (1820–96) was graduated from the University in 1838 with an A.B. degree, and in 1882 the LL.D. degree was bestowed upon him. He was an outstanding attorney and served in the Confederate Senate, 1862–64, and as attorney general for the Confederacy, 1864–65. From 1879 until 1894 he was a member of the Board of Trustees.

The commencement exercises in 1840 included an oration in Latin on an unannounced subject plus several others on topics of contemporary concern.

This table showing the number of matriculates and the number of graduates from 1798 through 1840 is from the trustees minutes 22 December 1840.

The program for the commencement exercises in 1841 was printed in Latin and the names of the graduates, in some cases, were Latinized. Among the graduates of that year were a number who later became distinguished in the state. John Willis Ellis of this class was governor of North Carolina in 1861 when he made the famous reply to the United States secretary of war: "You can get no troops from North Carolina."

Calvin H. Wiley (1819–87), of Guilford County, was graduated from the University in 1840. He received the M.A. degree in 1845 and the honorary Doctor of Divinity degree in 1881. He was a lawyer for a brief time, served in the General Assembly, 1850–52, and in 1853 he became the first superintendent of common schools of the state, attaining distinction through the establishing of a superior system of public education. The position was abolished after the Civil War and Wiley, an ordained Presbyterian minister, became an agent of the American Bible Society, living first in Tennessee and from 1874 in Winston, North Carolina. He was a leading figure in the organization of the graded schools of Winston and was an active trustee of the University from 1874 until his death.

Robert Rufus Bridgers (1819–88), of Edgecombe County, was graduated from the University in 1841 with first distinction. He became a member of the House of Commons in 1844 for the first of several terms, was a member of the Confederate Congress, 1864–65, and served as a member of the Board of Trustees, 1858–68, 1879–88. He was president of the Wilmington and Weldon Railroad, a planter, manufacturer, and lawyer.

Josiah G. Turner (1820–1901) was a student in the University, 1842–43. He served in the General Assembly in the 1850s, and as captain of an Orange County company in the Civil War. Wounds prevented him from continuing in the army, and he became a member of the Confederate Congress in 1864. The next year, at the end of the war, he was elected to the United States Congress but was denied a seat.

A Society of the Alumni of the University was organized on 31 May 1843 when thirty-one graduates of classes ranging from as early as that of 1801 to as recent as 1842 gathered in Gerrard Hall for this purpose. The incumbent governor, John Motley Morehead of the class of 1817, was present. This is the first page of the minutes of that meeting.

ORDER OF PROCESSION, &c.

ON

THE DAY PRECEDING COMMENCEMENT.

June 5th, 1844.

THE bell will ring at 9 o'clock, as the signal for assembling in front of the South Building. At 10, the procession, formed in double file, will move toward the Chapel in the following order:

1. Musicians.
2. Members of the Freshman class.
3. Members of the Sophomore class.
4. Members of the Junior class.
5. Graduating class.
6. Alumni.
7. Citizens of Chapel Hill and its vicinity.
8. Strangers and Visiters.
9. Teachers of Schools.
10. Parents and Guardians.
11. Clergy.
12. Faculty.
13. Trustees.
14. Governor of the State and President of the University.
15. Orator of the day, attended by Committee.

Every member of the College will be expected to join in the procession. While passing the monument of President Caldwell, the members of the procession will uncover their heads. Upon reaching the Chapel, the double file will open, and the procession enter in reversed order. There must be no passing in or out, except during the intervals of the exercises. No umbrellas must be raised in the procession; and neither sticks nor canes be used in applauding the speakers.

The entire space on the right of the aisle leading from the front entrance will be occupied by the Trustees, Faculty and Students of the University. The centre tier of boxes to the left will be reserved exclusively for the Ladies. The range of seats on each side of this tier, and the galleries, will be appropriated to the accommodation of visiters.

The Marshall and his Assistants, stationed immediately in front of the seats occupied by the Ladies, will be prompt and vigilant in pointing all persons to their appropriate places; and the authorities of the College will expect and require ready obedience to their commands.

VIRGINIUS H. IVY, Marshall.
SAMUEL J. CALVERT,
EUGENE J. HINTON, } Assistant
THOMAS T. SLADE, } Marshals.
LEONIDAS TAYLOR,

The faculty minutes of 1 June 1843 contain a record of the work of the members of the senior class of that year. The grading scale was "vg"—very good, "g"—good, "vr"— very respectable, "r"—respectable, "t"—tolerable, "b"—bad, and "vb"—very bad. None of the class merited the grade "vb."

The elaborate plans for the procession to the chapel at commencement in 1844 included some very specific rules designed to regulate the behavior of those present.

Charles Force Deems (1820–93), a native of Baltimore and an ordained Methodist minister, was professor of rhetoric and logic, 1842–48, but he also taught Latin and Bible. He afterwards served various churches in North Carolina, edited church papers, and wrote books on religious subjects. For five days just before the Battle of Gettysburg he preached to Confederate troops. His own son, a native of Chapel Hill and a Confederate officer, was killed at Gettysburg. In 1879 the Reverend Mr. Deems established a loan fund for needy students at the University in memory of his son. This is the oldest such fund at the University and it is still available. In 1865 he moved to New York City where he was minister of The Church of the Strangers. Cornelius Vanderbilt in 1870, because of his admiration of Deems, presented him with a church. In 1881 William H. Vanderbilt, son of Cornelius, enlarged the Deems Fund at the University by a substantial gift.

Members and selected friends of the senior class in 1844 received this engraved invitation to a ball at the Eagle Hotel "complimentary to the Graduating Class."

The minutes of a faculty meeting on 2 August 1844 contain a class schedule. There were no Saturday classes but a 4 o'clock session was scheduled for each Sunday afternoon, undoubtedly for religious instruction. Regular classes were also scheduled for 7 o'clock in the morning, Tuesday through Friday.

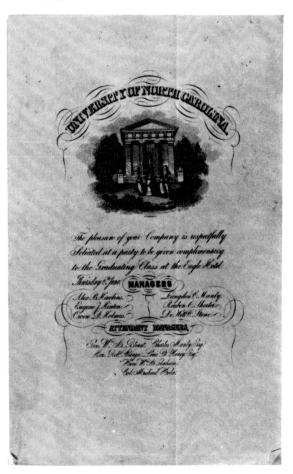

Alexander Jackson Davis (1803–92), recently of the New York architectural firm of Town and Davis (which had designed the North Carolina state capitol), was employed by President Swain in 1844 to aid in enlarging and beautifying the campus. Davis was responsible for enlarging Old East and Old West and for designing Smith Hall (Playmakers Theatre). He also drew up plans for campus walks and for plantings to conceal such undesirable views as the stables behind the hotel on Franklin Street adjacent to the campus. Davis served the University at intervals until just a year or two before the Civil War.

This etching is the earliest known general view of the campus. It dates from soon after 1837, when Gerrard Hall was completed.

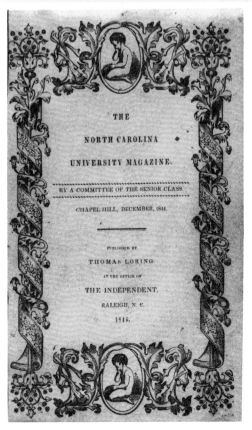

The senior class in 1844 undertook to establish a literary magazine for the University, but after a dozen issues it expired for lack of financial support. During its short life, however, it published a number of interesting pieces including a poem on the "Auld Poplar Tree in the Campus" in which reference is made to the "Trustee fathers" who visited it when they were about "to choose a place for Learning's seat."

Professor William Horn Battle (1802–79), a graduate with the class of 1820, had a distinguished legal career before he returned to Chapel Hill in 1845 as professor of law. He was a judge of the supreme court at the time and in addition to practicing law he had previously served as a superior court judge, been a member of the General Assembly, and a reporter for the supreme court. He continued on the bench until 1865 when, in the disordered times following the Civil War, his seat on the bench was declared vacated. Three years later he resigned his professorship to take up the practice of law in Raleigh. When his son, Kemp P. Battle, became president of the University, Professor Battle returned to Chapel Hill to take up his former position in which he continued until his death.

Professor Charles Phillips (1822–89), a graduate in the class of 1841, remained at the University as a tutor of mathematics until 1853, when he became professor of civil engineering. He held this post until the reorganization of the University in 1868, when he joined the faculty at Davidson College. With the reopening of the University in 1875, he returned to Chapel Hill and served as professor of mathematics until he retired in 1879 because of ill health. A highly respected citizen, he continued to reside in Chapel Hill during the remaining ten years of his life.

Judge William Horn Battle's law office in the yard of his home was the scene of the first law classes in the University. Students in the University who read law under him did so with the approval of the faculty but they paid an additional fee of $50.00 to Battle. Their course required two and a half years to complete. Judge Battle also had an "independent" class whose members were not associated with the University; they paid a fee of $100 and completed their course in two years.

The second President's House stood near the location of the present one at the southeastern corner of Franklin Street and Raleigh Road. It had been the home of Mrs. Helen Hogg Hooper when she married President Joseph Caldwell in 1809, and he moved in with her. The University acquired the house only after his death in 1835, but his successor, David L. Swain, chose to live from 1835 to 1849 in the Thomas Taylor house, which stood just across Raleigh Road on the site of present Spencer Hall. In the latter year, however, Swain decided to move into the University-owned house and lived there until he was removed from office in 1868. This house burned on Christmas morning 1886. The Taylor house was acquired by the University at some later time in the nineteenth century but was demolished in 1924 to make way for Spencer Hall.

The Episcopal Church, originally called The Church of the Atonement, was constructed with slave labor between 1842 and 1846, adjacent to the campus. Within a few years its name was changed to Chapel of the Cross. Professor William Mercer Green (1798–1889), who taught rhetoric and logic in the University between 1838 and 1849, was the first rector of the church. Several faculty members were instrumental in the formation of the parish. Ladies of the church soon provided nursing service for University students who became ill.

Shortly after the death of President Joseph Caldwell in January 1835 a monument was erected to him on campus near the site of present New West. It was cut from sandstone on a farm near the campus but the quality of the stone was soon discovered to be inadequate for the purpose. When President Polk was on campus in 1847 he and other former students of Caldwell, including Secretary of the Navy John Y. Mason who accompanied the president, proposed that the University alumni subscribe to a fund to provide a new monument. Funds came in slowly, but at commencement in 1858 an impressive ceremony was held to dedicate the new marble obelisk. For many years it was customary for the commencement procession to pass the Caldwell Monument and men uncovered their heads as they passed. President Caldwell, Mrs. Caldwell, and Professor William Hooper, Mrs. Caldwell's son by her first marriage, are buried on the east side of the monument.

President James K. Polk, a graduate of the class of 1818, returned to Chapel Hill in 1847 to attend commencement. For this occasion the trustees directed among other improvements that all of the buildings on campus "be rewashed with a coat of Hydraulic cement and the doors, windows, posts and sills be repainted." Miss Nancy Segur Hilliard, proprietor of the Eagle Hotel, had this annex constructed especially to receive President and Mrs. Polk and their party. The metal plate installed afterwards above the doorway, reads: "Erected to receive Pres. Polk when he revisited his *Alma mater*." The Eagle Hotel, which stood on the present site of Graham Memorial, was burned in November, 1921.

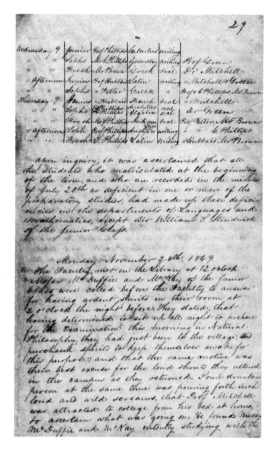

The minutes of a faculty meeting on 23 November 1849 contain a schedule for examinations for the fall term.

Students at the University in the 1840s and 1850s engaged the poetic services of George Moses Horton, a slave belonging to a nearby Chatham County farmer. For 25¢ he would compose short poems that students sent to their sweethearts. For 50¢ Horton would compose an acrostic. He received early encouragement in his literary efforts from Mrs. Caroline Lee Hentz and from President Caldwell. In addition to his earnings as a poet he also sold fruit and vegetables around Chapel Hill. At the end of the Civil War he went North with the Union Army.

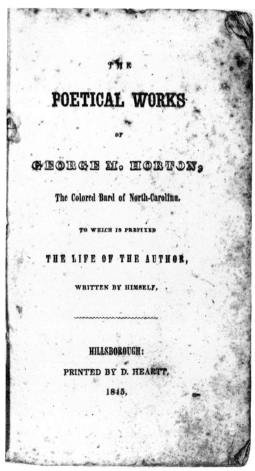

President Swain was deeply interested in beautifying the campus, and Professor Mitchell, who was superintendent of buildings and grounds, convinced him that the rail fences, which frequently fell or were knocked down, might be easily replaced by rock walls. Mitchell, from Connecticut and familiar with "stone fences," personally demonstrated the construction of a section. The bountiful supply of large attractive rocks in the vicinity of Chapel Hill made it possible to enclose the campus with handsome and useful rock walls. Roaming livestock was then kept at a proper distance from class and dormitory. Late in 1844 Mitchell was reimbursed $500 for his expenses and the work of his servants. Some of the old dry rock walls still stand around the old campus.

Watch fobs were popular articles of adornment for the male student of the 1850s, as well as at other times. This one, consisting of a piece of heavy black ribbon and the fragile gold emblem of the Dialectic Society, is among the University keepsakes now in the North Carolina Collection.

Thomas C. Fuller (1832–1901) was a student at the University from 1849 until 1851 when he left to enter business in Fayetteville. He later studied law and became an attorney and a judge. He enlisted in the Confederate Army as a private but was soon elected lieutenant and displayed traits of bravery and gallantry in battle which endeared him to the men under his command. In 1864 he was elected to the Confederate Congress and served until 1865, the youngest man in the congress.

The topics selected by the "declaimers" from the sophomore class at the 1850 commencement offered something
for everybody. With famous speeches by noted men from
the sixteenth to the nineteenth centuries, the leading
young men of the class probably impressed their guests
with their delivery. Except for two of them, who died
soon after graduation, all but one served in the Confederate Army and several went on to hold important positions of responsibility in North Carolina and elsewhere.

A view of Smith Hall from the west made about 1860
shows the windows that gave light to the basement,
which was a reading room. At one time in the 1850s the
basement was used as a chemistry laboratory. At a later
time law classes were held here and at another time
showers for the use of students were installed. The finish
of the building is also apparent here. It was covered with
stucco marked off in squares to resemble large building
stones.

DECLAIMERS

For Wednesday Evening, June 5th.

(Selected from the Sophomore Class.)

1. **WILLIAM M. CARRIGAN,** *(Alamance,)* BADGER, on the Slavery Question.
2. **WILLIAM D. BARNES,** *(Florida,)* HOLMES, on the death of Adams.
3. **LEGH R. WADDELL,** *(Pittsboro',)* PHILIPS, on Circulation of the Bible.
4. **JAMES J. SLADE,** *(Georgia,)* Defence of NORMAN LESLIE.
5. **THOMAS H. GILLIAM,** *(Gates Co.,)* Prosecution of same in Moot Court.
6. **JOHN M. DENNIS,** *(S. Carolina,)* WARREN, on the Boston Massacre.
7. **THOMAS C. LEAK,** *(Richmond Co.,)* EVERETT, on the Indian.
8. **THOMAS B. BURTON,** *(Halifax Co.)* STORY, on Classical Learning.
9. **JOSEPH A. MANNING,** *(Virginia,)* CLAY, on his Compromise.
10. **BASIL M. THOMPSON,** *(Chatham, Co.,)* MILTON's Moloch.

Alexander Jackson Davis's sketches for the library and
ballroom. Completed in 1851 and named Smith Hall for
General Benjamin Smith, early benefactor, this building
is one of the most beautiful on campus. The capitals of
the classical columns are carved with ears of corn and
sheaves of wheat. While it housed the small collection of
books comprising the University library it was also used
as a ballroom. Tradition says that at the end of the Civil
War when Union troops occupied Chapel Hill, cavalry
horses were stabled here.

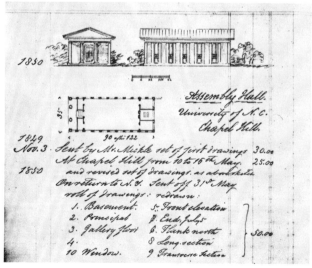

The campus about 1850 clearly showed that the University buildings had been erected in the midst of the woods.

ITY OF NORTH CAROLINA.
Chapel Hill.
vid.L.Swain.L.L.D.President.

(*See facing page*) Elisha Mitchell (1793–1857), a native of Connecticut and a graduate of Yale, was appointed professor of mathematics and natural philosophy in the University of North Carolina through the interest of William Gaston, then in Congress. Mitchell reached Chapel Hill in January 1818. He had studied theology in Connecticut and soon after he was settled in his new position he was ordained by the Orange Presbytery, and he preached in Chapel Hill for the remainder of his life. As a teacher Mitchell excelled and exerted a great influence over many young men who studied under him. In 1825 Mitchell became professor of chemistry, mineralogy, and geology in which capacity he made many expeditions around the state. He published many articles reporting his discoveries and he also prepared a number of manuals for the use of his students. His interest in natural beauty prompted him to supervise the laying of rock walls around the campus, and as superintendent of buildings and grounds he was responsible for the planting of trees and shrubs that improved the appearance of the campus. At one time or another, he was also acting president, bursar, magistrate of police, town commissioner, and justice of the peace, to cite but a few of his varied positions in the community. His curiosity about North Carolina took him frequently to the mountains where he was interested in establishing the fact that the highest mountain east of the Mississippi lay in this state and not in New Hampshire. In this he succeeded, but in his ramblings he slipped and fell to his death in a pool of water in June 1857. His body was recovered and later buried atop the peak he had discovered to be the highest in eastern America—now named Mount Mitchell.

Professor Mitchell's watch which he had in his pocket when he fell to his death.

A mortar and pestle from Elisha Mitchell's scientific laboratory are now among the University keepsakes.

A second observatory was built some time after the first was abandoned and burned in 1838. It was located south of the present Phillips Hall, where it stood until about 1900. It was used by Professor Mitchell as an observatory and meteorological laboratory. The instruments acquired by Dr. Caldwell were installed on the third floor where four windows in each side of the roof and two windows at each end permitted observations.

The old hand bell used to signal the changing of classes in the University in the 1850s.

This twentieth century etching by Louis Orr depicts the classic dignity of the building known as the Playmakers Theatre after Smith Hall was remodeled for this purpose in 1924.

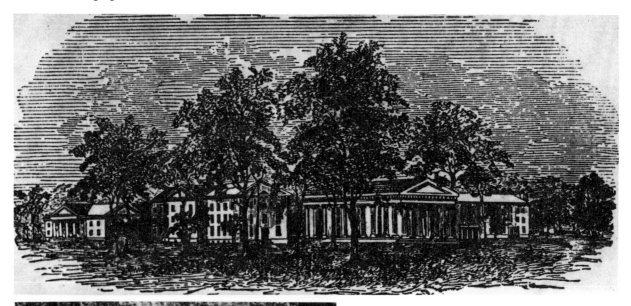

This 1854 view of the campus from the south shows the recently completed Smith Building on the right.

Samuel Field Phillips (1824–1903), member of the class of 1841, joined the faculty in 1854 as a professor of law. This was his office in which he taught both University students and independent students until 1859; it is still standing at the corner of East Franklin and Hillsborough Streets.

An attempt was made in the 1850s to change the orientation of the campus from north to south. This drawing was perhaps intended to sway some who objected. The original engraving is a "pretty" picture in vivid color. The absence of chimneys on South Building is remarkable, since there were more than twenty-five fireplaces in the students' rooms in that building. Perhaps chimneys would have detracted from the neat appearance of the picture.

Nine freshmen, appearing before the faculty on 14 April 1854, were charged with "disturbing the recitation by groaning in concert and rolling marbles along the bench." They confessed "to more or less participation in the disorders," the faculty minutes report, and the previous offenders among the group were suspended. First offenders were treated more leniently—their parents were informed of their conduct.

(*Above*) This view, published in 1855, shows three young trees planted in a row before Old East and three more before Old West. They perhaps were the results of President Swain and Professor Mitchell's efforts to beautify the campus, and may be cited as a precedent for the late twentieth century custom of planting trees in a row. In this case, however, old trees were left standing, whereas in the 1970s the suggestion has been made that any trees not in a straight row are declared diseased and soon removed.

(*Below*) This view of the campus as it appeared about 1852 suggests that the campus grass was not well kept. There appears to be a bench under one of the trees in front of South Building. The lightning rods attached to the chimneys of South Building were a practical safeguard that was popular at the time. The wooden belfry near the center of the small campus was burned in 1856 as a prank by a group of students.

Zebulon Baird Vance (1830–94) was a student at the University, 1851–52, and during part of this time was editor of the *University Magazine* to which he contributed many unsigned articles. He served in Congress from 1858 until the eve of the Civil War. During the war he was governor, 1862–65, and afterwards again from 1877 until 1879. He also served in the Confederate Army as a colonel. After the war he was a senator from North Carolina during the period 1879–94. At the end of the war he addressed the students on "The Duties of Defeat" in which he made an eloquent plea for the reestablishment of peace and good relations among all of the people of the country. In 1875 when contributions were being sought to enable the University to reopen Vance contributed $100. In 1890 he was awarded the honorary LL.D. degree by the University.

William Bingham (1835–73) was graduated with first honors in the class of 1856. He joined his father in conducting the Bingham School near Hillsborough and served as a principal from 1865 until his death. During the Civil War he conducted the school as a military academy and held the rank of colonel in the militia. Bingham was the author of popular Latin and English textbooks that were used in many schools in North Carolina.

Chapel Hill was a healthy place and apparently few students became ill. For those who did need attention, however, help was at hand. Students nursed each other or were nursed by Leroy Couch, a Chapel Hill resident, until members of the family could come. Faculty wives and ladies from the village also helped. The ladies of the Episcopal Church also provided this service. Finally, in 1858, an infirmary, called "The Retreat" by students, was erected on the lot where Spencer Hall now stands, just east of the Chapel of the Cross. It was a small two-room structure designed by Alexander J. Davis, the architect of more impressive buildings on campus, and served its purpose for thirty-six years.

William Badham, Jr. (1835–73) from Chowan County served as a captain in the Confederate Army and later practiced law in Edenton.

Daniel Iverson Brooks (1832–56) from Forsyth County died two years later.

John Williams Graves (1836–72) from Caswell County was a captain in the Confederate Army and afterwards practiced law.

Joseph Adolphus Engelhard (1832–79) entered the University from Mississippi but remained in North Carolina where he became a lawyer and journalist. He was a major in the Confederate Army and served as secretary of state, 1877–79. The town of Engelhard in Hyde County was named for him.

The class of 1854 produced a little book that must be considered a forerunner of a class annual. Charcoal sketches were made of each member and published, one to a page. There was no printed text, only pictures, and those shown here are typical of the group.

William Leak Ledbetter (1831–70) from Anson County was a physician and served as a captain in the Confederate Army.

William Stephens Long (1831–70) from Yanceyville became a planter and a civil engineer.

John Duncan Shaw (1833–1913) from Richmond County was a lawyer and served as a major in the Confederate Army.

James Allen Wright (1836–62) from Wilmington was a captain in the Confederate Army and lost his life at the Battle of Mechanicsville in June 1862.

Saturday. Jan. 27th. 1855.

The Faculty met at 10 o'clock. A.M.
Messrs Crump, Gaines, Hargrave, W. Lea, Ringo, Swain and Young appeared before them. A drinking party given by the friends of the candidates for the offices of Marshall and Managers of the Ball at the next commencement, was discovered by the Faculty at 10 o'clock yesterday evening to be holding its revels in the South Building. After dispersing the party, the Faculty immediately visited the students rooms to ascertain the condition of the young men. The above mentioned students were believed to be more or less intoxicated. They were now called upon to make answer to the charge.

Messrs Crump, Gaines and Hargrave were found to have participated in the drinking of spirits, but were not convicted of intoxication. The other four according to their own statements and the testimony of the Profs who saw them, were guilty of intoxication and suspended three weeks. Letters to the parents of the three former were directed to be written.

Mr Patrick was summoned to appear with the rest and found by Prof C. Phillips to be too much intoxicated this morning to come and answer the charge of being intoxicated last night.

The Faculty adjourned
A. G. Brown clk

On Friday night, 26 January 1855, friends of the candidates for the posts of marshal and managers of the coming commencement ball were discovered to be holding "revels" in South Building. After the young men were dispersed by the faculty, the faculty called on them in their rooms where they were found "to be more or less intoxicated." At a faculty meeting the following morning four students who admitted to being drunk were suspended for three weeks. One reveler, David Settle Patrick, was found by the faculty "to be too much intoxicated this morning to come and answer the charge of being intoxicated last night." Yet the same Patrick, in 1869, became a member of the University faculty as professor of Latin language and literature and bursar.

The report submitted to parents at the end of the term in 1857 contained two pages. On the first page was general information about an act designed to regulate sources of possible temptation to students and other efforts to control student behavior. Entries on the second page informed the parents of the conduct and scholarship record of their son. In this case Richard Stanford Webb of the class of 1859 was reported absent from prayers sixteen times, yet he became a Methodist minister and served as a chaplain in the Confederate Army.

UNIVERSITY OF NORTH CAROLINA,
Chapel Hill, June 12, 1857.

Dear Sir:
Permit me to request your immediate and earnest attention to the provisions of the Revised Statute in relation to the University.

AN ACT CONCERNING THE UNIVERSITY.
Chapter 113.

1. Any license, granted to retail spirituous liquor, wine or cordials at Chapel Hill, or within two miles thereof, shall be void. ,
2. No person shall erect, keep, maintain or have at Chapel Hill, or within two miles thereof, any tippling house, establishment or place, for the sale of wine, cordials, spirituous or malt liquor.
3. No person in the State, without permission in writing from the President of the University, or some member of the Faculty, shall sell, or offer to sell or deliver to any Student of the University, or to any other person, any cordial, wine, spirituous or malt liquor for the purpose of being used, or with knowledge that the same will be used, at Chapel Hill, or within two miles thereof by any such Student.
4. No person, at or within two miles of Chapel Hill, shall give or furnish any electioneering treat or entertainment.
5. No person shall set up, keep or maintain at Chapel Hill, or within five miles thereof, any public billiard table, or other public table of any kind, at which games of chance or skill, by whatever name called may be played.
6. No person, without permission in writing obtained therefor from the President of the University, or some member of its Faculty, seven days beforehand, shall exhibit at Chapel Hill, or within five miles thereof, any theatricals, sleight of hand or equestrian performances, or any dramatic recitations or representations, or any rope or wire dancing, natural or artificial curiosities, or any concert, serenade or performance in music, singing or dancing.

7. Any person who shall offend against any of the provisions of this chapter, hereinbefore recited, shall be deemed guilty of a misdemeanor.
8. Any contract or agreement by any Student of the University, being then a minor, with any shopkeeper, merchant, trader or other person, upon the sale of any wine, cordial, spirituous or malt liquor, or of any goods, wares or merchandise, or any article of trade, or with the keeper of any livery stable, shall be void, unless the same, if made at or within two miles of Chapel Hill, be made under the written permission of the President of the University, or some member of its Faculty; or if made at a greater distance from Chapel Hill, under the written consent of the person who may have the control and authority over such Student.
9. Every contract made with a Student of the University, contrary to the provisions of the preceding section, shall be void, and may be avoided on account of any of the matters therein contained, on the plea of the great alienage: on the trial whereof, if it appear that the defendant was, at the time of the alleged contract, a Student of the University, it shall be presumed that he was, at the making thereof, a minor.
10. Every such contract shall be incapable of being confirmed, and any promise or obligation given by such Student, after his arrival at full age shall be void.

To give full sanction and efficacy to the provisions of the criminal law, the Trustees have ordained, that any Student who may be seen publicly intoxicated, or in whose room ardent spirits may be found, shall be forthwith suspended or dismissed, as the circumstances of the case may seem to require. This ordinance has been and will be faithfully carried into execution in every instance of ascertained violation.

The merchants of Chapel Hill, with a unanimity highly creditable to them, have announced their determination to abandon the credit system heretofore pursued, and to sell goods to Students for cash paid upon the delivery of the articles or on an order from the parent or guardian. The Faculty have confidence, that this pledge will be faithfully redeemed, and that there is no danger that reckless expenditures will be encouraged by them. With respect to shopkeepers, confectioners and itinerant dealers, they are not authorized to give any assurances, and parents and guardians must adopt such precautionary measures as they may deem proper.

If you wish therefore that no contracts shall be entered into, here, in your name or on your account, please say so in a written communication to the Bursar, and make such remittances, to him from time to time, as may be indispensable, to meet necessary expenditures. Your silence upon the subject will be regarded as an intimation that no particular supervision upon his part is expected or desired.

The Rev. Elisha Mitchell, D. D., is the Bursar of the Institution. He will receive any sum of money that you may remit to him for the purpose, pay the tuition, board, and other necessary expenses, without any charge to you, for commissions, and transmit an account of expenditures at the close of each session.

* Every Student is required to attend Prayers thirteen times a week, and Divine Worship in the College Chapel, in the forenoon of every Sabbath. The Freshmen and Sophomores have fifteen, the Juniors seventeen, and the Seniors fourteen Recitations a week. All absences, whether unavoidable or not, are recorded, and a very simple computation will show the proportion of duties performed or omitted.

During the half-session, which closed on Friday evening last, (a period of ten weeks,) Mr. _R. St. Webb_ has been absent from Prayers _16_ times, from Recitations _2_ times, and from attendance on Divine Worship _1_ times— None of these absences, _from Prayers,_ from Recitations, and _____ from Divine Worship, were unavoidable, but were purposely repeated, by permission to visit his friend at home.

His relative grade of scholarship in his class *is respectable in composition & Mathematics, very respectable in Latin, good in the other departments.*

With respect to the necessary expenses of a Student, the Faculty entertain the opinion, that exclusive of the supplies of clothing ordinarily obtained from home, more than three hundred dollars a year is not necessary either to the comfort or reputation of any one.

Yours, very respectfully,

DAVID L. SWAIN, *President.*

page 80

Student behavior became such a serious problem that the trustees, on 4 January 1856, adopted an ordinance prohibiting students from keeping dogs and various forms of weapons either on campus or in Chapel Hill.

Ordinances.
Be it Ordained &c
No Student shall keep a dog or fire arms, or gunpowder. He shall not carry, keep, or own, at the College, or within the village of Chapel Hill a Bowie knife, Dirk, Sword, Sword Cane, or other deadly weapon: nor shall he use fire arms without permission from the President: And if any Student shall offend herein he shall be suspended for a period not less than three weeks, or be dismissed, at the discretion of the Faculty.

William J. Martin (1839–96), a native of Richmond and a graduate of the University of Virginia, joined the University faculty in 1857 as successor to Professor Elisha Mitchell. As professor of chemistry, mineralogy, and geology, he increased the laboratory work offered in these sciences. In 1861 he was granted a leave of absence to serve in the Confederate Army and rose to the rank of lieutenant colonel. He returned to his teaching duties in 1865 but resigned in 1867 just before the difficulties of the Reconstruction. He taught briefly in Tennessee and then joined the faculty of Davidson College. President Kemp P. Battle described Professor Martin as "one of the most lovable men this State ever had."

This daguerreotype from the Hamilton family papers in the Southern Historical Collection is the earliest known view of the student body. In 1853 there were fifty-nine students enrolled; in 1854 there were sixty; in 1857, seventy-one. The photo is undated, but since it shows fifty-eight young men, it may have been made in any of those years.

The class of 1859 apparently was the next after 1854 to issue a collection of portraits. By then it was possible to use a photographic process with the pictures printed on thin sensitized paper and bound together in a purple leather cover. These four are rather better than the average photograph in this little book as most of them are so faded that they cannot be satisfactorily copied today.

Robert Walker Anderson (1838–64) was from Wilmington and received the A.B. degree in 1858. He remained in Chapel Hill as a tutor in Greek and it apparently was for this reason that his picture appears with the class of 1859. In 1861 he was granted a leave of absence for service in the Confederate Army. He was killed at the Battle of the Wilderness.

Edward H. Davis from Elizabeth City served as a lieutenant in the Confederate Army.

Lucius Frierson was born in 1840 in Columbia, Tennessee, served with the troops from his native state during the Civil War, and became a banker in Birmingham, Alabama.

Charles W. McClammy (1839–96) was from New Hanover County. He served as a major in the Confederate Army and later was a member of the North Carolina General Assembly and of congress.

Diploma awarding the M.A. degree in 1856 to Needham Bryan Cobb, A.B., 1854, teacher and Baptist minister. Graduates of the University who were active in learned professions might apply for this degree several years after graduation.

New East Building

As early as 1855 the trustees began planning two new large dormitories since the existing facilities could accommodate less than half the student body. New East and New West Buildings, adjacent to the two older buildings with similar names, were completed in 1859. William Percival, a Richmond architect, planned these new buildings, and they attracted considerable attention because furnaces in the basement of each building were to provide hot water heat to each room. The idea was good, but this particular system was faulty and never worked properly. Makeshift flues had to be added as shown in this picture of New West.

New West Building

1. JAS. P. COFFIN, Batesville, Ark.
2. JAS. G. WHITFIELD, Whitfield, Ala.
3. SXDNEY SMITH, Dallas, Texas.
4. Mrs. WELLS THOMPSON, Bay City, Texas.
5. Mr. WELLS THOMPSON, Bay Ciry, Texas.

6. JNO. M. FLEMING, Raleigh, N. C.
7. JNO. E. BEASLY, Memphis, Tenn.
8. D. P. McEACHERN, Red Springs, N. C.
9. Dr. J. P. BACOT, Florence, S. C.
10. JAS. P. TAYLOR, Columbia, Texas.

11. R. H. BATTLE, Raleigh, N. C.
   (Only surviving Teacher.)
12. F. D. KOONCE, Richlands, N. C.
13. E. D. FOXALL, Tarboro, N. C.
14. C. N. MORROW, Mebane, N. C.

REUNION OF CLASS OF 1859
— AT —
CHAPEL HILL, N. C., June 1st, 1908.

Twelve members out of eighty-nine who were
graduated in 1859 returned for a class reunion in
1908.

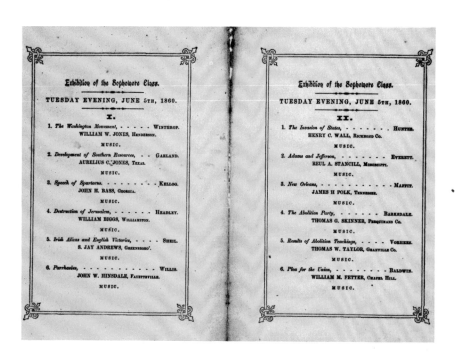

Exhibition of the Sophomore Class.

TUESDAY EVENING, JUNE 5TH, 1860.

I.

1. *The Washington Monument,* . . . . . WINTHROP.
   WILLIAM W. JONES, HENDERSON.
   MUSIC.

2. *Development of Southern Resources,* . . GARLAND.
   AURELIUS C. JONES, TEXAS.
   MUSIC.

3. *Speech of Spartacus,* . . . . KELLOG.
   JOHN H. BASS, GEORGIA.
   MUSIC.

4. *Destruction of Jerusalem,* . . . . . . HEADLEY.
   WILLIAM BIGGS, WILLIAMSTON.
   MUSIC.

5. *Irish Aliens and English Victories,* . . . . SHEIL.
   S. JAY ANDREWS, GREENSBORO'.
   MUSIC.

6. *Parrhasius,* . . . . WILLIS.
   JOHN W. HINSDALE, FAYETTEVILLE.
   MUSIC.

Exhibition of the Sophomore Class.

TUESDAY EVENING, JUNE 5TH, 1860.

II.

1. *The Invasion of States,* . . . . HUNTER.
   HENRY C. WALL, RICHMOND CO.
   MUSIC.

2. *Adams and Jefferson,* . . . . EVERETT.
   REUL A. STANCILL, MISSISSIPPI.
   MUSIC.

3. *New Orleans,* . . . . MAFFIT.
   JAMES H POLK, TENNESSEE.
   MUSIC.

4. *The Abolition Party,* . . . . . . BARKSDALE.
   THOMAS G. SKINNER, PERQUIMANS CO.
   MUSIC.

5. *Results of Abolition Teachings,* . . . VORHEES.
   THOMAS W. TAYLOR, GRANVILLE CO.
   MUSIC.

6. *Plea for the Union,* . . . . BALDWIN.
   WILLIAM M. FETTER, CHAPEL HILL.
   MUSIC.

In view of the conditions of the
times and the approaching Civil
War the topics chosen for their
declamations by members of the
sophomore class in 1860 are
unusually interesting. Only two
of the young men who spoke
on that Tuesday evening in
June remained in Chapel Hill to
complete their work. Most of
them left the campus in 1861 to
join the Confederate Army, but
all of them eventually saw
service. Only one was killed
during the war.

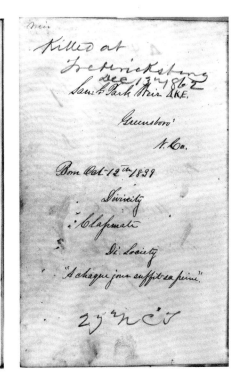

Typical pages from autograph albums of the early
1860s on which someone later recorded the unfortunate fate of two University graduates.

In the absence of a yearbook, autograph books were
popular in the late 1850s and in the 1860s. They
were handsomely bound in colored leather.

This view of the campus made in or soon after
1861 shows the newly completed New East and
New West and the belfry atop South Building
which was completed in September 1861.

A great many alumni of the University served in the Confederate Army. For some of those whose pictures appeared in the class publications of 1854 and 1859, pictures in Confederate uniform are also available. The effects on these young men of a few years, including several at war, become clear when the pictures are seen side by side.

John Barr Andrews, class of 1854, and a captain in the army, was killed at Richmond on 23 July 1863.

Richard Henry Battle, class of 1854, was a lieutenant when this picture of him in uniform was made.

John Marion Gallaway, class of 1854, was a major.

Louis Charles Latham, class of 1859, was a major.

William Laurence Saunders, class of 1854, was a colonel.

The trustees, at a meeting at the Executive Mansion in Raleigh in October 1863, authorized President Swain to correspond with President Jefferson Davis seeking exemption from conscription for University students until the end of the session.

Walter Clark (1846–1924) was graduated from the University in 1864. Before entering the University he had attended a military academy at Hillsborough and at the beginning of the Civil War, when Clark was just fifteen years of age, he was made drillmaster at an army camp near Raleigh. He accompanied troops to war in Virginia, but in 1862 he returned to the classroom. In June 1864 Clark was graduated at the head of his class and was immediately commissioned a major in the Confederate Army. After the war he studied law and practiced that profession. He became a justice of the North Carolina Supreme Court in 1899 and was chief justice from 1902 until his death.

The Civil War brought changes to the University. The student body of hundreds was replaced by a handful—boys under eighteen, young men exempt from service for physical reasons, and wounded veterans. The younger members of the faculty were gone and only old men and clergymen remained. Those left in Chapel Hill were constantly saddened by news of the deaths of former students. Revenues declined drastically, faculty salaries were cut, and there were severe shortages of supplies and workmen. As the war drew to a close the campus must have presented an empty and shabby appearance to one who had known its prewar bustle. Nevertheless, the devastation of battle had not been felt, no buildings had been destroyed, and classes continued in operation. But even greater changes came in the last month of the war.

Confederate cavalry under General Joseph Wheeler entered Chapel Hill on April 14, closely pursued by Federal troops. At first, plans were made to defend the village and campus, and rifle pits were dug on the southern slope of Point Prospect overlooking the road to Raleigh. Reports of the superiority in numbers of approaching Union troops, however, caused General Wheeler to change his mind and abandon his plans. At 8 o'clock on the morning of April 17, the day after Wheeler's departure, the thirty-year-old Union general, Smith B. Atkins, rode into Chapel Hill at the head of four thousand cavalry. Most of the students had left before the occupying troops arrived and classes were discontinued. When commencement exercises were held on 31 May and 1 June 1865 only four of fifteen members of the senior class were present.

Guards from the Federal Army were detailed to protect University property but horses were stabled in the University library, Old West, and South Building. Reports of damage on the campus vary, but apparently there was some. The surrounding countryside was not included in Sherman's agreement to protect the University, and livestock, personal property, and other possessions were freely taken by the occupying forces.

When General Atkins called upon President Swain on 19 April 1865 he met Swain's daughter, Eleanor. There occurred one of the legendary cases of "love at first sight" and in Chapel Hill on August 23 the daughter of the president of the University was married to the Union general whose forces occupied the town and campus. During the ceremony and for a total of three hours, University students tolled the South Building bell and afterwards they hanged President Swain and General Atkins in effigy. The University almost overnight lost many of its old friends and gained a host of powerful enemies. There were some who denounced the University as a stronghold of "unreconstructed Rebels" who abhorred the idea of a return to the Union, and they applauded the apparent destruction of the University because it had been a "pestilential hotbed of slavocracy." On the other hand, to the "unreconstructed Rebels" the marriage of the president's daughter to a Union general indicated that the University was a center of Unionism and disloyalty, or at the very least of people guilty of fraternizing with the enemy.

UNIVERSITY OF NORTH CAROLINA.

ORDER OF PROCESSION

THURSDAY, JUNE 6TH., 1867.

MUSIC.

FRESHMAN CLASS.
SOPHOMORE "
JUNIOR "
CITIZENS.
ALUMNI.
VISITORS.
FACULTY OF THE UNIVERSITY.
GRADUATING CLASS,
TRUSTEES OF THE UNIVERSITY.
GUESTS.
GOVERNOR OF NORTH CAROLINA.
PRESIDENT OF THE UNIVERSITY.
PRESIDENT OF THE UNITED STATES.

The procession will form in front of South Building at 9 1-2 A. M.

No Seats for Gentlemen in the Chapel until the Procession enters it.

J. S. BARLOW.   Chief Marshal.
J. S. BATTLE.
G. G. LATTA.   } Ass't. Marshals.
W. S. PEARSON.

The "unreconstructed Rebels" among the student body enjoyed one last bit of revenge. Without consulting anyone, the managers of the commencement ball on 7 June 1866 named former President Jefferson Davis, Generals W. R. Cox, J. C. Breckinridge, Robert D. Johnson, Robert E. Lee, and Governor Zebulon B. Vance as honorary managers. The names of these high officers in the Confederacy were engraved on the invitations and distributed before word of it got out. President Swain and the trustees were thrown into panic at the thought of what form the reaction against the University might take.

President Andrew Johnson, a native of Raleigh, attended the commencement of 1867 and was well received. He was accompanied by a number of Federal officials who were cordially welcomed and, in turn, spoke kindly of the University. President Johnson was initiated into the Dialectic Society and other officials were accepted in the Philanthropic Society. The admission of General Daniel E. Sickles into the Philanthropic Society, however, was prevented by "a small minority . . . in order to emphasize their hostility to the Reconstruction Acts." Sickles was commander of the military district in which North Carolina had been placed by these acts.

There were only three seniors present to receive their degrees at the commencement of 1866. Other members of their class had previously left to join the army; some had been killed in action; one died in a northern prison; and others had not yet been able to return to the University. The full fury of Reconstruction had not yet struck and sophomores could speak on such topics as "The Bonnie Blue Flag," "Memory of the Confederate Dead," and "Women of the South." Perhaps the final speech of the evening, "Right of a State to choose her Representatives," anticipated events in the immediate future.

The University endowment had been lost as a result of the Civil War, enrollment dropped off afterwards, buildings were falling into disrepair, and the faculty was leaving. In the summer of 1868 Governor W. W. Holden sent a guard of black soldiers to Chapel Hill to take possession of the campus. They used some of the dormitories as stables. Under the new constitution, ratified in March 1868, Governor Holden and the "Reconstruction" board of trustees removed President Swain on 23 July 1868. On 11 August Swain was thrown from his carriage when his unruly horse bolted, and with President Swain's death on 27 August, it has been said, "the deathknell of the antebellum University of North Carolina" was sounded. The new board of trustees appointed Solomon Pool (1832–1901) to be the president of the University. Pool was a graduate of the University in the class of 1853 and had been a member of the mathematics faculty since that year, but his close association with the unpopular Holden and his lack of administrative ability doomed his administration to failure. Trees were cut on campus and used for firewood. A "demonstration farm" was laid out on the land cleared south of South Building. Furnishings, rugs, and books from University buildings were removed to the homes of new faculty members. So few students were on campus in the spring of 1869 that a leading Chapel Hill merchant advised Pool to resign. Pool is said to have replied with defiance: "I would not resign for $50,000. If no whites will come here, I will have negro students." The Reconstruction government had taken over the University, but Reconstruction legislatures provided no financial relief at all. In a period of poverty, with the potential clientele of a Republican-sponsored school likely to come from the poorer classes, it was unlikely that any school that depended on student revenue could succeed.

UNIVERSITY OF NORTH CAROLINA.

SOPHOMORE COMPETITORS.

WEDNESDAY EVENING, JUNE 6th, 1866.

I.

1. Vallandigham on "The Great Civil War",
   FABIUS H. BUSBEE,   Raleigh, N. C.
2. Emmett's Last Speech,
   AUGUSTUS W. GRAHAM,   Hillsboro, N. C.
3. Irish Aliens and English Victories,   (Shield,)
   WILLIAM D. HORNER,   Granville, N. C.
4. Women of the South,   (Anonymous,)
   ISAAC R. STRAYHORN,   Hillsboro, N. C.
5. Memory of the Confederate Dead,   (Hilliard,)
   GEORGE G. LATTA,   Knoxville, Tenn.
6. Eulogy on Lafayette,   (S. S. Prentiss,)
   WILLIAM S. PEARSON,   Morganton, N. C.

II.

1. "The Bonnie Blue Flag,"   (White,)
   EDWIN W. FULLER,   Louisburg, N. C.
2. Address in behalf of the Greeks,   (Lacy,)
   ISAAC H. FOUST,   Randolph, N. C.
3. The Sublime and Beautiful,   (Anonymous,)
   JAMES W. HARPER,   Lenoir, N. C.
4. The Ball at Brussels,   (Byron,)
   J. BURGWYN McRAE,   Savannah, Ga.
5. The Crisis of Life,   (Anonymous,)
   WILLIAM H. S. BURGWYN,   Northampton, N. C.
6. Right of a State to choose her Representatives, (Prentiss,)
   PAUL B. MEANS,   Cabarrus, N. C.

UNIVERSITY OF NORTH CAROLINA.

ORDER OF EXERCISES FOR

COMMENCEMENT DAY.

FORENOON.

THURSDAY JUNE 7th, 1866.

The procession will form in the usual order, in front of the South Building, at 9 A. M. and proceed to Girard Hall, passing the monument of President Caldwell, with uncovered heads.

The annual address before the two Literary Societies will be delivered at 10 A. M.

AFTERNOON.

The procession will form at 3 o'clock and proceed to Girard Hall, and at 4 the Commencement Exercises will begin.

1. PRAYER AND SACRED MUSIC.
2. SALUTATORY ORATION,
   GEORGE SLOVER,   New Berne. N. C.
3. ORATION, SUÆ QUISQUE FORTUNÆ FABER EST.
   ABNER H. ASKEW,   Hertford, Co. N. C.
4. VALEDICTORY ORATION,
   WILLIAM C. RENCHER, Pittsboro, N. C.
5. ANNUAL REPORT TO THE TRUSTEES.
6. CONFERRING DEGREES.
7. BENEDICTION.

R. W. MEANS,   MARSHAL.
J. G. YOUNG,
W. H. REEVES,
G. M. ROSE,

Solomon Pool

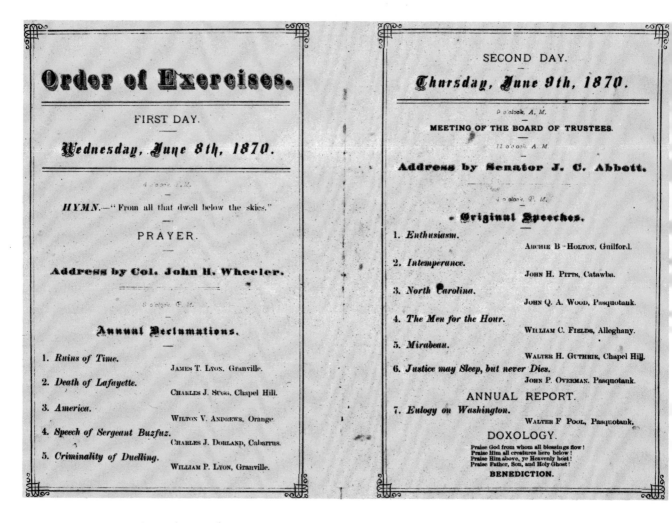

Order of Exercises.

FIRST DAY.

Wednesday, June 8th, 1870.

4 o'clock, P. M.

HYMN.—"From all that dwell below the skies."

PRAYER.

Address by Col. John H. Wheeler.

8 o'clock, P. M.

Annual Declamations.

1. *Ruins of Time.*
   JAMES T. LYON, Granville.
2. *Death of Lafayette.*
   CHARLES J. STGG, Chapel Hill.
3. *America.*
   WILTON V. ANDREWS, Orange.
4. *Speech of Sergeant Buzfuz.*
   CHARLES J. DORLAND, Cabarrus.
5. *Criminality of Duelling.*
   WILLIAM P. LYON, Granville.

SECOND DAY.

Thursday, June 9th, 1870.

9 o'clock, A. M.

MEETING OF THE BOARD OF TRUSTEES.

11 o'clock, A. M.

Address by Senator J. C. Abbott.

4 o'clock, P. M.

Original Speeches.

1. *Enthusiasm.*
   ARCHIE B. HOLTON, Guilford.
2. *Intemperance.*
   JOHN H. PITTS, Catawba.
3. *North Carolina.*
   JOHN Q. A. WOOD, Pasquotank.
4. *The Men for the Hour.*
   WILLIAM C. FIELDS, Alleghany.
5. *Mirabeau.*
   WALTER H. GUTHRIE, Chapel Hill.
6. *Justice may Sleep, but never Dies.*
   JOHN P. OVERMAN, Pasquotank.

ANNUAL REPORT.

7. *Eulogy on Washington.*
   WALTER F. POOL, Pasquotank.

DOXOLOGY.

Praise God from whom all blessings flow!
Praise Him all creatures here below!
Praise Him above, ye Heavenly host!
Praise Father, Son, and Holy Ghost!

BENEDICTION.

At the commencement of 1869 the B.A. degree was conferred on only one student and he was from Chapel Hill, a young man who had attended the University during 1863–65. Commencement exercises were held in 1870 but there is no indication that any degrees were granted. None of the young men whose names appeared as participants ever received degrees from the University. One old faculty member commented that by this time the University had "sunk to the level of an old-field school." The trustees had the good judgment to end the farce. At a meeting in November 1870 it was decreed that all faculty salaries should cease on 1 February 1871. In early January 1871 there were four students on campus, but by January 29 only two remained. On a blackboard in one of the classrooms someone wrote: "February 1, 1871. This old University has busted and gone to hell to-day."

During 1903–4 the northern section of the present Coker Arboretum was laid out and planted by Professor W. C. Coker. The area formerly was swampy and was used as a pasture by local residents but it has now been developed and planted with more than four hundred trees, shrubs, vines, and other plants native to or adapted to North Carolina.

III
1870 to 1920

In 1870 the Democratic party regained control of the state government, and in 1873, by the legislative process, eight amendments to the Constitution of 1868 were adopted and approved by a vote of the people. Among these was one removing the power of the State Board of Education to elect trustees of the University and placing that power in the General Assembly. Two University alumni who were also brothers-in-law are credited with the success of this move in the legislature—Montford McGehee, class of 1841, a Democrat, and Richard C. Badger, class of 1859, a Republican. In January 1874 a new Board of Trustees was elected and many of the trustees who had been removed in 1868 after long years of service were now returned. The new board met in February when former governor William A. Graham was elected president of the board and committees were appointed to undertake the work of reopening the University. Suits at law were instituted to reclaim University property; requests for the contribution of funds were sent out; the University seal, books, and papers were secured; and the campus and buildings were inspected. Under the immediate supervision of Paul C. Cameron work was undertaken to repair the buildings. At a meeting of the trustees in May 1875 the course of study in the University was organized in six "colleges." The first two named were agriculture and engineering and the mechanic arts through which the University qualified for the Land Scrip Fund. The other colleges were natural sciences, literature, mathematics, and philosophy. In June, when repairs were sufficiently along and the promise of funds was materializing, the trustees met again to elect the faculty. Seven were chosen, three of whom, John De-Berniere Hooper, John Kimberly, and Charles Phillips, had been on the faculty earlier. Andrew Mickle, a Chapel Hill merchant who had lost his business during the war, was made bursar. Former governor William A. Graham was offered the presidency but declined because of ill health. Before the end of the summer this loyal and devoted son of the University was dead.

When the trustees met again in June, requirements for admission and the course of study were set, and it was determined that the University would open on the first Monday in September 1875. Meeting again just a few days before the formal opening, the trustees named Dr. Charles Phillips to be chairman of the faculty. Houses were assigned to the married faculty, and those not married were given rooms in the dormitories. The faculty met on September 4 and classes began on the sixth. On September 15 formal ceremonies were held to mark the occasion. The young ladies of Chapel Hill decorated Gerrard Hall, and portraits of the great men of the University were hung on the walls. A band from Salisbury came to Chapel Hill to provide music and numerous distinguished alumni attended. Former governor Vance and Judge William H. Battle, who had earlier been a member of the faculty, participated in the program of the day. The history of the University was reviewed and old times, not strictly history, were recalled. A hymn, written especially for the occasion by Mrs. Cornelia Phillips Spencer, was sung. The Dialectic and Philanthropic Societies were reinaugurated.

The University was poor financially but it was rich in tradition from the past and enthusiasm for the future.

Mrs. Cornelia Phillips Spencer (1825–1908), the daughter of Professor James Phillips, loved Chapel Hill and the University as few have done before her time or since. She was married in 1855 to James Monroe Spencer of Alabama, an honor graduate of the class of 1853. After his death early in 1861, leaving his widow with a small daughter, Mrs. Spencer returned to Chapel Hill. During Reconstruction she devoted her best efforts to bring about "the overthrow of the foul gang that were polluting the University halls and for the restoration of the University to its own." Her personal letters to leaders of the state and her articles and letters in the state press, particularly her regular contributions to the *North Carolina Presbyterian*, had the desired effect. The lion's share of the credit for the reopening of the University in 1875 has always been hers. When a telegram arrived in Chapel Hill for Mrs. Spencer late in March 1875 bringing news of the passage of a legislative bill to give the University the sum of $125,000, which the old Board of Education had lost through bad investments, Mrs. Spencer quickly rounded up some of her friends and they climbed the stairs to the attic of South Building to ring the bell announcing the good news.

The University of North Carolina.

THIS institution will be re-opened on the 1st MONDAY OF SEPTEMBER NEXT, the term endinding 2nd Thursday in June 1876, with a vacation of two weeks at Christmas. It has been re-organized on the eclectic system, combining, however, three curricula of Arts, Science and Agriculture. Instruction will be given in the branches of learning usually taught in the best Colleges. Special instruction provided in Agriculture and the Mechanic Arts. An able faculty has been appointed. The buildings throughly repaired for the reception of several hundred students.

For circulars and explanatory of the above apply to　KEMP P. BATTLE,
Secretary Board of Trustees,
Raleigh, N. C.

An announcement of the reopening of the University appeared in a number of papers in the state. This one is from the *Hillsborough Recorder* of 11 August 1875.

UNIVERSITY
OF
North Carolina.

NOTICE.

ALL persons having books or other articles belonging to the University of North Carolina, or to the Dialectic or Philanthropic Societies, are notified to deliver them at once to Andrew Mickle, Esq., Bursar of the University.

By order of the Board of Trustees.

KEMP P. BATTLE,

july 21 4t.　　　　　　Sec'y.

This notice in the *Hillsborough Recorder* for 21 July 1875 suggests how desperate the search was for University property taken away during the period when the buildings were abandoned.

Francis Donnell Winston (1857–1941) was the first student to enroll in the University in 1875. A native of Windsor, he had attended Cornell the year before and was graduated from the University in 1879. He later practiced law, served in both the house and the senate of the General Assembly, and was lieutenant governor, 1905–9.

Kemp Plummer Battle (1831–1919), a member of the class of 1849 who had been a tutor of mathematics from 1850 until 1854, was made president of the University in 1876. He served until 1891 when he became professor of history, in which position he continued until his death. He had been active among the small group of alumni who took the lead in reopening the University, and his personal canvass of the state for funds among alumni and patriotic men who had never attended the University netted $20,000, which was essential to the reopening. His devotion to the University and its history was deep and sincere and he inspired this same feeling in others. He was the author of a two-volume *History of the University of North Carolina*, published in 1907 and 1912, and based on a careful study of the minutes of the trustees and other sources. All subsequent students of University history have been indebted to him for his pioneering work, as much of what he wrote was based on his personal knowledge or gained through interviews with men and women who had played leading roles in the University's past.

Among the first employees of the University when it reopened in 1875 was Wilson Swain Caldwell. He had been a slave of President Swain before the war and for a time afterwards was known as Wilson Swain. Since his father had been one of President Caldwell's slaves, he later took the surname Caldwell. He was a diligent supporter of the University and was loved and respected by the students. His concern for their welfare was legendary. His skill in lighting fires in their fireplaces before they arose each morning was the envy of many students. He sometimes reported serious infractions of University rules that he observed, but he also knew when to refrain from reporting a friendly game of cards. At his death students appropriated the old discarded Caldwell monument for him. Erected in the western section of the Chapel Hill cemetery, it bears a marble plaque to him and three others of his race who also served the University faithfully.

William Battle Phillips (1857–1918), the son of Professor Charles Phillips, was graduated from the University in 1877, delivering a senior oration on "Women in Politics." He became professor of chemistry in 1879. His Ph.D., awarded in 1883, was the first earned doctorate at the University.

Thomas Dunstan, a Chapel Hill barber who trimmed the locks of many of the students, called himself "Professor of Tonsorial Art." With his horse, Nellie Bly, he also provided essential drayage service between 1875 and 1900, and he operated fish traps jointly with other Chapel Hillians.

SEA-GIFT.

A NOVEL.

BY

EDWIN W. FULLER,

Author of "THE ANGEL IN THE CLOUD."

———•———

NEW YORK:
E. J. HALE & SON, PUBLISHERS,
MURRAY STREET.
1873.

Edwin W. Fuller (1847–76) of Louisburg was a student at the University, 1864–65, and afterwards attended the University of Virginia. He was fond of sports, especially hunting, fishing, and horseback riding, and in both universities he was a member of Delta Psi fraternity. His literary talent was recognized quite early, and he wrote poems and short stories that were published while he was still a student. His novel *Sea-Gift* was written in 1865 when he was eighteen, but it was not published until 1873. It is a moving and nostalgic story of the Civil War, and students returning to the University after it reopened read it eagerly as did those who came after them for many years. Numerous events in Fuller's novel were identified with events that had occurred on the campus and there were even those who thought they recognized University people in his characters. It was a means by which the students could return to a past in which they took pride. Fuller had written this novel when he was about their own age and his early death at the age of twenty-eight added to their empathy with him and the story he told.

By 1878 the faculty had grown to eleven in addition to President Battle. This picture was widely sold among friends and alumni of the University and a number of copies in attractive walnut frames have survived.

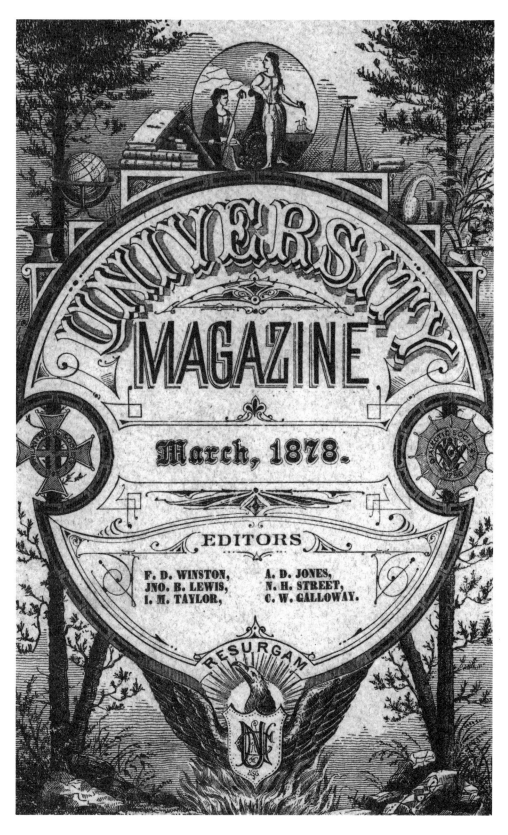

The *University Magazine*, begun in 1844, survived for only a year, but in 1852 it was revived and continued until April 1861 when the Civil War ended many normal pursuits. In 1878 it was begun again with the front cover as shown above. The present *Carolina Quarterly*, now in its twenty-third volume, claims descent from these early publications.

Thomas W. Harris (1839–88) from Chatham County, a graduate of the University in 1869, a Confederate major and M.D. of the University of New York who had spent two years in hospital work at the École de Médecine in Paris, established the School of Medicine in Chapel Hill in 1879. It was essentially a private school, like the law school, but its basic science courses were taught in the University. Dr. Harris was professor of anatomy and materia medica until he resigned in 1885. The School of Medicine was discontinued until 1890 when Dr. Richard H. Whitehead joined the faculty.

Charles Brantley Aycock (1859–1912) was graduated with the class of 1880, but he also studied law during 1879–80. He became superintendent of schools in Wayne County and a practicing attorney. From 1901 until 1905 he was governor of North Carolina and worked so diligently and successfully for public schools that he wrought a far-reaching educational revolution.

Members of the Philanthropic Society, 1883–84.

Zeta Psi fraternity in the spring of 1883. *Front row*, *left to right*: W. S. Wilkinson, W. J. Battle, J. R. Monroe, Max Jackson, L. B. Grandy; *back row*, *left to right*: N. H. D. Wilson, Jr., S. C. Weill, C. T. Grandy, Hayne Davis.

Members of the Dialectic Society, about 1884.

The street through the old campus, now known as Cameron Avenue, must have developed first as a simple path. It is shown here as a very narrow road on one half of a pair of stereoscopic pictures. Note the plank laid between two large trees on the left to make a bench beside the road. The other view shows a somewhat wider street passing in front of Memorial Hall. The street was known as College Avenue until about the time Memorial Hall was completed when it was named Cameron Avenue in honor of Paul C. Cameron. Students often complained in turn of the mud or the dust through which they were forced to walk here. At the west end just beyond the first President's House, the street ended at a field beyond which were woods. It was not until June 1927 that the trustees authorized the paving of Cameron Avenue.

Professor Walter Dallam Toy (1854–1933) became professor of modern languages in 1885 and taught until his death. He also served as secretary of the faculty from 1901. A very popular teacher and author of textbooks, he was director of summer school, chairman of the faculty committee that managed the Commons, and arranged entertainment for the students.

The 1885 baseball team.

Thomas Hume (1836–1912) was professor of English language and literature in the University from 1885 until his retirement in 1907 because of poor health. A native of Virginia and a Baptist minister, he had studied at the University of Virginia where he was one of the founders of the first college Young Men's Christian Association in America, and in Chapel Hill he continued his work with the YMCA. He was described as a lecturer of unusual charm and was much in demand as a public speaker both in North Carolina and elsewhere. It has been said that "he kindled in many a student an interest in literature hitherto unfelt and unexpressed." Under his leadership a Shakspere Club was organized in 1886 and continued until his retirement. For the first year the club also published *The Journal of the Shakspere Club* and afterwards contributed articles on the subject to other student publications. Professor Hume was also one of the founders, in 1893, of the Philological Club, an organization that is still active.

Eben Alexander (1851–1910) was professor of Greek from 1886 until his death, except for the period 1893–97 when he was United States minister to Greece, Rumania, and Serbia. At various times he was also supervisor of the library and served as dean of the University from 1903 until his death. The Eben Alexander Prize in Greek, established in 1887 and awarded annually to the undergraduate who presents the best rendering into English of selected passages of Greek not previously read, is still awarded. At Professor Alexander's death his widow presented the University with some four hundred classical volumes from his library.

Class of 1886.

Phi Kappa Sigma fraternity about 1886. *Front row, left to right*: S. S. Jackson, I. H. Manning, J. H. Baker, Haywood Parker, H. W. Rice; *back row, left to right*: L. M. Bourne, L. J. Battle, J. C. Englehard.

Samuel Sloan, an architect from Philadelphia who had designed the Executive Mansion in Raleigh, was selected to design an auditorium for the University. This is his drawing of the building that soon came to be known as Memorial Hall.

Memorial Hall as it appeared some years after its completion and dedication on 3 June 1885. Paul C. Cameron lent the trustees $8,000 toward its construction, but the sum was never repaid and at his death his heirs were given the privilege of naming ten students to receive free tuition in the University. The original estimate of the cost of this building was $20,000, but as work progressed the cost mounted steadily until it reached $45,000. It was a marvel of beams and trusses, there being no inside support for the roof from the floor, but the building proved to be unsatisfactory acoustically as well as structurally. The slate roof was too heavy and by 1929 the building had become unsafe for use and was abandoned. This building was originally intended to be a memorial to President Swain but plans were changed so that it honored Swain as well as the sons of the University who fell in the service of the Confederacy and "all others connected with the University, who, by honorable lives, in civil or military service, deserve commemoration here." A marble plaque in Swain's memory occupied the highest spot on the wall of the hall while other plaques to other honored men and women surrounded it and occupied other places in Memorial Hall.

ROLL OF CONFEDERATE DEAD
OF THE UNIVERSITY OF
NORTH CAROLINA.
1821.
LEONIDAS POLK, LIEUTENANT-GENERAL.
1832.
CHARLES C. NELMS, LIEUTENANT-COLONEL.
1834.
WILLIAM W. AVERY, A VOLUNTEER.
1835.
CLARKE M. AVERY, COLONEL.
1836.
LUCIUS J. JOHNSON, MAJOR.
OLIVER H. PRINCE, CAPTAIN.
1837.
ISHAM W. CARROTT, BRIGADIER-GENERAL.
THOMAS RUFFIN, COLONEL.
1838.
LAWRENCE O'B. BRANCH, BRIGADIER-GENERAL.
THOMAS H. LANE, SERGEANT.
GASTON MEARES, COLONEL.
1839.
CLEMENT G. WRIGHT, LIEUTENANT-COLONEL.
1840.
ROBIN AP C. JONES, CAPTAIN.
JAMES H. McNEILL, COLONEL.
1841.
JOSIAH E. BRYAN, PRIVATE.
TRISTRIM L. SKINNER, MAJOR.
THOMAS T. SLADE, CAPTAIN.
1842.
WILLIAM L. JOHNSON, CAPTAIN.
1843.
JOHN A. BENBURY, CAPTAIN.
EDWIN L. DUSENBURY, PRIVATE.
PETER G. EVANS, COLONEL.
ELIAS C. HINES, CORPORAL.
J. JOHNSTON PETTIGREW, BRIGADIER-GENERAL.
THOMAS I. SHARP, CAPTAIN.

JOHN H. STONE, PRIVATE.
JOHN H. WHITAKER, MAJOR.
1844.
JAMES J. IREDELL, MAJOR.
EDWARD M. SCOTT, CAPTAIN.
1845.
GEORGE T. BASKERVILLE, CAPTAIN.
EDWARD MALLETT, LIEUTENANT-COLONEL.
JOHN A. WHITFIELD, CAPTAIN.
1846.
JOEL C. BLAKE, CAPTAIN.
1847.
GEORGE B. ANDERSON, BRIGADIER-GENERAL.
ISAAC E. AVERY, COLONEL.
JOHN A. AVIRETT, CAPTAIN.
JAMES CHALMERS, PRIVATE.
BENJAMIN R. HUSKE, MAJOR.
JOHN R. WADDILL, LIEUTENANT.
1848.
CHARLES E. BELLAMY, SURGEON.
THOMAS M. GARRETT, COLONEL.
JOHN H. McDADE, CAPTAIN.
LEMON RUFFIN, PRIVATE.
MILTON A. SULLIVAN, CAPTAIN.
WILLIAM M. WALKER, CAPTAIN.
1849.
JAMES F. BELL, COLOR SERGEANT.
WILLIAM M. CARRIGAN, LIEUTENANT.
GAVIN H. LINDSAY, LIEUTENANT.
JAMES T. McCLENNAHAN, SERGEANT.
JOHN HENRY MOREHEAD, COLONEL.
JOHN T. TAYLOR, CAPTAIN.
1850.
CLINTON M. ANDREWS, COLONEL.
JOHN B. ANDREWS, CAPTAIN.
JESSE AVERITT, SERGEANT.
D. WHITING HUSTED, LIEUTENANT.
J. GLENN JEFFREYS, LIEUTENANT.

ROLL OF CONFEDERATE DEAD
OF THE UNIVERSITY OF
NORTH CAROLINA.
1858.
THOMAS C. HOLLIDAY, CAPTAIN.
JAMES P. JENKINS, LIEUTENANT.
AURELIUS C. JONES, PRIVATE.
JOHN T. JONES, LIEUTENANT-COLONEL.
JAMES S. KNIGHT, LIEUTENANT.
HARRISON P. LYON, LIEUTENANT.
RICHARDSON MALLETT, LIEUTENANT.
WILLIAM T. NUCKOLLS, CAPTAIN.
AUGUSTUS M. PARKER, PRIVATE.
OLIVER T. PARKS, LIEUTENANT.
CHARLES E. RIDDICK, LIEUTENANT.
JESSE G. ROSS, PRIVATE.
JESSE W. SILER, LIEUTENANT.
RUFUS S. SILER, LIEUTENANT.
JAMES M. SMITH, PRIVATE.
SAMUEL T. SNOW, LIEUTENANT.
REUEL A. STANCIL, PRIVATE.
ARCHIBALD T. STATON, LIEUTENANT.
SIMON H. TAYLOR, PRIVATE.
1859.
ARCHIBALD H. ARRINGTON, PRIVATE.
LEONARD W. BARTLETT, CAPTAIN.
W. LEWIS BATTLE, LIEUTENANT.
ELIAS BUNN, LIEUTENANT.
EDWARD J. CHILTON, PRIVATE.
JOHN CARLINGTON, PRIVATE.
WILLIAM M. GUNNELS, PRIVATE.
LEONARD A. HENDERSON, CAPTAIN.
JOHN M. KELLY, MAJOR.
NEILL R. KELLY, LIEUTENANT.
NATHANIEL A. OGILBY, PRIVATE.
GEORGE M. QUARLES, PRIVATE.
LAWSON W. SYKES, CAPTAIN.

FELIX TANKERSLY, LIEUTENANT.
WILLIAM B WHITFIELD, PRIVATE.
1860.
JOSEPH H. ADAMS, SERGEANT.
EDWARD R. ATKINSON, PRIVATE.
DeWITT C. BUCK, PRIVATE.
SEABORN W. CHISHOLM, PRIVATE.
GEORGE M. CLARK, MAJOR.
JOSEPH B. COGGIN, LIEUTENANT.
VIRGINIUS COPELAND, LIEUTENANT.
REUBEN R. DeJARNETTE, PRIVATE.
RICHARD M. FOOTMAN, PRIVATE.
WILLIAM P. GILL, LIEUTENANT.
SAMUEL WILEY GRAY, CAPTAIN.
JOHN A. GREEN, SERGEANT.
NEVERSON C. MANER, PRIVATE.
CLARENCE D. MARTIN, SERGEANT.
WILLIAM R. McKETHAN, PRIVATE.
WILLIAM H. H. MILLS, PRIVATE.
EDWARD A.T. NICHOLSON, CAPTAIN.
JESSE H. PERSON, LIEUTENANT.
SETH B. SPEIGHT, PRIVATE.
CHARLES VINES, JR., LIEUTENANT.
1861.
JOSEPH H. BRANCH, PRIVATE.
THEOPHILUS H. HOLMES, JR., LIEUTENANT.
ROBERT C. McREE, SERGEANT MAJOR.
HENRY C. MILLER, JR., PRIVATE.
NAPOLEON B. OWENS, PRIVATE.
EDWARD L. RICHARDSON, PRIVATE.
NATHAN J. SNEAD, PRIVATE.
1862.
JOHN R. HAUGHTON, PRIVATE.
FREDERICK NASH, PRIVATE.
1863.
JAMES J. PHILLIPS, PRIVATE.
1864.
WILLIAM H. C. WEBB, LIEUTENANT.

Marble plaques high on the wall on each side of
the stage in Memorial Hall list the students who
lost their lives fighting for the Confederacy. Included were members of the classes from 1821
through 1864. These tablets, now in the new
Memorial Hall, were installed in the first building
of that name before its dedication in 1885.

ROLL OF CONFEDERATE DEAD
OF THE UNIVERSITY OF
NORTH CAROLINA.
1850.
LEONIDAS J. MERRITT, LIEUTENANT.
JOHN T. WHEAT, CAPTAIN.
CAREY WHITAKER, CAPTAIN.
BRYAN WHITFIELD, CAPTAIN.
1851.
WILLIAM L. ALEXANDER, CAPTAIN.
WILLIAM BAILEY, CAPTAIN.
HENRY L. BATTLE, PRIVATE.
RICHARD BRADFORD, CAPTAIN.
WILLIAM H. BUNN, CAPTAIN.
JOHN S. CHAMBERS, LIEUTENANT.
THOMAS NEWTON CRUMPLER, MAJOR.
JAMES H. FITTS, PRIVATE.
JOHN M. MICKLE, CAPTAIN.
JAMES C. MOORE, LIEUTENANT-COLONEL.
THEOPHILUS PERRY, MAJOR.
PETER P. SCALES, CAPTAIN.
MAURICE T. SMITH, LIEUTENANT-COLONEL.
THOMAS McG. SMITH, MAJOR.
PETER E. SPRUILL, PRIVATE.
OWEN A. WADDELL, MAJOR.
JAMES A. WRIGHT, CAPTAIN.
1852.
WILLIAM ADAMS, CAPTAIN.
GEORGE A. BAXTER, CAPTAIN.
OWEN N. BROWN, MAJOR.
FRANCIS D. FOXHALL, LIEUTENANT.
ROBERT E. JAMES, SERGEANT.
DANIEL W. JOHNSON, CAPTAIN.
DANIEL McDOUGALD, CAPTAIN.
DUNCAN E. McNAIR, CAPTAIN.
MONTFORD S. McRAE, SERGEANT.
E. GRAHAM MORROW, LIEUTENANT.
WILLIAM A. OWENS, COLONEL.
STARK A. SUTTON, CAPTAIN.

JAMES N. TURNER, CAPTAIN.
SHUBAL G. WORTH, CAPTAIN.
1853.
JOHN ANTHONY, CORPORAL.
THOMAS O. GLOSS, CAPTAIN.
ANDREW J. FLANNER, PRIVATE.
HUGH W. ARDNER, PRIVATE.
JAMES W. HORNE, SERGEANT.
JOHN W. MAYFIELD, LIEUTENANT.
GEORGE T. MORGAN, PRIVATE.
HENRY MULLINS, CAPTAIN.
JOHN D. RANKIN, SERGEANT.
EDWIN S. SANDERS, CAPTAIN.
WILLIAM E. WILSON, PRIVATE.
1854.
ROBERT L. ALLEN, PRIVATE.
JOHN W. BALLARD, CAPTAIN.
JESSE S. BARNES, CAPTAIN.
EDWARD S. J. BELL, LIEUTENANT.
HUGH T. BROWN, CAPTAIN.
THOMAS COWAN, JR., CAPTAIN.
JOHN L. FULLER, PRIVATE.
WILLIAM H. GIBSON, LIEUTENANT.
FREDERICK H. JENKINS, CAPTAIN.
JAMES B. JORDAN, PRIVATE.
WILLIAM C. LORD, CAPTAIN.
WILLIAM B. McKINNON, PRIVATE.
JULIUS A. ROBBINS, CAPTAIN.
WILLIAM H. WHITAKER, PRIVATE.
DAVID YOUNG, PRIVATE.
1855.
SOLOMON W. ALSTON, ASSISTANT SURGEON.
ROBERT W. ANDERSON, LIEUTENANT.
BENJAMIN I. BLOUNT, LIEUTENANT.
JAMES G. BUSTIN, SERGEANT.
THOMAS D. CLAIBORNE, LIEUTENANT-COLONEL.
JOHN T. COOK, SERGEANT.
HENRY R. DANIEL, LIEUTENANT.
ROBERT T. HARRIS, CAPTAIN.

ROLL OF CONFEDERATE DEAD
OF THE UNIVERSITY OF
NORTH CAROLINA.
1855.
WILLIAM M. HOLT, LIEUTENANT.
N. COLLIN HUGHES, CAPTAIN.
GEORGE B. JOHNSTON, CAPTAIN.
WILLIAM P. MANGUM, LIEUTENANT.
JAMES L. McCORMIC, CAPTAIN.
JOHN G. PURCELL, LIEUTENANT.
EDWARD L. RIDDICK, PRIVATE.
EDWARD F. SATTERFIELD, PRIVATE.
WILLIAM W. SILLERS, LIEUTENANT-COLONEL.
AUGUSTINE B. WASHINGTON, PRIVATE.
THOMAS LOWE WATSON, LIEUTENANT.
DAVID C. WHITAKER, LIEUTENANT.
JOSEPH A. WILLIAMS, CAPTAIN.
1856.
ISAAC T. ATTMORE, PRIVATE.
JUNIUS C. BATTLE, CORPORAL.
STERLING H. BRICKELL, CAPTAIN.
GEORGE P. BRYAN, CAPTAIN.
CHARLES BRUCE, JR., CAPTAIN.
THOMAS W. COOPER, LIEUTENANT.
ADDISON HARVEY, CAPTAIN.
JAMES D. HUNT, CAPTAIN.
ROBERT H. LINDSAY, PRIVATE.
JAMES B. McCALLUM, LIEUTENANT.
ROBERT J. McEACHERN, CAPTAIN.
JOHN W. MEBANE, CAPTAIN.
CHARLES B. MURPHY, PRIVATE.
WILLIAM T. NICHOLSON, CAPTAIN.
WALTER C. Y. PARKER, CAPTAIN.
JAMES L. ROBBINS, PRIVATE.
IOWA M. ROYSTER, LIEUTENANT.
EDWARD G. STERLING, PRIVATE.
JOHN D. TATUM, PRIVATE.
JAMES H. TAYLOR, PRIVATE.
JOHN F. THOMPSON, PRIVATE.

SAMUEL P. WEIR, LIEUTENANT.
WILLIAM A. WOOSTER, LIEUTENANT.
1857.
LAWRENCE M. ANDERSON, LIEUTENANT.
WILLIAM H. AUSTIN, SERGEANT.
HENRY K. BURGWYN, JR., COLONEL.
JAMES E. BUTT, LIEUTENANT.
THOMAS COWAN, PRIVATE.
JOHN H. D. FAIN, CAPTAIN.
JAMES W. W. FEREBEE, CAPTAIN.
BENJAMIN L. GILL, LIEUTENANT.
THOMAS S. HILL, PRIVATE.
JOSEPH V. JENKINS, PRIVATE.
H. FRANCIS JONES, LIEUTENANT.
JOHN McDONALD LAND, PRIVATE.
JARVIS B. LUTTERLOH, LIEUTENANT.
GEORGE S. MARTIN, CAPTAIN.
WILLIAM WHITMEL MARTIN, MAJOR.
GEORGE W. McMILLAN, PRIVATE.
STEPHEN D. RICHMOND, LIEUTENANT.
DAVID W. SIMMONS, JR., LIEUTENANT.
THOMAS LUCIUS SMITH, LIEUTENANT.
MASSILLON F. TAYLOR, CAPTAIN.
JAMES N. THOMPSON, PRIVATE.
NATHAN B. WHITFIELD, CAPTAIN.
HENRY C. WILLIAMS, ENSIGN.
JOHN W. WILSON, LIEUTENANT.
E. ELDRIDGE WRIGHT, CAPTAIN.
1858.
EDWARD H. ARMSTRONG, CAPTAIN.
JOSEPH H. BASON, SERGEANT.
LUTHER R. BELL, PRIVATE.
JAMES J. CHERRY, CAPTAIN.
JOSEPH D. CHERRY, PRIVATE.
WELDON E. DAVIS, CAPTAIN.
JOHN H. DOBBIN, PRIVATE.
JOHN G. GAINES, CAPTAIN.
JOHN L. HAUGHTON, PRIVATE.

Paul C. Cameron (1808–91), student, 1824–25, and recipient of the LL.D. degree in 1889, was a member of the Board of Trustees, 1858–68 and 1875–91. A generous benefactor of the University, he was chairman of the building and executive committees of the trustees at various times.

Student publications as early as 1844 advocated the establishment of a physical education program and the plea continued into the 1850s, but there was no official response. Critics of the University who condemned dancing, particularly in a University building, were responsible for the erection of the first gymnasium. Smith Hall served as both a library and a hall for dances and President Battle agreed that dancing in the library was improper. The trustees decided that the commencement ball of 1884 would be the last in Smith Hall, and they joined in a scheme to erect a gymnasium, which could also be used as a ball room, adjacent to the campus but on private property. A site just east of modern Peabody Hall, opposite the first President's House, was purchased and a building designed by Samuel Sloan, architect of Memorial Hall, was erected. Dr. Richard H. Lewis of Raleigh was instrumental in raising funds. Opened at the beginning of the fall, 1885, session, it was a long wooden building that provided a hall one hundred by forty-five feet.

Stephen B. Weeks (1865–1918) was graduated with highest honors in 1886, received the M.A. degree the following year and a Ph.D. the year after that. He has been called "North Carolina's first professional historian" and was professor of history at Trinity College for several years. He also served on the staff of the United States Bureau of Education and in schools operated by the United States Indian Service in New Mexico and Arizona. In spite of his removal from his native state, he continued to collect North Caroliniana as he had done since his youth. His policy of collecting not only books and periodicals, but also pamphlets, proceedings of organizations, broadsides, maps, newspapers, and other published materials was most unusual. At his death the trustees of the University purchased his collection and it became the nucleus of the present North Carolina Collection.

The University faculty, 1887.
Seated, left to right: R. H. Graves,
N. B. Henry, A. W. Mangum,
Kemp P. Battle, John Manning,
Thomas Hume; *standing, left to
right*: F. P. Venable, G. F. Atkinson, J. L. Love, W. D. Toy, J. A.
Holmes, J. W. Gore. For a picture
of a group of distinguished faculty
members in 1971 at approximately
the same site, in a similar pose,
see *page 303*.

A fraternity, probably Phi Gamma
Delta, about 1888.

Class of 1888.

John Sprunt Hill (1869–1961), a graduate with the class of 1889, served the University faithfully as a trustee from 1904 until his death. The University honored him with the LL.D. degree in 1933. His gifts to his alma mater were generous and unselfish, often made quietly but always to meet a pressing need. His generosity benefited the campus beautification program begun in 1923; his interest made it possible to remodel the old Carnegie Library into a music building; he constructed the Carolina Inn adjacent to the campus and in 1935 gave it to the University. His magnanimous gift of extensive business property along Franklin Street to provide a permanent endowment for the North Carolina Collection has been responsible for the growth and development of this scholarly resource for the University community and the people of the state in general.

Class of 1889. Derbies had replaced the top hats of the previous year, but high-top shoes were still the fashion. As in so many pictures of this period, it is evident that the campus lawn was not well tended. Weeds are nearly shoe-top high at this spot across the way from Memorial Hall.

The Order of Gimghouls was organized in 1889 by five members of the class of 1891 as a secret junior and senior social organization. This lodge was built in 1896 at the corner of Rosemary Lane and Boundary Street and served until the present Hippol Castle, popularly known as Gimghoul Castle, was occupied in 1926 on Piney Prospect a short distance east of the campus, overlooking Raleigh Road and the land to the east. Ideals of chivalry and knighthood play a role in the order and the chief officer is styled Rex.

Zeta Psi fraternity in the spring of 1890. Gates in the stone wall, such as the one seen here, were frequently broken, permitting livestock to roam the campus. The student at the left, R. H. Johnston, is wearing a finger ring—the earliest instance observed of this form of personal adornment. Seated on the gate post to the right is C. S. Mangum, later a distinguished member of the medical faculty in the University from 1896 until his death in 1939.

The first Medical School in Chapel Hill was established in 1879 under the direction of Dr. Thomas W. Harris, but he resigned in 1885 to devote full time to private practice. The school was revived in 1890 under the leadership of Dr. Richard H. Whitehead who was named professor of anatomy, physiology, and materia medica in 1889. He became dean of the medical department in 1901 and continued in this capacity until he removed to the University of Virginia in 1905. This view of Dr. Whitehead in 1890 with the first-year class in anatomy was made just across the rock wall that marked the southern boundary of the campus. This spot was in front of what is now the University Library between Bingham and Dey halls, in thick woods well removed from the prying eyes of the curious.

This view of Memorial Hall and New West, about 1890, shows the old Caldwell monument near the west corner of New West, before it had been moved to the Negro section of the cemetery. The flag pole on the center section of Memorial Hall, as shown in the architect's drawing, does not appear in later pictures. Note also the numerous paths worn across the campus.

The road to Raleigh in 1890 was almost as wide and straight as it is today. A trip to the state capital then took a little longer but was considerably less hazardous.

The home of Mrs. Ralph H. Graves, widow of Professor Graves, about 1890 at the present site of the Carolina Inn. Mrs. Graves operated a very popular boarding-house and many generations of students remembered the good food she served.

This scene in Battle Park in 1892 could be duplicated today. About forty-five acres on the southern and southeastern edges of the campus have been preserved with woodland paths, streams, a variety of wildflowers, and native trees. The park was named for President Kemp P. Battle who cleared the paths through the woods behind his home and gave sentimental and romantic names to many spots there—Trysting Poplar, Anemone Spring, Fairy Vale, Wood-Thrush Home, Dogwood Dingle, and Flirtation Knoll, among others.

South Building in 1892 with the cupola that had been added in 1861. The worn paths to the well suggest its importance as a source of water. The steps without a rail at the west door of South Building lead to the conclusion that few ladies in the long dress of those days ever entered the building. Surely, if they had, a handrail for their assistance would have been provided.

This exterior view of Gerrard Hall about 1890 shows the portico that was removed, 1900–1901. There was no entrance to the hall from the portico, but it was a popular setting for photographing small groups. The interior shows the decorations for some special occasion after 1901, the year in which the old stiff-backed pews were removed. The North Carolina centennial banner from the 1876 exposition at Philadelphia hangs above the rostrum, and the bust of President Caldwell sits on the corner shelf to the right.

George Tayloe Winston (1852–1932) had been a student at the University but left in 1868 when it began to decline. He later completed his undergraduate work at Cornell with highest honors. He returned to Chapel Hill with the reopening of the University in 1875 as professor of Latin and German and assisted in revising the curriculum along more modern lines, with elective courses of study and high standards of scholarship. With the retirement of President Battle in 1891 to become professor of history, Professor Winston was elected president, the first professional teacher to hold that position since Caldwell. During the five years of his administration the income of the University more than doubled and the number of students almost trebled. An active alumni association was organized and speakers from the University began to go out into the state to conduct programs for various groups and organizations. Under President Winston's direction the society libraries were consolidated with the University library, a permanent library endowment was secured, and a professional librarian was appointed. He left North Carolina in 1896 to become president of the University of Texas but the climate disagreed with him, and in 1899 he returned home to become president of the North Carolina College of Agriculture and Mechanic Arts, now North Carolina State University in Raleigh.

John Motley Morehead (1870–1965), native of Spray (now Eden) and a graduate of the University in 1891, was a chemist and cofounder of Union Carbide. In addition to his extensive business interests he was United States minister to Sweden, 1930–33. Among his many gifts to the University are the Morehead Planetarium and $17 million for a scholarship program. He also joined Rufus Lenoir Patterson, class of 1893, in giving the Morehead–Patterson Memorial Bell Tower in 1930.

The gymnasium, erected during 1884–85, was enlarged and remodeled in 1898 to become Commons Hall. It served as the University dining hall until Swain Hall was erected in 1913, but the old building was used for dances and banquets from 1898 until it was torn down about 1915–16.

Blacks have long served the University community. Although the records are not always specific, their labor was surely essential in the construction of University buildings—it certainly was for Person Hall, the second building on campus. Black men cut firewood and made the morning fires in students' rooms, provided fish and wild game for the tables, cleaned rooms, tended the campus, and provided transportation. One even produced affectionate poems for the students to send to their ladies. At least two blacks operated restaurants in Chapel Hill that the students patronized. Black women prepared meals and washed and ironed clothes. These men and women were recognized and remembered fondly by the young men whom they served. The three pictures here are from President Kemp P. Battle's photograph album. Ben Boothe, pictured here with a few eggs in a hat, entertained the students in a variety of ways. He died in 1891. Identified only as "Uncle Jerry," the second man has a basket of what appears to be shelled peas or peanuts and a quart tin for measuring them. Finally, Eli Merritt, who worked in Old West.

Commons Hall ready for a meal to be served. Student waiters received their meals free of charge, but those who paid were charged only $8.00 a month, according to a report of 1906. Surplus receipts were used for improvement in the food or adding to the equipment.

The first intercollegiate football game in which the University participated seems to have taken place in 1888 and was with Wake Forest, who won. This picture is believed to be of the football team of 1890.

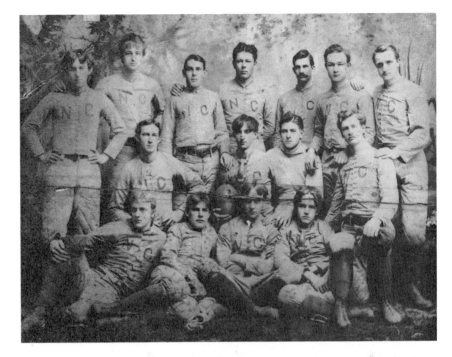

Singing was taught briefly at the University in 1878, but the Glee Club was not established until 1891. This picture of the Glee Club made in 1892 is the earliest known. Professor Karl P. Harrington, director of the group, is shown seated, fourth from the left.

Person Hall, the second oldest building on the campus, was enlarged in 1886 by the addition of a wing to the west side of the original structure built in 1797. In 1892 another extension to the west was added to match the original eastern section in order to provide additional laboratory space for the Department of Chemistry.

Chemistry laboratory in the central section of Person Hall about 1892 with a glimpse of the interior of the west wing through the open door.

Members of the Order of Gimghouls, 1892.

Ball managers, 1892.

Old West in the 1890s when it was about seventy years old. A water plant was authorized by the trustees in March 1893, and it was completed soon after the middle of September. In February 1894 President Winston announced that the arrangements for water supply, baths, urinals, closets, and sewerage had been completed. The fire hydrant in the center of this photograph and the evidence of newly filled trenches leading by it suggest that the water system was new. It might also be noted that the grass on the campus was not well kept at this time.

A young lady on the path from Franklin Street to Old East pauses to be photographed during a stroll with her doll carriage about 1892.

The assembly room of the Dialectic Society in New West, 1892. Note the oil-burning lamps in the chandeliers and the heater with the long pipe in the background.

The post office in Chapel Hill in 1892 was at the southwest corner of the present downtown post office lot. The nattily dressed young man by the building is posting a letter while through the door at the left a few post office boxes gleam in the early afternoon sun. The signs posted on the two trees advertise iced drinks in many flavors at A. Kluttz's and at Yearby's.

The law class in 1892 with Professor John Manning seated in the center.

Tennis was introduced to the campus in 1884 when Dr. Francis P. Venable built an excellent court near the president's house. This picture of students at play was made about 1892.

In the late nineteenth century there were many pleasant paths and rural roads in the vicinity of Chapel Hill along which students, townspeople, and visitors strolled. One of the favorites led east of the campus to Piney Prospect. This photograph made in 1892 shows a young lady pointing out the road to Raleigh at the foot of the hill on which Gimghoul Castle is now located. Level land stretches east as far as the eye can see, and to the left of the young ladies one can today see the tower of Duke Chapel.

A string orchestra and chorus composed of students and faculty in the 1890s gathered at the east end of Gerrard Hall to have this picture made.

Five members of the faculty early in February 1893 incorporated the University Press, a print shop rather than a publishing body. Its purpose was to engage in commercial printing and to issue official publications and journals of the University. *The Tar Heel* was among its first jobs, but within a few months it was also issuing other journals. Before long, it also began to issue the *Record*, the president's report, the catalogue, and similar documents. Programs, posters, library call slips, and stationery for the University departments came from the University Press, which occupied three adjoining rooms on the first floor of New West, shown here. A great many students, among whom were some who later held positions of importance in the University and the state, earned a large portion of their expenses by working in the press. In 1901 the University took over the operation of the establishment and installed it in a one-story brick building just west of Memorial Hall. Within a dozen years the University's requirements for attractive printing could no longer be filled by this small press and most printing was done thereafter by commercial printers in Durham, Raleigh, and elsewhere. In 1922 The University of North Carolina Press was established and the old University Press, then operated as a private business on Franklin Street, became the University Printery.

Class of 1893.

Fraternities had come into existence on the campus by 1851. Delta Kappa Epsilon was organized in that year, and soon there were others but all disappeared before the end of the Civil War. Several petitions for the establishment of fraternities were denied after the University reopened, but in 1877 or soon afterwards several were formed without official permission. These four pictures of fraternity members were made about 1892. The fraternities represented are: *top*, Delta Kappa Epsilon and Phi Gamma Delta; *bottom*, Theta Nu Epsilon and Sigma Nu. A careful examination of the hats, suits, shirts, and particularly the ties worn by these young men suggests that male fashions were changing. Members of Theta Nu Epsilon seem to be wearing uniform dark coats and white trousers. The very wide ties worn by two members of Sigma Nu are especially interesting.

The staff of the University Press about 1898 outside the shop in New West.

THE TAR HEEL.

VOL. I. UNIVERSITY OF NORTH CAROLINA, FEBRUARY 23, 1893. **NO. 1.**

The Tar Heel,
University of North Carolina.

EDITORS.
CHARLES BASKERVILLE,
WALTER MURPHY,
A. C. ELLIS,
W. P. WOOTEN,
PERRIN BUSBEE,
J. C. BIGGS,
A. H. McFADGUE.

Editor in Chief
CHARLES BASKERVILLE,
Managing Editor,
WALTER MURPHY,
Business Manager,
A. H. McFADGUE.

THURSDAY, February 23, 1893.

CHURCH DIRECTORY.
Baptist Church.
REV. J. L. CARROLL, D. D.
Preaching every Sunday, morning and night. Sunday School at 9:30 a. m. Prayer meeting every Wednesday night.

Presbyterian Church.
REV. J. E FOGARTIE.
Preaching every Sunday, morning and night; except the first Sunday in each month. Sunday School at 10:30 a. m. Prayer meeting every Wednesday night.

Methodist Church.
REV. N. M. WATSON
Preaching every Sunday, morning and night Sunday School at 10:30 a m. Prayer meeting every Wednesday night.

Episcopal Church.
REV. FREDERIC TOWERS.
Sunday services at 7, 11 and 7 o'clock. Weekly services at 4 p. Friday. Sunday School 4 p. m During Lent services daily at 4 p. m

UNIVERSITY DIRECTORY.
University Choir.
PROF. KARL P. HARRINGTON, Leader.
Organists, J. A. MAXWELL and CHAR. ROBERSON.

UNIVERSITY MAGAZINE,
SIX TIMES A YEAR.
EDITORS.

PHI.	DI.
W. P. Wooten,	W. P. M. Currie
J. E. Ingle, Jr.,	J. M. Cheek,
A. H. Koonce,	T. J. Wilson.

Business Manager,
Prof. Collier Cobb.

UNIVERSITY LIBRARY.
DR. EBEN ALEXANDER, Librarian,
F. L. WILCOX Student Librarian.
Open every day except Sunday, from 11:30 to 1:30 and from 3 to 5. Open Sundays from 3 to 6 p. m.

University Reading Room
Open every day. Leading papers published in Union and State on file.

University Press Association.
H A. Rondthaler, president,
Dr. B Whitaker, Secretary.
Julian Engle Dr. B. Whitaker,
H. A. Rondthaler, Walter Murphey, Executive Committee.

Object is to further the disbursement of news relating to the University.
Meets at the call of the president.

University Atheetic Association.
H. B. Shaw, president.
J. L Pugh, sec'y. and treas.
Meets regularly the second Saturday in September and January Other calls subject to the president

University Foot Ball Team.
Michael Hoke, captain,
Charles Baskerville, Manager.

University Base Ball Team.
Perrin Busbee, captain,
W. R. Kenon, manager.

University German Club.
J· C. Biggs, president,
C. R. Turner, sec'y. and treas.
Meets at the call of the president. Leader selected for each German.

University Glee Club.
E. Parson Willard, president and leader.
Charles Roberson, manager.
Prof. Karl P. Harring.or director.

Shakespere Club.
Dr. Thomas Hume, president,
J. M. Cheek, sec'y. and treas.
Meet in the Y. M. C. A. hall the third Tuesday night in each month. Library open one hour each day.

Elisha Mitchell Scientific Society.
Prof. J. A. Holmes, president,
Prof. J. W. Gore, vice-president,
Dr. F. P. Venable, secretary and treasurer.
Meets in Person hall second Tuesday night in each month.
Journal issued twice a year.

Historical Society.
Dr. Kemp Battle. president and corresponding secretary.
H. M. Thompson, secretary and treasurer.
Meets at the call of the president.

Philanthropic Society. (Secret)
Meets every Friday night in Phi. hall new east building.

Dialectic Society. (Secret)
Meets every Friday night and Saturday morning in Di. hall new west building.

The Order of Gim Ghoulds. (Secret) Junior.
The society meets in February. October. Banquet Thursday night of commencement.

Fraternities. (Secret)
Sigma Alpha Epsilon, Kappa Alpha, Zeta Psi Alpha San Amega, Sigma Nu, Phi Kappa Sigma, Phi Delta Theta, Phi Gamma Delta Sigma Phi. Beta Thata Pi Delta Kappa Epsilon, meet in their respective halls every Saturday night.

Y M. C. A.
F. C. Harding, president,
George Stephens, secretary and treasurer,
R. E. Zachary, organist.
Meets four times a week in Y. M C. A. hall. Members appointed to lead. Hand books issued every September.

Philological Society.
Dr. Eben Elexander, president.
Prof. Karl P. Harrington, secretary and treasurer,
Meets first Friday night in each month.

The Hellenian. (Annual)
Published by the Fraternities,

THE TAR HEEL.
A weekly paper published at the University of North Carolina, under the auspices of the University Athletic Association, devoted to the interest of the University at large.

Issued every Thursday morning. It will contain a summary of all occurrences in the University and village of Chapel Hill.

Space will be assigned for the thorough discussion of all points pertaining to the advancement and growth of the University.

A brief account each week of the occurrences in the amateur athletic world, with especial attention to our own athletic interests, and progress in Football, Baseball, Tennis, etc.

All society news, personals and every subject of interest both to the students and citizens of the village, will be treated each week.

The columns will be open to discussion on all appropriate subjects with an endeavor to do full justice to everyone. The chief and his assistants will decide as to appropriateness of articles--no anonymous articles will be accepted without antho. nam ⁚ing known to the chief, which will be in confidence, if desired.

Advertisers will note that this is the *best, quickest,* and *surest,* means by which they can reach the students. For notes see or write "Business Manager of TAR HEEL" Chapel Hill. N. C, or drop him a card and he will call.

Subscription one Dollar and a half per session. This spring 75cts.

SALUTATORY.
The growing demands of the University have shown the need of a weekly paper. The University Athletic Association regarding itself as the means by which such a need could be supplied, at a stated meeting elected a board of editors (chief and five subs.) and a business manager.

With this apology only, the first issue of the first volume of the TAR HEEL makes its appearance.

This new venture is necessarily entered upon by the present board with no little trepidation, nevertheless with a determination, to make a success which can only be done through the indulgence and assistance of our faculty and fellow-students. Therefore we invite honest criticism and any aid in the advancement of this new project will be thoroughly appreciated.

THE LEGISLATIVE COMMITTEE VISIT THE UNIVERSITY.
The following members of the legislature composing the visitation committee arrived at the University on a special train Friday morning, February 3rd:

Messrs. Battle, chairman; Cheek Aycoke, James, Pou, of the senate; and Messrs. Holt (chairman) Euse, Parker, Starnes, Walker, Ward, of the house.

After breakfasting, the regular chapel exercises were attended, then visits were made to the reading room, libraries and various lecture rooms where classes were assembled. The numerous laboratories were inspected as well as some of the students' rooms. In the afternoon meetings of both the societies were held and the gentlemen who were not alumni were made honorary members. Just after prayers the boys called repeatedly for speeches from our visitors, a majority of whom responded most felicitously and gave words of encouragement for the future outlook of the university, from a legislative appropriation standpoint. All saw the need of a sufficient appropriation to fully equip, this the most useful and important of all the State properties, and give to a university of whose past brilliant record and whose future prospects are such as would make any State in the union proud to be the possessor of such an heritage to hand to posterity, a sufficient appropriation to put the university on a financial basis equal to its rapid expansion and growth. When some of the committee expressed their deep regret at not having had an opportunity of receiving an education, in their youth, we could not but feel that it was a duty that was owed to future generations, and which has been due to those that have passed away, that the supreme law making power in the State, ought to make tuition at the university free to North Carolinians as is done at the University of Virginia to Virginians and the only way to do this is to appropriate a sufficient amount to keep the university up, until resources from outside States and the technical courses shall make itself sustaining, and, too, we could not but think what a shame and loss it was to North Carolina, that it had failed, to open the doors of the university, in the past to such sterling manhood as represented the legislature on the committee. The body of the students were well pleased with our friends, if they are a fair sample of our legislators this year. North Carolina is in good hands. They know the needs of the University.

The first issue of *The Tar Heel* appeared on 23 February 1893 under the auspices of the University Athletic Association.

Football team, 1893.

University faculty and students, 1893–94.

A baseball game about 1893–94 on the old athletic field south and east of Smith Hall.

The staff of *White and Blue*, a newspaper that began in 1894 and was discontinued the next year. It was published by nonfraternity men who objected to the excessive coverage of sports by *The Tar Heel* to the exclusion of news of other campus activities. When *The Tar Heel* agreed to a broader coverage of campus events, *White and Blue* ceased publication.

Baseball team, 1894. The University won ten out of fourteen games that year.

The faculty about 1895. President Winston perhaps kept his hat on as a badge of office while the faculty was uncovered.

Edwin A. Alderman (1861–1931), native of Wilmington and graduate of the University in the class of 1882, succeeded George T. Winston as president of the University in 1896. Since 1893 he had been professor of history and philosophy of education and librarian. While he was president he also was professor of political and social sciences, but in 1900 he left Chapel Hill to become president of Tulane University, and in 1904 he became president of the University of Virginia. Under President Alderman's administration in Chapel Hill, women were first admitted to the University. It was he who redesigned the shelter over the well in front of South Building to make it the beautiful symbol it has become. He had the main doorway of South Building redesigned, based on the doorway at Westover, the colonial Byrd home in Virginia; he also had vines planted to cover the walls of several buildings and in other ways attempted to beautify the campus.

Dr. R. H. Whitehead, dean of the Medical School, suggested in 1894 that the University should have a small infirmary in which sick students might be treated instead of being sent home. The death of William Preston Bynum, Jr., from typhoid fever in the summer of 1893 was believed caused by this unwise practice. A small three-room cottage was erected in 1895 to replace the Retreat that had ceased to be used in 1891, but so few students were sick that visiting trustees were often housed there. This building stood near the present auditorium of Hill Music Hall. After a new infirmary was erected in 1907 the old one was purchased by Dr. Eric A. Abernethy, moved to Columbia Street, and with extensive additions occupied as a home.

A heavy snow in December of 1896 gave students an opportunity to enjoy a diversion. They built snow people larger than life size and at least two cameramen turned out to photograph one of them. Unfortunately the original picture is too faded to copy, but this pen and ink sketch is based on it. The interesting feature here is the large tripod camera beside one of the students.

This photograph of another snowman made during the same 1896 snowfall is better preserved.

There can be no doubt that this is the class of 1896. In addition to painting the numbers on the door and columns of Smith Hall, the library, they have laid out books to form the numerals.

The Glee Club, 1896, with the director, Professor Karl P. Harrington, at the right. This picture was made on the south portico of Gerrard Hall.

The Hellenian, so called because it was issued by the Greek-letter fraternities, first appeared in 1890. It was the nearest thing to the modern annual yearbook to be published for the students, but it was sponsored by the fraternities and featured them. There were no pictures at first, but before *The Hellenian* ceased publication in 1900, group pictures, a few pen and ink sketches, and an occasional special picture appeared. In 1901 the first *Yackety Yack*, representing all segments of the University, was published. This picture of the editors of *The Hellenian* of 1896 was made beside the Methodist Church. It is interesting for many reasons, not the least of which is that it reveals that eleven out of twelve of the editors adopted the latest fashion of parting their hair in the middle. The spats and the high-top shoes with pointed toes must also have been the latest style in footwear.

The class of 1897. Here for the first time several of the students are wearing overcoats that appear to have black velvet collars.

William Starr Myers, class of 1897, seated in a rocking chair before the fireplace in his campus room in February 1897. A tennis racket hangs on the wall and behind him is a wardrobe in which his clothes hang.

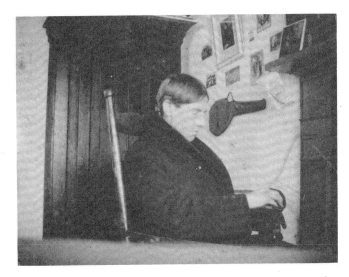

The faculty in 1897. A number of young, new faces appear for the first time in this photograph. Melting snow chilled the day and a carpet runner was brought out to protect the feet of the older men seated on the front row. The chairs were brought out of Gerrard Hall for the occasion, and many of these comfortable chairs may still be found around the campus and in the library.

These "before" and "after" pictures explain better than words what President Alderman's ideas, formulated in the fall of 1897, wrought on the Old Well. He recorded that the new structure was "derived largely from the Temple of Love in the Garden at Versailles."

Alumni Building, begun in 1898, was the first building to be erected on the campus since New East and New West in 1859. It was constructed largely with funds subscribed by alumni and was designed to provide offices, class-rooms, and laboratories.

Staff of *The Tar Heel* in 1898. The young lady is Mary MacRae, first woman registered at the University. *Standing, left to right*: E. D. Broadhurst, W. E. Cox, R. E. Follin, R. D. W. Connor, P. DuP. Whitaker; *seated, left to right*: P. C. Whitlock, Mary MacRae, and P. D. Gold.

The football team of 1898, champions of the South. It won nine games and lost none. *Front row, left to right*: C. B. Buxton, Warren E. Kluttz, S. E. Shull, F. M. Osborne, J. W. Copeland. *Middle row:* H. J. Koehler, H. B. Cunningham, F. O. Rogers, E. C. Gregory, E. V. Howell. *Back row:* J. B. Martin, F. F. Bennett, Miller, Coach William A. Reynolds, I. A. Phifer, Ernest Graves, R. Samuel Cromartie, E. G. McIver, J. C. Mac-Rae. Miller is not identified in records of the time; there were five students of this name enrolled in 1898.

The Central Hotel on East Franklin Street, shown here as it appeared about 1898, was popular with students and visitors to town and campus. It stood about where the Battle-Vance-Pettigrew buildings are now.

The editors of the *University Magazine* in 1898 posed beside the rock wall with New West faintly visible in the background. Standing second from the right is R. D. W. Connor, later a member of the history faculty and the first archivist of the United States, a position to which he was appointed in 1934.

The Spanish-American War in 1898 was much smaller than the Civil War, of course, but University students in a number of cases went direct from campus to camp in this war just as they had done earlier. William Johnson Hannah (1867–1936) from Cataloochee was a law student in Chapel Hill when he left in 1897 to enter the army as captain of Company H, First North Carolina Volunteers. He appears on the left as a student in the University and on the right in uniform.

William Belo Lemly (1875–1962) of Salem was graduated in 1896 and worked as business manager and assistant editor of a hometown newspaper before being commissioned a second lieutenant in the Marine Corps in 1898; he remained in the Marine Corps after the war and rose to the rank of colonel. He appears here as a student with his Sigma Alpha Epsilon pin on his vest and as a newly commissioned Marine Corps officer.

Thomas Stringfield (1872–1954) of Waynesville was a
student in the University during 1894–95, but left to take
his medical degree at Vanderbilt University. His education was interrupted by the Spanish-American War,
however. He appears here as a student and before his tent
in camp, seated on the right. He was a lieutenant in the
First North Carolina Infantry.

The Carr Building, begun in 1899
and dedicated at the June commencement of 1900, was constructed largely with funds given by
Julian S. Carr of Durham, who had
been a student in the University,
1862–64. His gift was described as
the largest of its kind ever given to
the University up to that time.
The Carr Building served as a
dormitory for men at first, but at
different times it has been used for
law students, for women students,
and more recently for foreign
students.

Aerial view of the campus, 1919.

The University library occupied Smith Hall from 1854 until 1907. These interior views suggest that it was as much a museum as a library. The full-sized copy of the Venus de Milo was a gift of the class of 1900. The bust of Governor Zebulon B. Vance remained in the University library until 1970 when it was transferred to the Dialectic Society chambers in New West. The death mask of Napoleon, visible atop the card file in the left of one of the pictures, is now in the care of the North Carolina Collection. The portrait of Henry Clay is now in the Ackland Art Center. The Willie P. Mangum, Jr., china displayed in glass cases near the window is in the library vault.

About 1902 a number of wells were dug around campus and pumps were installed in them both for the convenience of students and as a source of water in case of fire. Gazebos sheltering the pumps became popular gathering places.

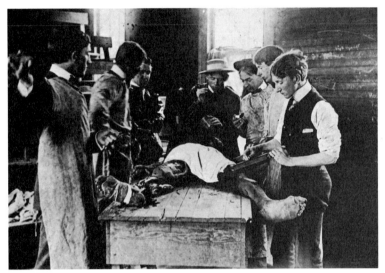

A dissecting hall for the Medical School was erected about 1900 in an almost inaccessible part of the campus where Venable Hall is now located. A picture of students at work inside was made soon after the building was completed. It was abandoned in 1911 when Caldwell Hall was built for the Medical School, and the deserted dissecting hall was burned in 1919 after the Carolina football team defeated Virginia.

Francis Preston Venable (1856–1934) who had been professor of chemistry since 1880, became president of the University in 1900, following the resignation of President Alderman. He served until 1914 when he returned to his former position in the Chemistry Department. Under Venable an extensive building program was inaugurated and among the new buildings erected was one to house Venable's former department—the first building ever erected on the campus by a direct appropriation of money from the General Assembly.

The University faculty, 1900, on the steps of Alumni Building, which had not yet been completed. This was a favorite spot for group pictures for many years. The young man second from the right, back row, is Archibald Henderson, a graduate student working toward his Ph.D., who became an instructor in mathematics in 1898. He later became a Kenan Professor and was one of the most distinguished members of the faculty when he retired in 1948.

Mary Ann Smith Building, erected in 1901 as a dormitory, was built with money from the estate of the daughter and heiress of Richard Smith, prominent Raleigh merchant.

Members of the German Club, 1901. In spite of their formal dress many of the students still wore their high-top lace shoes. The student seated on the front row, right, however, wears low-cut dress slippers—the first footwear other than high-top shoes noted in any of the student pictures.

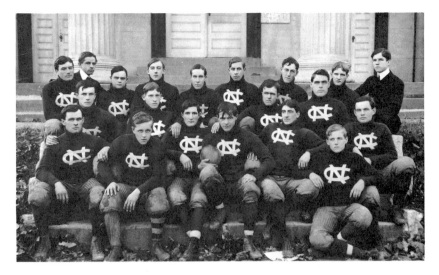

The football team, 1902. Based on the pictorial evidence available in a fairly long and complete file of annual football pictures, parting the hair in the center never completely caught on with this student group. Most of them parted their hair slightly to the side or else wore their hair in such a devil-may-care style that no part was to be seen.

Guitar and Mandolin Club, 1902.

The stands on the old athletic field, predecessor of the Emerson and Kenan stadiums. The field lay south of the old library (Smith Hall) and probably was cleared of trees in 1876. The stands probably were erected about 1884 at the time of the first intercollegiate athletic contest in which a University team participated, and they were burned after 1909.

Delta Kappa Epsilon fraternity, 1902 or 1903. The young man seated in the front row at the left has the stub of a cigar in his right hand, while the one seated in the wicker chair is wearing a ring, a form of personal adornment heretofore observed in only one student picture. In this photograph and in others for this year the collars are uniform, the old-fashioned wing-tip collar having been entirely discarded.

Commencement marshals, 1902, were members of the class of 1903. G. Lyle Jones, fifth from the left, was chief marshal. Others were Robert W. Herring, Harry P. Stevens, Jacob Tomlinson, James L. Morehead, Joshua J. Skinner, and David Z. Cauble.

Alpha Theta Phi Society, 1902–3, the honor society that preceded Phi Beta Kappa on the University campus. It was organized in 1894 and in 1904 its members were transferred to Phi Beta Kappa.

The Pipe of Peace and Fellowship was passed around and smoked by the graduating seniors of 1906 and then turned over to the rising senior class. This ceremony was continued until about 1921. The original pipe is now among the University keepsakes in the North Carolina Collection.

James Horner Winston (1888–1968) of Oxford was graduated with an A.B. degree in 1904. The first University student to receive a Rhodes Scholarship, he was awarded the A.B. degree in jurisprudence from Oxford University in 1907.

The football team, 1905.

The Order of the Golden Fleece was organized in 1903 as a means of recognizing academic standing and other characteristics of high personal attainment by undergraduates. This picture, made in the spring of 1904, is the first taken of members of the Golden Fleece. They are, *bottom*, *left to right*: William P. Jacocks, Ralph H. Harper, Phillips Russell, Albert L. Cox, Alfred W. Haywood; *top*, *left to right*: R. W. Herring, Roach Stewart, Sidney S. Robins, William J. Gordon, William Fisher, and Neill Ray Graham.

The first chapter of Phi Beta Kappa at the University, 1905. An earlier scholarship society, Alpha Theta Phi, established in 1894, was dissolved in 1904 when it was admitted to the national society of Phi Beta Kappa as the Alpha Chapter of North Carolina.

Funds for the construction of Bynum Gymnasium were given in 1904 by Judge William Preston Bynum of Charlotte as a memorial to his grandson and namesake, William Preston Bynum, Jr., class of 1895, a member of the University football team who had died of typhoid fever at the close of his sophomore year. It was formally presented at commencement in 1905.

The main floor of Bynum Gymnasium was well stocked with apparatus for exercise, while the balcony served as an indoor track. Bynum ceased to be used as a gymnasium in 1937 when Woollen Gymnasium was opened, and was extensively remodeled for office use.

The indoor pool at Bynum Gymnasium was a marvel to
the students and they made good use of it for a number
of years until it was declared unsanitary because there
were no filters or circulating pumps.

The YMCA building, begun in 1904 and dedicated in
June 1907, was long an important center of student
activity. The YMCA had been organized on campus
in May 1860 and reorganized in September 1876 with
headquarters in South Building. The new YMCA building had an excellent auditorium on the south side of the
building straight through the front door and many public
meetings were held there. (The boxcar visible at the left
of this picture was on a temporary track laid to carry
material to the site of some new buildings on the east side
of the campus in the 1920s.)

The new chemistry building, completed in 1906, contained space for three times the number of students who could be accommodated in the former quarters in Person Hall. The Chemistry Department remained here until it moved to Venable Hall in 1925. At that time the Department of Pharmacy was installed here and the building named Howell Hall after Edward Vernon Howell, first dean of the School of Pharmacy.

In 1868, when University affairs were in turmoil, the executive committee supported the admission of women, but the whole Board of Trustees refused to accept this idea. It was not until 1897, in more settled times, that the trustees passed an ordinance admitting women to the postgraduate courses. President Battle noted in 1912 that "the experiment has not met with much success. The attendance has averaged only about half a dozen a year, but of these there have been some brilliant students." Miss Mary S. MacRae was the first of five young women to register, and in 1898 Miss Sallie Walker Stockard received the first earned degree to be awarded to a woman. By 1906 there were enough women on campus that they organized the Women's University Club, and in 1907 they had their picture made together.

The male editors of the 1906 and 1907 editions of the *Yackety Yack* took note of the presence of women among the student body by means of cartoons. Their drawings suggest that the men stood in awe of the female beauties, but that they were pleased nevertheless.

In 1879 a railroad 10.2 miles long was completed from University Station on the North Carolina Railroad to the western edge of Chapel Hill in what is now Carrboro. Two daily trips were made to connect with the train running between Goldsboro and Greensboro, and it usually took between an hour and an hour and ten minutes to make the run as the wood-burning engine had to stop several times each way for fuel. Between ten and twelve hundred passengers rode this train each month. During the course of construction on the campus in the 1920s the line was extended so that building materials could be delivered closer to the sites where they would be used. Passenger trains then came onto campus, stopping between Memorial Hall and the Carolina Inn site, to pick up and deliver students at Christmas or to take the football team to games away. This picture, made early in the twentieth century, shows Brakeman Marcus D. Prigden, Engineer J. P. Nesbitt, Captain Fred Smith, popular conductor, and Fireman G. M. Ramsey.

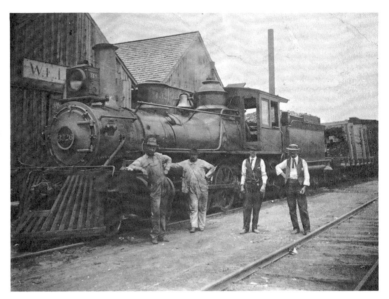

Abernethy Hall, the third University Infirmary, was erected and opened in 1907 and continued in use until the Navy erected a new one in 1942. Abernethy Hall has since been used for various offices including those of the Playmakers at one time and of the University Extension Division.

In 1907 the third President's House was erected on the campus. It is located on East Franklin and Raleigh Streets near the site of the second President's House that burned in 1886. It was occupied by presidents of the University of North Carolina until 14 November 1932 when Frank Porter Graham ceased to be president of the University on this campus alone and became president of the Consolidated University. He did not vacate the President's House and his successors in that office have continued to occupy this house. Other quarters have been provided for the chief executive officer of The University of North Carolina at Chapel Hill.

On 1 June 1907 the cornerstone was laid for a new library building to replace the long inadequate Smith Hall. President Venable secured a gift from Andrew Carnegie for the construction of the building subject to the providing of a similar amount for the library's upkeep and future expansion. Alumni and friends generously met the call and a number of library endowments were established at that time. Within less than two decades this building proved inadequate for the library, and through the generosity of the John Sprunt Hill family of Durham this building was remodeled for the Department of Music. An auditorium was added to the building and an organ costing $30,000 was installed. A new library was opened in 1929.

A reading room in the Carnegie Library. Portraits of Presidents Caldwell, Swain, Battle, and Winston hang on the rear wall.

Circulation desk and card catalogue of the library in December 1921.

The University campus in 1907.

Edwin Mims (1872–1959) was professor of English only from 1909 until 1912, but he had earlier been on the faculty of Trinity College, Durham, and had a wide range of experience in teaching, writing, and editing. He made a deep impression upon his students and the state during the brief period he was in Chapel Hill. He inaugurated extension lectures away from the University, a service that grew and expanded in the years ahead.

Davie Hall, completed late in 1908 to house the Departments of Biology and Botany, was later occupied by the Department of Botany alone. It was adjacent to the Coker Arboretum.

Caldwell Hall, completed and dedicated in 1912, was designed to house the School of Medicine. It provided space for a library, laboratories, and lecture rooms, and released space formerly occupied by this department in Person Hall and in New West.

A dormitory in three sections was begun in May 1912 on property recently purchased by the University. On the site of the former Central Hotel on Franklin Street, Battle-Vance-Pettigrew Dormitory was completed by the end of the year.

Peabody Hall for the School of Education was begun in 1912 and dedicated early in May 1913. Funds for its construction came to the University from the George Peabody Fund, established in 1867 "for the promotion and encouragement of intellectual, moral or industrial education among the young" of the southern and southwestern states.

Students waiting for the train to leave the campus at the beginning of the Christmas vacation, 1912.

Swain Hall was erected in 1913, on the former site of the first President's House, to serve as a dining hall with double the capacity of old Commons Hall across the street. It was named for President David Lowry Swain, and, as Professor Archibald Henderson expressed it, "suffered the unhappy, but inevitable, fate of receiving at the hands of the students the uncomplimentary cognomen of 'Swine Hall.'" Swain Hall served its purpose well until it was replaced by Lenoir Hall in 1939. Swain Hall is the home of the Department of Radio, Television, and Motion Pictures and studios for the University educational television station are here. The eighty-foot standpipe, visible at the left rear corner of Swain Hall, was erected in the 1890s as a part of the University water system, which also served the town. No longer used, the standpipe was taken down in the 1940s.

The North Carolina Division of the United Daughters of the Confederacy decided at their convention in 1909 to honor University students who had served the South during the Civil War by erecting a monument on campus. Funds were raised through their organization and came also from friends and alumni of the University. Dedication and unveiling exercises were held on 2 June 1913 with Governor Locke Craig, class of 1880, as principal speaker. The monument faces north, not far from Franklin Street near Battle-Vance-Pettigrew.

The Pickwick Theatre on Franklin Street, in operation by 1912, was a very popular place of entertainment for the students. The interior view is from an advertisement in the 1913 *Yackety Yack*. The photograph of the entrance probably was made during the year 1918–19.

PICKWICK THEATER
HIGH-CLASS MOTION PICTURES
Instrumental Music

Only highest-class pictures shown   Complete change of program

Open from 6.30 p. m. to 10.30 p. m.

S. J. BROCKWELL, Manager

Unexcelled Automobile Service at Your Command·at All Hours

S. J. BROCKWELL

Half time at the 1913 Carolina–Wake Forest football game in Chapel Hill.

Governor Locke Craig speaking to the North Carolina students at half time at the Carolina–Virginia football game at Charlottesville, Thanksgiving Day, 1913.

The University catalogue for 1881 described the facilities of the School of Natural Philosophy; among its apparatus was "a fine Holtz Electrical Machine, capable of giving an electric spark twenty inches in length." By 1894 the University boasted a physical laboratory "with standard instruments of precision for electrical testing and measurements. An electric light plant has been installed," the catalogue for that year explained, "chiefly for instruction in electric engineering." An early laboratory for the physical sciences had been in Person Hall but afterwards was located in South Building. By the early decades of the twentieth century it was in the basement of Alumni Building where this photograph was made.

A student studying in his room on the first floor of Carr Building during the year 1914–15.

It was announced in January 1915 that Captain Isaac Emerson, class of 1879, had provided funds for a new playing field and a modern grandstand. Within a year the new athletic park was completed and called Emerson Field. Baseball, football, and track were accommodated here. Dressing rooms, a ticket office, and other facilities were available underneath the stadium. With the growing popularity of football as a spectator sport, Emerson Stadium soon became inadequate. A new stadium for football was dedicated in 1927, and Emerson Field was used almost exclusively for baseball until the 1960s. Emerson Stadium was demolished in the spring of 1971.

A cab drawn up before Carr Building, 1914.

Edward Kidder Graham (1876–1918), member of the class of 1898, served as University librarian during 1899–1900 and then became professor of English. After nine years he was made dean of the College of Liberal Arts and served from 1909 until 1913 when he became acting president. In 1915 he became president, but in 1918 he fell victim to the influenza epidemic that swept the country.

Dignitaries gathered on campus for the inauguration of President E. K. Graham, 1915. Episcopal Bishop Joseph Blount Cheshire is on the left.

The inauguration of Edward Kidder Graham, successor to President Venable, in Memorial Hall, 21 April 1915. The United States flag and the North Carolina flag are draped behind the speaker's platform.

In 1915 the families of Henry and Sol Weil of
Goldsboro established the Weil Lectures on Ameri-
can Citizenship and former President William
Howard Taft delivered the first lecture in that
year. President Taft is shown here on the front
porch of the President's House, flanked by Judge
Henry Groves Connor and President Edward K.
Graham.

Two University presidents, Edward K. Graham
and Kemp P. Battle, in springtime academic
procession in 1917. President Battle by this time
was known affectionately as "Old Pres."

Swimming in Purefoy's Mill Pond on Morgan Creek, 1915. Few provisions were made on campus for the spare-time activity of students, and long hikes through the woods to popular swimming holes were common. Bathing facilities were far from adequate on campus and a weekly visit to a pond or a creek was an established routine for many students.

"A Gentleman and four students," the 1915 *Yackety Yack* labeled this picture. They are Robert W. Winston, Jr., Dr. John M. Booker (the "gentleman" of the *Yackety Yack* caption), Allen Mebane, Freddie Manning, and Austin H. Carr.

The shout "Mail is up!" brought students rushing from campus to the post office on the south side of East Franklin Street.

This informal gathering of student musicians about 1917 was a forerunner of the many popular student bands of the 1920s and 1930s, many of which enjoyed national fame.

This advertisement from the 1916 *Yackety Yack* tells its own story.

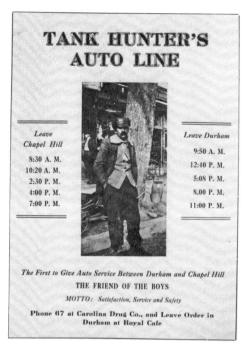

Commencement, 1917, with President E. K. Graham leading the procession. Evidence of the preparation for World War I may be seen on every hand.

Virginius Faison Williams of Faison, a member of the class of 1917, practices a speech in the Philanthropic Society Hall. Many public figures in North Carolina received valuable experience in public speaking while they were members of one of the literary societies on campus.

The University of North Carolina student batallion, 1917.

Members of the faculty as well as students joined the Army during World War I. Here four professors pose on Emerson Field, *left to right*: Andrew H. Patterson, professor of physics; Charles S. Mangum, professor of physiology, anatomy, and medicine; T. Felix Hickerson, professor of mathematics and engineering; and James B. Bullitt, professor of histology and pathology.

Parking on campus in the fall of 1917 was no problem. This snapshot was made from his window in Old East by W. G. Wilson, Jr., of Smithfield, member of the class of 1918.

A Liberty Loan parade on Franklin Street during World War I.

A fast getaway after chapel in Gerrard Hall provided time for a snack or a hasty review of a lesson before the next class. This picture was made just before World War I.

Bright sunshine following a light snowfall in the winter of 1918 brought out soldier and civilian to plaster the front of Gerrard Hall with snowballs. Required chapel attendance was unpopular and few opportunities were lost to express an opinion.

Albert Coates (1896–1989), from Johnston County, was a member of the class of 1918 who went to Harvard for a degree in law. He returned to the University to serve as a professor of law from 1923 until his retirement in 1968. His "monument" is the Institute of Government, which he founded in the early 1930s.

The class of 1918, posing in front of the entrance to South Building, was composed of soldiers and civilians, three women, and one Japanese. This is the earliest pictorial evidence of a foreign student at the University. Kameichi Kato, the Japanese, formed a society designed to foster better relations between Americans and Japanese, a step that the Emperor personally approved.

Rupert Crowell from Candler, member of the class of 1918, was "riding high," one of his classmates commented, in this sporty roadster.

Bulletin boards have long lured the amateur artist and cartoonist, and this one in front of Gerrard Hall in 1919 was no exception. The locked box at the lower right corner suggests how desperate one editor was— "Write Something for YOUR Magazine" says the inscription on the front.

A tall sophomore and a short senior posed in 1918 for a classmate. Thomas Wolfe of Asheville and E. A. Griffin of Goldsboro made an interesting pair. When he pasted their picture in his University album, W. G. Wilson, Jr., could not resist the obvious label: "The Long and Short of it."

W. G. Wilson, Jr., who made this snapshot for his University album labeled it: "One of Bill Folger's famous end runs." The tall sycamore tree at the west end of Emerson Stadium, which offered welcome shade to students for more than half a century, slowly died in the late 1960s and in 1970, for the first time, put out no leaves. When Emerson Stadium was razed in 1971 the sycamore tree was also removed.

The north side of Franklin Street about 1919.

The class of 1918 planted a rooted shoot from Davie Poplar at a spot near the parent tree and tagged it "Davie Poplar, Jr." The young tree is now full grown, but the old tree still stands. President Kemp P. Battle, who died less than a year later, posed beside the newly planted tree.

A student motor parade on Franklin Street near
the end of the second decade of the twentieth
century.

A group of young lady visitors outside
Memorial Hall at commencement time about
1918.

George C. Pickard, left, poses about 1919
with the operator of a mowing machine on
campus. Pickard became supervisor of buildings and grounds about 1910.

Phillips Hall, completed in 1920, was designed to be the home of the School of Applied Science. Mathematics, physics, and engineering classes had previously been scattered around the campus wherever space could be found, but they were now brought together. A new wing was added in 1925 and another in 1927, and the interior has frequently been changed to accommodate different programs. In the 1960s a large addition to the south side of Phillips Hall provided space for the computer sciences.

Chapel Hill in the 1920s was still isolated. This view of the road approaching Chapel Hill from Durham shows little improvement over its condition in the colonial period when the last royal governor of North Carolina, Josiah Martin, commented that the roads in the vicinity of Hillsborough were nearly impassable. Rocks in the road were still frequent obstacles in the 1920s as they had been in the colonial period.

Up the hill from Durham and into the village, the Durham road became East Franklin Street, but it was little better than a rural road of the time. Professor George M. McKie of the English Department lived here at the very edge of Chapel Hill.

The intersection of East Franklin and Hillsborough Streets on an early winter afternoon
in the 1920s was wide, free of rushing traffic,
and marked by wheel tracks of wagons and
buggies.

The Chapel Hill Post Office, familiar to
students of the twenties and thirties, on East
Franklin Street across the campus from
Battle-Vance-Pettigrew dormitories was first
occupied in December 1919. By 1936 the
volume of mail was too great to be handled
in this small building and a new addition was
constructed behind this one. Postal workers
then moved into the new area and the old
post office was torn down to make way for
a new one connected to the addition.
In this way the postal service was neither
interrupted nor moved from the site.

Sunday afternoon scholars on the fraternity house porch. *Left to right*: reading the comic section is Beemer C. Harrell, class of 1917, who was a graduate student during 1918–20; Thomas Wolfe, class of 1920, dozing over a closed book; and James Newland Brand, class of 1922, preparing for a Monday morning class.

Constructed during 1920–21, Steele Dormitory was the first building to face the newly planned South Quadrangle. It was named for Walter Leak Steele (1823–91), class of 1844, a trustee for many years, member and secretary of the Secession Convention of 1861, and active in the reopening of the University in 1875. Steele Dormitory was last used for its intended purpose in 1957, then the interior was remodeled to accommodate University administrative offices. It is one of the few buildings on campus without chimneys, either real (but abandoned) or decorative.

Fraternity Row in the 1920s extended along the north and west borders of the campus. Ten frame houses had provided homes for the fraternities until early January 1919 when three of them burned in a fire that also threatened the north end of the library. Fraternity membership among the student body rose from 17 percent in the 1910–19 decade to 25 percent in the 1920s, and the fraternities began to consider finding more adequate quarters. The trustees purchased property on the west side of South Columbia Street which they exchanged for the sites along Fraternity Row, and by October 1926 the new Fraternity Court on Columbia Street was completed.

The Delta Kappa Epsilon fraternity house on Fraternity Row, used in later years by the Orange-Person-Chatham County Public Health Department.

With the increased enrollment of women in the 1920s, Mrs. Marvin H. (Inez Koonce) Stacy (1886–1961), widow of Dean Stacy, played an increasingly important role. She was made adviser to women in 1919 and was responsible for improving facilities on campus for women. In 1942 she was given the title "dean of women," a more apt description of her duties for many years, and she held this office until her retirement in 1946.

This picture postcard view of a corner of the arboretum in the early 1920s will be difficult for students of a later time to recognize. Much of the open space has disappeared, and trees and shrubs have grown. The building on the left is Caldwell, a corner of Bynum Gymnasium is visible, and next is a glimpse of Carr Building. On the right is Davie Hall as it appeared before the wing was added to the north side during 1925–26.

Following World War I housing for students on campus and for faculty in town became difficult to find. The construction of new dormitories solved the problem for students, but the trustees also turned their attention to faculty needs. In January 1920 the use of endowment funds was authorized to purchase sites and to construct ten houses. Carpenters were brought over daily by automobile from Durham when work was begun in the late spring. By making use of pre-fabricated houses, new homes were ready for the faculty when classes started in September. These houses, shown here in a twelve-inch snow on 27 January 1921, were constructed on Park Place facing Battle Park. They were removed in 1971 and a carefully landscaped, prize-winning parking area established on the site.

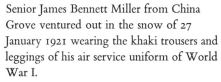

Senior James Bennett Miller from China Grove ventured out in the snow of 27 January 1921 wearing the khaki trousers and leggings of his air service uniform of World War I.

Melting snow on 2 February 1921 added to the beauty of this walk in the arboretum. Snow seems always to have tempted campus photographers to snap scenes that otherwise would have been considered commonplace.

The mineralogy laboratory in New East during the spring quarter of 1921.

Another walk in the arboretum of the 1920s during a warmer season.

Geological field trips into the country around Chapel Hill have been traditional, at least since the days of Elisha Mitchell. This student in 1921, wearing his old army campaign hat, rests as he contemplates the numerous specimens surrounding him.

A group of young faculty members and their friends gathered at the home of Mrs. W. F. Prouty on 13 May 1921 for a party. *Left to right*: Walter Bryan Jones, instructor in geology; Miss Ernestine Kennette, member of the library staff; Charles I. Silin, instructor in French; Miss Adeline Denham, a student who was also working in the North Carolina Collection at the library; Miss Ione Markham, who worked in the Extension Division of the library; J. B. Linker, an instructor in mathematics; Miss Nell Pickard, a 1921 graduate of the University who would teach in the Durham City Schools in the fall; John Theodore Krumpelmann, instructor in German; Miss Nina Mae Cooper; and Earle H. Peacock, professor of accounting.

On 12 October 1921 the cornerstone was laid for the first of four new dormitories to be erected on a new quadrangle east of Caldwell Hall. Grimes, Mangum, Manly, and Ruffin dormitories were then in the edge of the woods that bounded the campus on the east. In this view the railroad, laid to deliver building material to the site, may be seen on the left. The persimmon tree at the southwest corner of Caldwell nearly always produced a bountiful crop.

In 1922 the Chapel Hill telephone exchange was located in this building behind the post office on Henderson Street just north of Franklin. In 1927 the University bought the telephone system from the town and soon afterwards tore down this building when a new exchange was constructed on nearby Rosemary Lane.

New classrooms, Saunders (*left*) and Murphey (*right*), were built in 1922 and Manning in 1923. An attempt was made to provide cool air for summer relief in Saunders and Murphey by the construction of air ducts from the basement, through which cool air was to be drawn up to various spots throughout the building. This idea was good but in practice it was no more successful than the antebellum plan to provide central heating in New East and New West. These buildings represented a further development of the area south of Steele Dormitory. Saunders provided space for history and social science, Murphey for language and literature, and Manning for law. They have subsequently been put to use by other departments.

The paving of the road to Pittsboro, leading south out of Chapel Hill, was well documented by an anonymous photographer. The six-mule team rests behind Peabody Hall, with Phillips in the background and the peak of Memorial Hall visible in the distance. The other view, looking up the hill toward the future site of the Carolina Inn, shows the railroad trestle over which trains to campus passed. Professor Howard W. Odum talked with some of the black workmen, especially those who passed his house as they worked, and from the stories he heard from them (particularly from one man who had lost an arm) he gathered information that he used in three novels.

"Proff" Koch and Paul Green pose in the edge of Battle Park at the site of the Forest Theatre. Frederick Henry Koch came to Chapel Hill in 1918 as professor of dramatic literature and soon afterwards organized the Carolina Playmakers. Paul Green of Lillington, class of 1921, joined the faculty as an assistant professor of philosophy in 1923 and became professor of dramatic art in 1936. Green had been a student under Koch and continued his dramatic work afterwards. In 1927 he won the Pulitzer Prize for drama.

A dormitory for women, Spencer Hall, named for Cornelia Phillips Spencer, was opened in 1924. Unlike the other dormitories on campus Spencer Hall included a dining room.

On Saturday morning 24 January 1925, Archer House on Columbia Street, used for the past several years as a dormitory for women, was badly damaged by fire. Furniture and personal possessions were quickly rescued by students and deposited across the street. Among the articles rescued from the burning building was the bathtub, an article of considerable fame. For several years the twenty-two young ladies living in the house had been complaining to University officials that one bathtub was not enough. *The Tar Heel* published denials of the rumor that the fire had been set by coeds smoking in the attic.

Head Cheerleader Vic Huggins in 1924 decided that the University should have a mascot such as State's wolf and Georgia's bulldog. Since Jack Merritt, a popular member of the football team, was known as "The Battering Ram," Huggins hit upon the idea of a ram as the Carolina mascot. He prevailed upon University Business Manager Charles T. Woollen to find $25.00 to buy one. Ordered from Texas, Rameses the Ram arrived in time for the U.N.C.–V.M.I. game at which the two teams battled to a standstill until late in the fourth quarter. Bunn Hackney then stepped back to the thirty-yard line and made a perfect dropkick for a 3–0 victory. Rameses' presence was credited with making the victory possible, and Rameses I became the first of a continuing line of rams to witness Tar Heel football games.

The Carolina Inn, built in 1924 by John Sprunt Hill, student at the University, 1885–89, and a law student, 1891–92, was opened in December as an important new center of activity at the University. Mr. Hill had built the Inn at his own expense when a corporation composed of alumni and friends of the University had been unable to raise the necessary funds. In 1935 Mr. and Mrs. Hill and their three children presented the Carolina Inn property as a gift to the University with the stipulation that the income be used first for the maintenance and upkeep of the Inn and second for the support of the University Library, especially the collection of North Caroliniana.

A chemistry laboratory in Howell Hall shortly before Venable Hall was completed in 1925 to house the Chemistry Department.

The Henderson County Club in 1924. County clubs were organized through the efforts of the North Carolina Club, which Professor E. C. Branson initiated in 1914. Members of the various county clubs engaged in research on their home counties, and often local citizens provided funds for the publication of their findings. Members of the county clubs were most often concerned with surveys designed to promote better public schools, public health, improved methods of county government, and other aspects of community life.

Smith Hall remained the home of the library until 1907 when a new library building was occupied. The Law School moved into Smith and remained there until Manning Hall was completed in 1923. During 1924–25 this handsome old building was remodeled as a theatre for the Carolina Playmakers, and it was dedicated for this purpose on 23 November 1925.

The interior of Smith Hall as a theatre.

The Chemistry Department had outgrown Person Hall even with two additions to the original building, and it later became too large for satisfactory accommodation in Howell Hall. In 1925 Venable Hall, the first building on the west side of the south campus, was completed and occupied by this department.

William T. Couch (1901–89), class of 1926, became acting director of the University of North Carolina Press in June 1925, a year before he was graduated. In 1932 he was made director, and he held this position for more than twenty years. Under his leadership the press grew in importance and influence, particularly in the Southeast. As a regional press publishing books of national interest it had no rival. The books published were both critical and commendatory of the South. He also encouraged native literary genius, and the press published an increasing number of books by North Carolina authors and books dealing with North Carolina, both fiction and nonfiction.

South Building was extensively remodeled during 1926–27. A massive portico was added to the south side. Workmen are shown putting finishing touches on the roof in this picture. A stone and brick wall and steps were erected a short distance from the building in 1929.

By 1921 Emerson Field was no longer adequate for accommodating spectators at University football games, and officials and alumni began to lay plans for the construction of a larger stadium. When William Rand Kenan, Jr., class of 1894, heard of the plans of the group to raise funds for this purpose, he revealed his recently developed plan to establish a memorial of some kind to his parents. He offered to build the stadium as such a memorial. His gift was accepted and on 24 November 1927 the Kenan Memorial Stadium was dedicated. It is situated in a natural bowl surrounded by a thick stand of pines and hardwood trees.

The field house at Kenan Memorial Stadium, also a gift of William Rand Kenan, Jr., was built at the same time the stadium was under construction.

Summer school registration in Memorial Hall in the mid-1920s. Freshly bobbed hair and short dresses of the "flapper era" were new on campus.

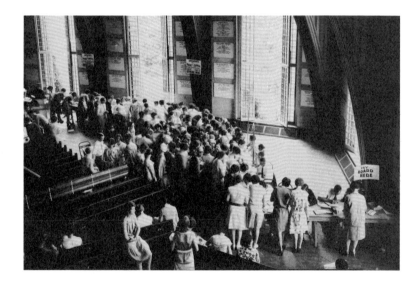

The evening meal in camp in eastern Tennessee on a field course in geology conducted by Professors W. F. Prouty and G. R. MacCarthy in the summer of 1927. Dr. Prouty is in the center, facing camera, and Dr. MacCarthy is on his left. The trip began at Knoxville, Tennessee, and ended at Sanford, North Carolina. There were nine students in the group and five of them wore white shirts for dinner, even in camp. "This was early in the trip," one of the students later commented, "and dress-for-dinner soon lost its appeal."

The high price of clothing in the spring of 1922 led to a student protest. A campaign to encourage the wearing of overalls met with favor and this group gathered in front of the Carnegie Library to demonstrate its support. Students were urged to put their suits in storage to be worn only on special occasions. The placard reads: "MOTH-BALLS Get 'em in Vance #8 Save that spring suit." One participant later recalled that some students violated the spirit of the protest when they wore tailor-made overalls.

Band leader Kay Kyser (1906–85), class of 1927, earned a B.S. degree in commerce as James Kern Kyser from Rocky Mount. He enjoyed an active extracurricular program and was a member of the Grail, the YMCA Cabinet, the Monogram Club, the Carolina Playmakers, the Inter-Fraternity Council, the Golden Fleece, and other organizations. He was also head cheerleader, as shown here in uniform.

In 1924 three new dormitories for men (Aycock, Graham, and Lewis) were built in the edge of Battle Park to form part of a new quadrangle. A fourth (Everett) was under construction in 1928 in the right background when this picture was made.

A new library building was completed and dedicated in October 1929. A large and impressive structure, it faced South Building and formed the south side of the large quadrangle. Built of limestone instead of brick, as were the other buildings on campus, it was admired for the beauty of its detail. Large and attractive reading rooms, space for such special resources as the North Carolina Collection and the Southern Historical Collection, well-equipped stack space, and carrels for graduate students encouraged greater use of the library by students.

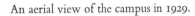

An aerial view of the campus in 1929.

In spite of the sound of hammers and saws and the presence of temporary railroad tracks to new building sites, life in the old section of the campus was undisturbed during the great building program of the 1920s. These two pictures, made about noon on a bright early spring day in the center of the campus, suggest how peaceful and quiet it was. The student walking away from South Building is wearing knickers, which were very popular that year.

With the physical enlargement of the University during the 1920s, the faculty also grew in numbers. But more important than numbers was the creative work of the faculty, the lasting impression they made upon students, and the esteem in which they were held by their fellow North Carolinians and their compatriots elsewhere in the world of scholarship. Men who had joined the faculty fresh from college themselves in the previous decade reached scholarly maturity during the twenties.

Marvin Hendrix Stacy (1877–1919), class of 1902, belongs in this group by virtue of the fact that he laid the groundwork for the opening of a new and great era for the University. Following President E. K. Graham's death from influenza, Dean Stacy became acting president. He had joined the faculty in 1902 as an instructor in mathematics, becoming professor of civil engineering in 1910. He was among those of the faculty who served well and with recognition without the doctorate. He had served as acting dean of the College of Liberal Arts since 1914 and in 1918 became dean and chairman of the faculty, in addition to continuing as professor of civil engineering. Under his direction the University adopted the quarter system, set up a new scale of fees, and made the transition from the war to the postwar years. Faculty and students returning from military service had to be accommodated. Stacy also laid plans for the next two academic years and prepared and submitted the budget for the next biennium. One week after his report was submitted to the executive committee, Stacy was dead from influenza and pneumonia. His proposals, however, were approved. They included the establishment of a school of commerce, a directorship of music, the expansion of the Law School, the construction of a woman's building, and the appointment of a health officer and a publications editor. All of these materialized in the twenties.

Sallie Marks (1891–1968) became the first female professor in the University in 1927, when she was named supervising principal of the elementary grades of the training school with the rank of assistant professor of education. She remained until 1934, then joined the faculty of Salem College. From 1938 to 1944 she held a professorship at the University of Chicago.

Harry Woodburn Chase (1883–1955), a native of Massachusetts, joined the University faculty in 1910 as professor of the philosophy of education and became professor of psychology four years later. When Dean Stacy became acting president in 1918, Chase became chairman of the faculty and acting dean of the College of Liberal Arts. Following Stacy's death Chase became acting president and in June 1919 he was elected president. President Graham and Stacy had already pointed the direction in which the University would progress in the future, but Chase saw that these plans for growth and expansion were followed. As they envisioned, he made the University a tool of the state; physical facilities were enlarged; young, enthusiastic faculty members were brought to Chapel Hill; and the support of students, alumni, and the General Assembly was enlisted. Chase's sound judgment, his good sense, and his fearlessness in the face of opposition that he deemed unjustified won him friends on campus and around the state. His undaunted support of his faculty in the face of unwarranted attack on them because of their scholarly publications or research was the marvel of friend and foe alike. His opposition to an antievolution bill introduced into the General Assembly in 1925 has been given a large share of the credit for its defeat. At the risk of jeopardizing the University appropriations bill, he spoke in support of academic freedom and won without losing the financial support so desperately needed. Chase declined a number of opportunities to accept other positions outside North Carolina until 1930 when he was offered the presidency of the University of Illinois, one of the nation's largest and most progressive state universities. With much regret on both sides—both his and that of the people of North Carolina—he departed, but ties of friendship bound him to Chapel Hill until his death in 1955.

Collier Cobb (1862–1934), who joined the faculty in 1892 as assistant professor of geology and mineralogy, taught several generations of students before his death. He delighted in telling new students that he had taught their fathers or grandfathers and often remembered a father's grade or a particular paper he had written. Cobb challenged the young to equal or better the father's grade. "Few professors at Carolina," it was said of him, "have ever been so close to the students, few so beloved by them."

William C. Coker (1872–1953) was the first professor of botany. He joined the faculty in 1902 and became Kenan Professor of Botany in 1920. He was noted as a scientist, a teacher, and a landscape architect. As a member of the buildings and grounds committee from 1913 until 1942 he was instrumental in beautifying the campus by planting trees and shrubs. The arboretum, which he began in 1903, is widely known for its natural beauty and for the great variety of plants growing there— the Coker Arboretum is his monument. A book by Coker, *The Saprolegniaceae, with Notes on Other Water Molds*, published in 1923, was the first to be issued by the newly established University of North Carolina Press. A faculty committee in a tribute to Professor Coker described him as "in every sense a gentleman—dignified but friendly, reserved but sensitive to the needs of others, often quietly opening up avenues of financial assistance to struggling students. He helped many young men through college by making them personal loans. Though he lost money on some, he never lost faith in people."

Robert D. W. Connor (1878–1950), class of 1899, joined the faculty in 1921 as Kenan Professor of History and Government after having organized and directed the North Carolina Historical Commission in Raleigh. He was a pioneer in many scholarly fields; he was an inspiring teacher, possessor of a keen sense of humor, and a devoted friend of the University. Except for the fact that he was a member of the Board of Trustees, which disqualified him, he almost certainly would have been made president of the University following President E. K. Graham's death in 1918; he was again considered for this post after President Chase's resignation. Professor Connor left the classroom in 1934 to become the first archivist of the United States, but in 1941 he returned to Chapel Hill and taught until his retirement in 1949. His ground-breaking research in North Carolina history, his many books and articles, and his public addresses created an interest in and appreciation for the history of this state which is perhaps unparalleled in any other Southern state.

Frank Porter Graham (1886–1972), class of 1909, had been general secretary of the YMCA and an instructor in history before becoming dean of students and assistant professor of history in 1919. In 1926 he was promoted to the rank of professor and in 1930 was elected president of the University succeeding Chase. President Graham and other friends of the University, including faculty as well as alumni, successfully mounted a campaign to secure more adequate financial support for the University. The result was increased appropriations and a bond issue for permanent improvements. In 1932 the University of North Carolina, State College at Raleigh, and Woman's College at Greensboro were joined to form the Consolidated University of North Carolina with Graham as president. Although his office remained in South Building and he continued to live in the house provided for University presidents, he was no longer the chief executive officer of the Chapel Hill campus alone. The title of dean of administration (Robert B. House) was eventually adopted for that position.

Edwin Greenlaw (1874–1931) joined the faculty as professor of English in 1913 and became a Kenan Professor in 1917 and dean of the Graduate School in 1920. Dean Greenlaw brought new ideals of scholarship to the University. Teaching, research, and publication found new encouragement, and under his leadership the University became the twenty-fifth member of the Association of American Universities. He was instrumental in securing greater library resources, establishing research fellowships and assistantships, securing grants-in-aid from foundations and other sources, and creating the University Press.

T. Felix Hickerson (1882–1968), class of 1904, joined the faculty in 1905 as an instructor in mathematics and by 1920 had become professor of civil engineering. When the School of Engineering was moved to Raleigh, Professor Hickerson remained in Chapel Hill as a member of the mathematics department. His published books on highway and bridge construction were used around the world, and during World War II the engineers who worked feverishly to build the Burma Road over impassable terrain used Hickerson's *Route Survey and Design* as their guide. A member of the Order of Gimghouls as a student, he continued to serve as a trustee afterwards and is given a large share of the credit for the construction of the unique Gimghoul Castle in 1926. He retired from the classroom in 1952 but continued his research and writing almost until the time of his death. Unmarried, he left his home, adjacent to the campus, and its furnishings to the University.

S. Huntington Hobbs, Jr. (1895–1969), class of 1916, was graduated one day and joined the University faculty the next. Beginning as an instructor in rural economics and sociology, he was professor of rural social economics by 1930 and editor of the *University News Letter*, a popular and influential organ for the betterment of North Carolina, from 1922 until 1956. In 1953 Dr. Hobbs estimated that six thousand students had taken his course— "North Carolina: Economic and Social." His influence in improving the economic and social conditions of the state was great; his work for rural electrification, agricultural diversification, industrialization, and highway and transportation developments bore good results. At the time of his retirement in 1967 he had been a member of the faculty for fifty years.

E. Vernon Howell (1872–1931) became professor of pharmacy in 1896 and was dean of the School of Pharmacy from 1901 until his death. Before this time pharmacy had been taught in Chapel Hill occasionally, more or less as had law and medicine—privately and in classes independent of the University. Howell, however, established the School of Pharmacy as a part of the University. He was a gifted teacher, a friendly man, and a beloved citizen of the community. As an authority in his chosen field he was without equal, and his published works were often consulted by his profession. It was reported that any question could be settled quickly by prefacing one's remarks with "Dean Howell says. . . ." It was Dean Howell who purchased the first automobile owned in Chapel Hill. He named it "Old Wheeze" and used it often to take his neighbors and students fishing or hunting.

Andrew H. Patterson (1870–1928), class of 1891, was active in student affairs when he was enrolled in the University. He was on the football team and managed the baseball team; he was president of the YMCA and the Dialectic Society; he was a member of SAE fraternity and a charter member of the Order of Gimghouls. After further education elsewhere and teaching experience at the University of Georgia, he became professor of physics at the University in 1908. Three years later he also became dean of the School of Applied Science; in 1922 engineering was removed from this school and a separate dean was appointed, but chemistry, medicine, and geology remained and with recently increased quarters the school grew. Professor Patterson served on more than half of the University's standing committees and his advice was constantly sought by members of other committees. He was ever the champion of the student and always gave him the benefit of any doubt. In the fight over the teaching of evolution, his publications and his comments were important. He held that no conflict existed between science and religion and that a bigoted attitude toward either was detrimental to progress in North Carolina. As a faculty member and as an administrator he helped build up a high standard of athletic excellence in the southern states and was one of the moving spirits in the organization of the Southern Intercollegiate Athletic Association.

Horace Williams (1858–1940), class of 1883, was librarian of the University during the 1880–83 period. In 1890 he became professor of mental and moral science and was made Kenan Professor of Philosophy in 1920. He was a teacher of idealist philosophy. He maintained that the spirit is the controlling element in human life and that individuals may be free in their actions. He encouraged his students to question and to think, and he trained a large and devoted number of followers. In his novel, *Look Homeward, Angel*, Thomas Wolfe clearly refers to Williams under whom he studied and whom he admired very much: "Eugene looked with passionate devotion at the grand old head, calm, wise and comforting. In a moment of vision, he saw that, for him, here was the last of the heroes, the last of those giants to whom we give the faith of our youth, believing that the riddle of our lives may be solved by their quiet judgment. . . ." As late as 1940, twenty years after Wolfe had left Chapel Hill, Horace Williams was spending much of his time in Graham Memorial lounge reading and talking with the young men of a new generation.

Louis Round Wilson (1876–1979), class of 1899, perhaps holds the record for length of service to the University. He became librarian in 1901 and retired in 1959. Between 1932 and 1942 he was dean of the Graduate Library School at the University of Chicago, but from his return in 1942 until his retirement he was professor of library science and administration. All in all he served for thirty-one years as librarian and at various times during that period was director of the Bureau of Extension and director and chairman of the Board of Governors of the University of North Carolina Press. He began to offer courses in library administration in 1904 and some years afterwards began to consider plans for the establishment of a School of Library Science. This plan developed during the administration of President Chase, and in 1929 a grant from the Carnegie Corporation insured the operating expenses of such a school for five years. In 1931 the school was formally opened, and Dr. Wilson became its director and Kenan Professor of Library Administration.

Thomas J. Wilson, Jr. (1874–1945), class of 1894, joined the faculty in 1899 and served continuously as instructor in Greek and Latin, associate professor and professor of Latin, and registrar and dean of admissions until his death. At various times he was also editor of the *Record*, secretary of the faculty, and advisory dean. "His job has been that of sitting in judgment as new students were admitted to the University," the *Alumni Review* reported in 1939. "Likewise he has recorded their grades and counseled with those students at the time of their academic difficulties. Indelible impressions have been formed by many students as they sat across Dr. Wilson's desk, and these experiences have become a part of rich alumni reminiscences."

Dudley DeWitt Carroll (1885–1971), native of Danbury, joined the University faculty in 1918 as professor of economics and the following year became the first dean of the School of Commerce which he helped plan and establish. Following President E. K. Graham's recommendation, the school required a broad liberal base of those who majored in commerce, and Dean Carroll maintained this objective faithfully. Dean Carroll was described as an indefatigable and prodigious worker and expected the students in his classes to follow his example. He also took part in municipal, county, and state government, serving as town councilman and as a member of the State Board of Conservation and Development among other positions. Although he retired from his position of leadership at the head of the School of Commerce in 1950, he continued to teach for six more years. Upon the foundations that he laid, the present School of Business Administration developed, and one of the buildings of this school is named in his honor.

The Morehead-Patterson Bell Tower, gift of John Motley Morehead, class of 1891, and Rufus Lenoir Patterson, class of 1893, is located in a formally landscaped plot, bordered by boxwood, south of the University library. Dedicated on 26 November 1931, at the Carolina-Virginia homecoming game, it rises to a height of 167 feet and contains a dozen bells weighing from 300 to 3,500 pounds each.

The Carnegie Library building was remodeled after the new library was occupied, and it became Hill Music Hall. John Sprunt Hill of Durham, class of 1889, provided funds for enlarging the old book-stack area into an auditorium and also gave funds for the purchase of a pipe organ.

Jack Wardlaw's orchestra posed on the stage of the new auditorium in Hill Hall in 1931. Formed on the campus in 1928, the orchestra was well received at engagements throughout the state. The musicians stayed together until 1941 and play-ed on many occasions in the eastern United States, including New York, Atlantic City, Washington, and Myrtle Beach. A number of other bands that formed about this time also enjoyed a national reputation, among them Hal Kemp's and Kay Kyser's.

George Thomas Barclay, class of 1934, was captain of the 1934 football team, which compiled a 7–1–1 record. Carolina's first All-American football player and an outstanding performer in the 1935 East-West Shrine Game, Barclay later served as coach at a number of institutions before returning to the University as head coach for the 1953–55 period.

James Moore Tatum (1913–59), class of 1935, played at Carolina but is best remembered for his outstand-ing coaching ability. After coaching at Maryland, where his teams amassed a 73-15-4 record over a nine-year period and he was voted national coach of the year in 1953, he returned to his alma mater in 1956 as head football coach.

Old Memorial Hall was found to be unsafe in 1929 and in January 1930 John Sprunt Hill, speaking for the building committee of the trustees, recommended that a modern fireproof building of greater dignity be erected. Shortly after this Memorial Hall was being razed.

By midsummer 1931 a new Memorial Hall had risen on the site of the old. The marble memorial plaques were installed on the walls of the new building, and since funds for new seats were not available the uncomfortable old heart-pine benches were set up again.

One of Edward Kidder Graham's desires for the campus was a student center in which dormitory residents could relax and entertain their friends. A committee of faculty members and alumni was formed soon after Graham's death in 1918 to raise funds for a student union. By the late spring of 1928 the sum of $155,351 had been raised, and the gift of $80,000 by an anonymous donor, later known to have been L. Ames Brown, class of 1910, enabled the committee to authorize construction to begin. Graham Memorial, shown here while work was underway, was completed in the autumn of 1931 and dedicated in January 1932.

Graham Memorial provided space for student relaxation with bowling alleys, a pool room, space for dances and recitals, and offices for student government and student publications. Student elections were frequently held here and campaign banners graced the columns each spring as election day approached. With the completion of a new student union in 1968 nearer the center of the expanding campus, not far from the Bell Tower, Graham Memorial was taken over temporarily by the Department of Dramatic Art.

The lounge room in Graham Memorial, with handsome oak-paneled walls, was often acclaimed "the most beautiful room in the United States south of Washington." Portraits of University faculty and presidents graced the walls, newspapers and popular magazines were available, and a variety of musical and dramatic programs were offered, particularly on Sunday afternoons and evenings.

Robert Watson Winston (1860–1944), class of 1879, returned to Chapel Hill when he was in his sixties "to be re-educated." He was a familiar figure on campus in the 1930s and early 1940s and is shown here in the lobby of Graham Memorial with Bill McDade, long a faithful servant of the University. Winston had been an instructor in Latin immediately after his graduation, but he afterwards studied law and became a judge of the superior court. He was the author of biographies of Andrew Johnson, Jefferson Davis, Robert E. Lee, Horace Williams, and others, and he spent much time in the University library engaged in research. His presence on campus was a living link with the past for many students who admired him and with whom he passed much time in pleasant and scholarly conversation.

An aerial view of the campus in the spring of 1932.

South Building about 1932 was still the center of the campus, large oaks from the eighteenth century survived, and the well, picturesque though it was, stood in the middle of unpaved, ungrassed, and well-trod ground.

Eight o'clock classes on a cold winter morning in the mid-1930s lured a few diligent students across campus. Most of them avoided the damp gravel walks after a recent light snow in favor of the grassy plots.

Members of Alpha Kappa Delta, sociology fraternity, 1931.

Don Jackson hits the line in the Maryland game, 12 October 1935. Andy Bershak is shown blocking out a Maryland tackler while Babe Daniel seeks someone to shove off his feet. At the extreme left Dick Buck appears quite angry about something.

Bill Conner, class of 1937, dozes on the porch of the Sigma Nu house in the spring of 1934. On the open page of the magazine under his left elbow is a picture of Hitler who had recently assumed dictatorial powers in Germany.

A group of graduate women pose on the steps of Archer House, 1936.

Student government council, 1936, in one of the upstairs offices in Graham Memorial.

Students and faculty of the School of Library Science, 1936. Dean Susan Grey Akers is on the front row, at right.

The Carolina Theatre on Franklin Street offered
the latest in motion picture entertainment in 1937
for an admission of 30¢.

Afternoon classes in the
1930s were rare and the
first afternoon show at
the local motion picture
house was referred to as
"Smith's 2 o'clock class."
The young man with
his left leg extended is
Walker Percy, future
author of *The Moviegoer*.

The Senior Ball, 1937, in the Tin Can.

The Department of Mathematics in which engineering courses had been taught, was divided in 1912 and the Department of Civil Engineering established. Electrical engineering was added in 1922 to create the School of Engineering, and the following year the Department of Mechanical Engineering was added to the school. The need for electrical engineers to operate the rapidly developing public utilities companies in the state and for highway engineers to aid in the extension of the state highway system was responsible for this development. In 1938 the School of Engineering fell victim to consolidation and was transferred to North Carolina State College. The mock tombstone erected in front of Phillips Hall suggests the attitude of many on the campus toward this move.

Woollen Gymnasium was erected during 1937–38 and was named by the trustees for Business Manager Charles T. Woollen. The need for a new gymnasium to replace the inadequate Bynum Gymnasium was first mentioned by Woollen in his 1923–24 report. When Bynum was completed in 1905 the student body numbered 600; the student body in 1938 was 3,508.

Walker Percy, class of 1937, was a science major as an undergraduate and went on from Chapel Hill to the Columbia University College of Physicians and Surgeons. Graduating with the M.D. degree in 1941 he began an internship in Bellevue Hospital, but he soon contracted tuberculosis and went to the mountains of New York for a period of recuperation. During the enforced idleness he read a great deal and began writing. He has contributed to *Harper's* and other magazines and has published novels that have been highly praised. *The Moviegoer*, published in 1961, won the National Book Award; *The Last Gentleman* appeared in 1966, *Love in the Ruins* in 1971, *The Message in the Bottle* in 1975, and *Lancelot* in 1977. He was awarded an honorary degree by the University in 1972.

Stacy Dormitory, completed in 1938 and named for Dean Marvin H. Stacy, stands between Everett and Graham dormitories and completes the lower quadrangle.

President Franklin D. Roosevelt, invited to Chapel Hill by the Carolina Political Union, spoke to a crowd of twelve thousand packed into Woollen Gymnasium on 5 December 1938. In a twenty-five-minute speech Roosevelt praised the progressiveness of the University and defended his own liberalism. Afterwards, as shown here, he was awarded an honorary LL.D. degree.

The staff of the North Carolina administrative headquarters of the Public Works Administration in the summer of 1936 shortly before it was consolidated into a district office in Atlanta. Among those pictured on the steps of Phillips Hall are Director Herman G. Baity (*third from right in the front row*), Florence Gee, Lillian Long, Thomas Rose, Carl Mengel, Billie Curtis, Betty Winston, and Elizabeth Lyne Thompson.

The medical and public health building under construction in 1938 was later named the MacNider Building for Dr. William deB. MacNider. It was the first of many buildings constructed on the southern limits of the campus where the Division of Health Affairs developed.

Whitehead Dormitory, built in 1939 and named for Dr. Richard H. Whitehead, professor of anatomy and early dean of the medical school, was occupied originally by medical students, but with the rush of students after World War II it was occupied by veterans and their wives. Afterwards it became a dormitory for women.

East Rosemary Lane about 1939.

Lenoir Hall, a dining hall named for General William Lenoir, first president of the Board of Trustees, was completed late in 1939 and opened to students returning after the Christmas holidays in January 1940. It replaced Swain Hall, which accommodated only 500, while Lenoir had seats for 1,300.

A tobacco auctioneer who lost a football bet in the U.N.C.-Duke game in November 1939 pays off by pushing a warehouseman from the warehouse to the Durham County courthouse.

Wallace E. Caldwell (1890–1961) joined the University faculty in 1921 as professor of history. His courses in ancient history and in historiography were very popular. His interest in archaeology, Masonry, and the Society of Mayflower Descendants brought him into contact with many North Carolinians who might otherwise never have known a professor. Professor Caldwell always enjoyed talking with his students at the end of a class period, and it was a widely held belief that this was one way to secure a good grade.

Professor Caldwell in a favorite pose at home.

Oscar J. Coffin (1887–1956), class of 1909, joined the faculty as professor of journalism in 1926 after having served as the editor of a Raleigh newspaper. He headed the department of journalism for a number of years and retired from teaching only after thirty years. Insisting upon accuracy, the proper use of the English language, and style, "Skipper" Coffin exerted a great influence on his students. The respect that he fostered for newspaper work lives on and he has been given much of the credit for the splendid daily and weekly newspapers that exist in the state.

The Institute of Government, through conferences, seminars, classes, and publications, trains and instructs officials in all levels of governmental activity as well as private citizens in the proper performance of their duties. It grew out of the law school classroom of Professor Albert Coates, class of 1918, who, with Mrs. Coates, supported and operated it at great personal sacrifice for a number of years. The story of the institute begins in September 1932 when six hundred officials, citizens, teachers, and students attended sessions on the campus. The building shown here was opened in 1939 through the generosity of many private donors. Early in 1942 the institute, by act of the trustees, became an integral part of the University. In the summer of 1956 the institute was moved into a new building on the eastern edge of the campus erected in part through a donation of the Knapp Foundation, Inc.

William M. Dey (1880–1961), a nephew of Professor Walter D. Toy, attended the University as a freshman but was graduated from the University of Virginia in his native state. He joined the faculty in Chapel Hill in 1909 as professor of romance languages and literatures and for forty years was chairman of the Department of Romance Languages. When the Division of the Humanities was organized in 1935, he became its first chairman and during the five years of his leadership gave it a tradition upon which to build. Professor Dey also served as faculty marshal from 1934 until 1946. Under his direction the Department of Romance Languages became one of the very best in the nation and the faculty grew from four men in 1917 to sixty at the time of his retirement in 1950.

Professor Fletcher M. Green (1895–1978) began his teaching career at Chapel Hill as a graduate instructor in 1922 and after receiving his Ph.D. in 1927 joined the regular faculty. Except for a few years at Emory University, he continued to teach until his retirement in 1966. His ability to inspire students and to win their loyalty created in them a feeling of friendship both for Professor Green and among themselves which has stood the test of time. He made historical scholarship exciting for his students, who served as professors, department chairmen, and deans in more than forty institutions of higher learning.

Professor J. G. de Roulhac Hamilton (1878–1961),
a native of Hillsborough, joined the history faculty
of the University in 1906 and was head of the
History Department from 1908 until 1930. Under
his leadership the department increased its faculty
from two to sixteen and became the leading center
for graduate research in the history of the South.
Professor Hamilton served on numerous faculty
committees, contributed to and edited journals
and historical publications, and was the author of
a number of books and monographs. A gifted and
inspiring teacher of both graduate and undergraduate students, he was also a pioneer in preserving
historical sources. In 1930 he was relieved of his
teaching duties to devote full time to the development of the Southern Historical Collection. Established in the new University library, this collection grew under his guidance into one of the most
important repositories of historical manuscripts
in the nation. Dr. Hamilton's long collecting trips
throughout the South earned for him the reputation of "ransacker for posterity," and he undoubtedly saved many records that would have been
lost forever had he not gathered them up, taken
them to Chapel Hill, and organized them for the
use of researchers. Even after his retirement in
1948 he continued to collect manuscripts and
frequently assisted scholars in using the resources
he had gathered.

Edgar W. Knight (1885–1953) was professor of
education in the University from 1919 until his
death, but his scholarly reputation far exceeded
the bounds of both his department and the subject
he taught. Tests and educational programs designed
by him were used by the United States in both
world wars. From 1934 until 1937 he was director
of the summer sessions of the Consolidated University. He visited China, the Scandinavian countries,
and Iraq in advisory capacities to the governments
of those countries. He was critical of superficial
educational activities and decried the mass production of Ph.D.'s. His numerous articles, pamphlets, books, and lectures, all carefully researched
and precisely written, were well received in many
quarters, but in others they hit home with such
great force that they were not always appreciated.
Sympathetic but firm with his students, Professor Knight was remembered with fondness by his
many students who recognized the debt they owed
him. Professor Knight's five-volume *Documentary History of Education in the South Before 1860*
has served to credit the antebellum colleges and
universities of the South with their just dues, long
ignored by those outside the region.

Robert B. House (1892–1987), class of 1916, returned to Chapel Hill in 1926 as executive secretary to President Chase and later to President Graham. In 1934, at the completion of the program of consolidation of the campuses at Chapel Hill, Raleigh, and Greensboro, House was named dean of administration at Chapel Hill. In 1945 this title was changed to that of chancellor, and as such he served until his retirement in 1957. From 1957 until 1962, when he reached the age of seventy, he served as professor of English and classics and proved to be a very popular teacher. During Chancellor House's administration a great many important buildings were constructed and the instructional program expanded. The General College was organized in 1935, physical education and athletic programs were enlarged, the Communication Center was established, many departments were organized—among them city and regional planning, art, dramatic art, statistics, radio, religion—and the Division of Health Affairs was created. Educational television was begun during this period, and the Faculty Council was established as the legislative body representing both the general faculty and all administrative divisions of the University.

Archibald Henderson (1877–1963), class of 1898, became a graduate instructor immediately after graduation and taught for the following fifty years until his retirement in 1948, at which time he was Kenan Professor and chairman of the Department of Mathematics. He is shown here in 1941 exhibiting his new chart for interpreting Einstein's theory of relativity. Dr. Henderson's wide range of interests, embracing both science and the arts, made him a scholar in the Renaissance sense. As a mathematician he wrote on many subjects, among them atomic theory, astrophysics, and relativity; as an international literary critic he contributed to leading periodicals in half a dozen languages. He was the official biographer of George Bernard Shaw, the great dramatic genius, and wrote eight books dealing wholly or in part with Shaw. He wrote a history of the University campus and a two-volume history of North Carolina, and he contributed scores of articles based on original research to leading historical and popular magazines. In 1945 he revived the defunct Historical

Society of North Carolina, established a century earlier. Many high honors were bestowed upon him including election as a Fellow of the Royal Society, and he enjoyed the friendship of prominent men around the world. Nevertheless, he always delighted in visits from friends and neighbors nearer home. He gladly shared his notes and knowledge on a variety of topics with those who called upon him to discuss their own research. His keen sense of humor and his seemingly endless stock of good stories delighted his colleagues on the faculty as well as the tradesmen in Chapel Hill. He was equally at home with either group.

William deBerniere MacNider (1881–1951) was
graduated with the first class to receive the Doctor
of Medicine degree from the University medical
school, which was operated in Raleigh for a brief
period after 1902. In Chapel Hill he was an assistant in biology during 1899–1900 and at the time
of his retirement in 1950 he had been a member
of the faculty for more than half a century. From
1936 until he retired, he was dean of the Medical
School. Dr. MacNider was widely known for
his research in pharmacology and was internation-
ally known for his special research in the process
of aging. His discoveries made in the study of
diseases of the kidney were particularly important,
and during World War I his findings enabled
British physicians to treat men who suffered from
nephritis in the trenches of France. Dr. MacNider
was also interested in the methods and problems
of medical education. It was said of him that his
greatest reward was the esteem and affection in
which he was held by students who passed under
his tutelage.

Marcus Cicero Stephens Noble (1855–1942), class
of 1879, joined the University faculty in 1897 as
professor of pedagogy and served as dean of the
school of education from 1913 until his retirement
in 1934. As a young man he participated in the
campaign that brought good public schools to the
state, and this interest continued for the remainder
of his life. From 1899 until his death he was chairman
of the board of trustees of the Agricultural and
Technical College at Greensboro; he was a member of the first board of trustees of the Normal
and Industrial School (which became the University of North Carolina at Greensboro); and for
many years he was chairman of the State Historical Commission. Professor Noble's friendly
greeting, his cheerful disposition, and his genuine
interest in people endeared him to many generations of University students, and even after he
retired, his presence on campus and in town made
him known to new generations. At the time of
his death, Louis Graves wrote that Professor
Noble was "deservedly admired for his achieve-
ments, but . . . he will be held most lovingly in
memory not because of anything he did for the
public at large but because in the close-knit life
of the village he was understanding and loyal and
kind."

Howard W. Odum (1884–1954) joined the faculty in 1920 as a Kenan Professor, the first to be added to the faculty in accordance with the regulations governing the Kenan Fund, which enabled the University to invite distinguished scholars from other institutions. He came to Chapel Hill as professor of sociology and almost immediately established the School of Public Welfare. In 1922 he established the scholarly journal, *Social Forces*, of which he was editor until his death. Two years later he formed the Institute for Research in Social Science and served as its director until 1944. As a teacher Odum attracted many promising students whose future work was important, particularly in the South. He also engaged in research and writing and in 1930 published *An American Epoch: Southern Portraiture in the National Picture*. Late the following year he began his monumental study of the South which resulted in the publication in 1936 of his classic *Southern Regions of the United States*. Much of the progress of the South during subsequent years has been traced to the understanding and stimulation fostered by this book. From 1937 until 1944 Odum was president of the Commission of Interracial Cooperation, and he later organized and was first president of the Southern Regional Council.

Julius Algernon Warren (1881–1956) was treasurer of the University from 1912 until his retirement in 1952. It was to Mr. Warren, and through this grill, that students paid their bills. This photograph is from a student's scrapbook of the time and he labeled it: "The Bursar Bursing."

Senior Week in the 1930s and 1940s was a time when seniors might be recognized on campus and perhaps even envied by lower classmen. There were extra cuts from class, picnics, beer parties in Battle Park, and other carefree occasions including Barefoot Day when seniors were invited to go barefooted, perhaps symbolic of a last retreat to childhood before assuming a serious role in the world of adults. Senior jackets, such as the one shown here worn by a member of the class of 1940, were an important part of the "uniform" of the week.

The north edge of the campus along Franklin Street in the early 1940s. The large oak tree in the center died during the late spring of 1971 and was removed in early August of that year.

It was customary in the 1940s for large groups of students to gather on the lawn of the president's house on numerous pleasant occasions—before a pep rally, after a football victory, on a concert afternoon. This picture is from Dr. Frank Graham's personal papers and probably was made in March 1949 at the time of his departure for the United States Senate. The light suggests early evening, and the leaves on the trees suggest those of spring. All of the men have on coats and ties, one or two of the women are wearing hats, and almost everybody seems to be singing.

An aerial view of the campus from the bell tower north in the summer of the early 1940s, perhaps 1942—the Horace Williams Airport in the background was under construction during 1941–42.

Officers and some of the members of the Carolina Political Union in Graham Memorial in the fall of 1940. Seated second from the right at the table is Professor E. J. Woodhouse, adviser to the group.

Football player Paul Severin deals during a friendly game in Graham Memorial in 1940.

The Naval ROTC Armory was erected in 1942 on Columbia Street and has been in continuous use for its original purpose.

High noon in Franklin Street on a hot May day in 1943. The Frank Sinatra movie at the Carolina Theatre was "Reveille with Beverly," which had just been released in April.

The first dress parade of Pre-Flight cadets at the University, 25 May 1942, in Emerson Stadium. The reviewers include Governor J. Melville Broughton, President Frank P. Graham, Chancellor Robert B. House, and Professor Wallace Caldwell.

Navy Hall on Country Club Road opposite the Forest Theatre was constructed in 1942 to provide social quarters for the Pre-Flight School. At the end of the war it was used as the Monogram Club and still later as the faculty club.

The Forest Theatre in the edge of Battle Park was first used in 1916, but it was redesigned and remodeled in 1940. In May 1943 it was formally dedicated on the twenty-fifth anniversary of Professor Frederick Koch's coming to the University. Professor Koch is shown here on the left.

Pre-flight cadets seated in Lenoir Hall patiently await the word.

Soon after the opening of the United States Navy Pre-Flight School at the University, Commander Oliver Owen Kessing, first commanding officer of the school, recognized the need for outdoor swimming facilities. In the fall of 1942 construction got underway on a pool south of Woollen Gymnasium. It was put into use in August 1943, and the trustees later named it Kessing Pool in honor of Commander Kessing who was decorated many times for his activities in the South Pacific.

Commander E. E. Hazlett, at the microphone, Josephus Daniels, and Captain W. T. Mallison in Kenan Stadium in October 1944.

Naval ROTC unit on parade in the arboretum in 1944.

Review of NROTC and Pre-Flight Cadets in Kenan Stadium, 11 December 1943, on the occasion of the visit of the British ambassador, Lord Halifax. The first line of companies is composed of the NROTC. Next are the Pre-Flight cadets, the V-12 Marine companies, and at the bottom with white caps are the V-12 Naval companies.

Memorial services for the late President Franklin D. Roosevelt in Kenan Stadium, April 1945. V-5 students are on the left.

Cadets in Bowman Gray Pool willingly obey their instructor's command to face the camera.

Gene Johnstone, *Yackety Yack* editor in 1945, and Margaret Going Woodhouse, business manager, at the Kappa Sigma house on V-J Day, 1945.

President Graham in his home chatting with students in 1946. President and Mrs. Graham held open house every Sunday evening and students dropped in for conversation and refreshments.

An autographing party at the Bull's Head Bookshop in the library on the occasion of the publication of *Mexican Village* by The University of North Carolina Press, 1945. At the left is Marion Fitz-Simons, illustrator of the book, Josefina Niggli, author, and guest Betty Smith.

Returning veterans swelled the enrollment figures in the University following World War II and long lines, such as this one in 1946, snaked their way into Woollen Gymnasium for registration.

The University housing office was hard pressed to provide accommodations for veterans. The Tin Can, erected in 1923 as an indoor athletic court, was filled with beds and lockers and put to a new use as this picture made in the fall of 1946 shows. In scenes reminiscent of earlier days when plumbing on campus was rare, towel-draped students were often seen dashing to Woollen Gymnasium for a shower.

Miller Hall, at the intersection of McCauley and Pittsboro Streets, and nearby Nash Hall were built about 1942 by the Navy for the V-12 program. After the war they housed veterans who had returned to the classroom. Later, with more dormitory space available, they were brick veneered, remodeled inside, and used by various departments as need for extra space arose.

Students at the head of the line for registration in September 1946. They took their places on the steps of Woollen Gymnasium at 6:30 in the morning.

Waiting in the cafeteria line at Lenoir Hall in the fall of 1946.

Temporary, prefabricated houses were erected in the woods south of the public health and medical buildings to provide quarters for married students, most of whom were veterans. They soon called this isolated community "Victory Village." Many of these temporary buildings, such as these erected during 1946–47, stood for well over twenty years.

Surplus army housing from Fort Bragg and other North Carolina military bases was moved to Chapel Hill and converted into apartments for married students. Many buildings such as these, together with the small individual units, formed Victory Village.

The soda fountain at the Book Exchange in the YMCA building did a rushing business between morning classes in 1946, but veterans were accustomed to lines and patiently awaited their turns.

Quonset huts also provided makeshift quarters for students.

Trailers provided accommodations for many families. This former officer, still wearing an army shirt and happy to be reunited with his family, did not object to the close companionship required in a trailer during the 1946–47 school year in Chapel Hill.

With the return of peace and the end of gasoline rationing, attendance at football games soon returned to and even exceeded the prewar level. This view of Kenan Stadium during the Carolina-Duke game in 1946 shows an overflow crowd of forty-four thousand. The score was Carolina 22, Duke 7.

Rain dampened everything but the Tar Heel spirit at this game in Kenan Stadium in the fall of 1946.

Connor Dormitory, built in 1946 and named for the Connor family, including Professor R. D. W. Connor and Judge Henry Groves Connor, housed graduate men for a time before it became a women's dormitory.

This view of the reserve reading room in the University library in 1947 leaves no doubt as to the seriousness with which students took their work. Veterans set new standards of scholarship in many classes and departments.

The aftermath of a final examination in 1947.

Students at work in the Carolina Playmakers scene shop, 1947.

Navy Hall became the Monogram Club, and the Circus Bar there became a favorite gathering place for snacks and friendly visits. The wooden circus figures on the wall and reflected in the mirror were carved by Carl Boettcher from a sketch made by William Meade Prince. These figures were later removed to the new Carolina Inn cafeteria, which opened in April 1970.

Professor Rupert B. Vance with Josephus Daniels (student of law, 1884–85), editor of *The News and Observer* and long a trustee of the University, at the twenty-fifth anniversary party of The University of North Carolina Press, 13 March 1947. Books by both of these men, published by the Press, had won the Mayflower Award as the best books by North Carolinians during the years in which they were published.

The prewar playing field across South Road from Woollen Gymnasium gave way to two new dormitories after World War II. On the right is Winston, completed in 1948, with a small portion of Connor, completed two years earlier, just visible behind it. Alexander, at the left of the court, was completed shortly before the war, and Joyner, parallel to Raleigh Street, was completed in 1948. All of these were originally occupied by men, but by 1967 all except Alexander had been converted to women's dormitories.

Among those attending the Press's twenty-fifth anniversary party were Chancellor Robert B. House, John Couch, Press Director Thomas J. Wilson, Robert Wettach, Hugh T. Lefler, Rupert B. Vance, L. R. Wilson, and Sturgis E. Leavitt. These men constituted the Board of Governors of the Press; some outstanding publications of the Press appear on the table before them.

In 1948 the Administrative Board of the Graduate School attended a barbecue dinner at Turnage's in Durham and others concerned with graduate education in the area were also present. Posing here are: Berthold L. Ullman and William M. Dey, members of the Administrative Board; A. K. King, associate dean; W. Whatley Pierson, Jr., dean; Donald B. Anderson of the North Carolina State College faculty and assistant dean of the Graduate School of the Consolidated University; Paul M. Gross, dean of the Duke University Graduate School; and William de B. MacNider of the Administrative Board.

Robert C. Ruark (1915–65), class of 1935, nationally syndicated newspaper columnist and novelist, returned to the campus in the spring of 1947 and chatted informally with students in the School of Journalism. Shown here with Ruark are, left, Professor O. J. "Skipper" Coffin and, right, Professor Walter Spearman. At far right in the background is Clarence E. Whitefield, class of 1944, who became alumni director of the University in 1970.

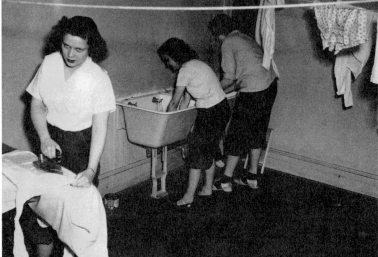

Coeds in 1948 share a necessary chore.

An exercise in serious concentration in the Graham Memorial lounge, 1949.

Professor Philip Schinhan instructs a student at the concert organ in Hill Hall in 1949.

One of the polling places for the 1949 student elections was in the lobby of Memorial Hall.

A class in economic statistics taught by Professor Dudley Cowden in 1949.

Lights in the windows of the bookstacks of the University library at 7 o'clock in the evening, 9 December 1949, meant that graduate students were diligently working in the carrels.

Members of the Interfraternity Council posed in Graham Memorial lounge in 1949.

Diagrams for the card section during the 1948 football season.

The "Beat Dook" parade along Franklin Street in 1949.

Charlie "Choo-Choo" Justice in the famous 22 jersey demonstrates for the cameraman, 1949.

"Choo-Choo" Justice, class of 1950, hears some advice in the ballroom of the Carolina Inn from Kay Kyser, class of 1927.

An Air Force ROTC review about 1949 on Emerson Field.

Late in 1949 in a studio in Swain Hall members of the radio department rehearse for the first broadcast of the series known as "The University Hour." The programs were transcribed and broadcast by more than twenty-five stations located throughout the state. The half-hour program being produced here is based on an incident in the career of Thomas Wolfe as a student at Chapel Hill. *Left to right:* Rhoda Hunter, instructor in radio, taking the part of the telephone operator; John Taylor, Chapel Hill student, and Tom Potter, Winston-Salem student, sound effects; Don Roberson, Asheville, announcer; John Ehle, Asheville student who wrote the Wolfe script (playing Thomas Wolfe); and Earl Wynn, director of the Communication Center (playing "Proff" Koch).

The University library, opened in 1929, was filled to overflowing twenty years later and in 1949 construction was underway on an addition that was designed to provide space for another twenty years' growth.

The housing shortage had become so critical by the spring of 1949 that many small trailers, some with a tarpaper-covered lean-to, were clustered around the bath house (on the left) at the edge of Victory Village.

A Tar Heel convertible on the streets of New York before the Carolina–Notre Dame game on 12 November 1949 attracts curious glances from bystanders.

Rupert B. Vance (1899–1975) came to Chapel Hill for graduate study and received his Ph.D. in 1928. He became a research associate in sociology in 1932 and was a member of the faculty from that time, being made a Kenan Professor in 1945. The author of a number of important books and articles, he engaged in research of national and regional significance, especially that relating to planning, social security, and population. His teaching specialities included human ecology, population, social theory, and social structure. One of his books, *Human Geography of the South*, received the Mayflower Award.

William Whatley Pierson, Jr. (1890–1966) joined the University faculty in 1915 as an instructor in history and at the end of five years, when he was just twenty-nine, he became a full professor. In 1930 he was appointed dean of the graduate school and continued in that post until 1957 when he returned to full-time teaching. He set high scholarly standards for teaching and research on the campus, and through his work with the Conference of Deans of Southern Graduate Schools, as secretary of the Association of American Universities, and as president of the Southern University Conference he inculcated a respect for the highest ideals of scholarship in other areas. Dean Pierson was an inspiring teacher who also engaged in productive research. On two occasions he also served as acting chancellor of the University at Greensboro.

Hugh T. Lefler (1901–81) joined the history faculty in Chapel Hill in 1935 after having taught at State College for several years. A specialist in colonial American history, he also taught North Carolina history and did it so effectively that he came to be referred to affectionately as "Mr. North Carolina." An enthusiastic teacher with a knack for making his enthusiasm contagious, he estimated that he had taught around twenty thousand students in the classroom and many hundreds in extension and correspondence courses. Textbooks by Professor Lefler have been used in the public schools and the colleges of the state for nearly thirty years, and his name is well known to most of the young people who have passed through the schools of North Carolina. Dr. Lefler published many books on various aspects of American history, and one of them, *North Carolina: The History of a Southern State*, received the Mayflower Award in 1954. He also headed a number of historical organizations and served on numerous boards and commissions. This portrait of Professor Lefler was given to the University by a group of his former students.

Sturgis E. Leavitt (1888–1976), *left*, professor of Spanish, and Almonte C. Howell (1895–1986), professor of English, were popular and highly respected members of the faculty until their retirements in 1960 and 1966, respectively. Both were deeply interested in foreign students. Dr. Leavitt specialized in Latin American studies and in seventeenth-century Spanish drama. In 1941, during the South American summer, he directed a "Winter Summer School" in Chapel Hill that was well attended by Latin American students; afterwards he directed other special sessions for students from Central and South America. He was president and chairman of numerous scholarly organizations and often represented the United States at international meetings. In recognition of his contributions to the understanding and appreciation of Spanish culture, he was made "Perpetual Honorary Mayor of Zalamea" in 1959 by that city of some nine thousand inhabitants in southwestern Spain. Dr. Leavitt was also active on the campus and served on numerous committees and boards and on the Faculty Council. Dr. Howell joined the faculty in 1920 as an instructor in English and attained the rank of professor in 1937. Two years later he also became an adviser in the General College and in 1943 he was made secretary of the faculty. Dr. Howell's friendly disposi-

tion contributed to his popularity as a teacher and perhaps was an important factor in his selection for work with foreign students. He also participated in international educational exchange programs, and at various times, under the sponsorship of the Department of State, he taught courses in English literature at universities in Korea, Paraguay, and Guatemala.

In February 1946 John Motley Morehead announced to the Board of Trustees that he was presenting the University one million dollars for the construction of a building to house his art collection and a planetarium. At the site of the new building between Graham Memorial and Alumni Building, ground was broken in late November 1947, and in May 1949 the planetarium opened with a preview for the faculty. Shown here is the front of the building facing west.

The Zeiss planetarium was shipped to Chapel Hill from Sweden and assembled in the big room of Woollen Gymnasium preparatory to installation in the new Morehead Planetarium. By means of a central group of projectors, this instrument projects the celestial bodies and their movements on the hemispherical ceiling in this large round room filled with comfortable seats. Many interesting, informative, and entertaining programs have been presented here, many of them very timely. Seasonal programs concerning Easter and Christmas have been especially popular, but programs on the moon and the possibilities of interplanetary exploration have also been presented to enthusiastic audiences. At various times the American astronauts have come to Chapel Hill to study celestial navigation in this room.

Courses in astronomy are conducted in conjunction with the facilities offered by the Morehead Planetarium and night observations are frequently made from the roof terraces of the building. Here a group of students and staff members is shown adjusting a telescope for use later in the evening.

The earliest of many groups of apartment buildings designed to relieve the housing shortage in Chapel Hill was Glen Lennox on the Raleigh Road, not too far down the plain beneath Gimghoul Castle. Well laid-out streets, comfortable apartments, and many trees made this a desirable home for many graduate students as well as for new faculty members who found a convenient temporary home here until they were able to move into a suitable house.

Some of the quonset huts erected on the tennis courts along Country Club Road were torn down in 1949 to make way for a new dormitory that went up in 1950. Named Cobb Dormitory in honor of Professor Collier Cobb, it was occupied by men until 1962 when it was converted into a women's dormitory.

Mangum Dormitory's entry in the "Beat Dook" parade in the fall of 1950.

A veteran in new white bucks and old GI undershorts conducts some important business by telephone. The slip of paper in his right hand undoubtedly contains the number he has just dialed.

A float in the Sadie Hawkins Day parade, 1950.

The trellis beside the arboretum is covered with great clusters of purple wisteria and sweet-smelling yellow jessamine in the spring. Every student who has rushed up this path to class or strolled along more leisurely later in the day has had the perfume so indelibly etched in his memory that any future whiff of wisteria and jessamine will bring this scene to mind.

Old trees on the campus have been nursed with great care as the patched wounds left by broken limbs on this elm tree show. It stood at the east end of the University library and provided space for more than just the one squirrel nest shown here. In the spring many students sat in the reference room and gazed out the high windows into the top at the opening buds, and a little later this tree provided cooling shade from the hot morning sun against the building. But this elm and many very large oaks nearby gave way to progress a few years later when the site was cleared for the construction of the undergraduate library. A noisy mockingbird and several cardinals shared this grove for several summers just before it was cleared. The cardinals left quietly, but the mockingbird complained loudly for several weeks before he disappeared.

William Donald Carmichael (1900–1961), class of 1921, *left*, and Gordon Gray (1909–82), class of 1930, *right*. Carmichael was controller of the Consolidated University from 1939 until 1952, when he became vice president and finance officer. He also served as acting president of the University on two occasions: 1947–48, when President Graham was in Indonesia, and 1949–50, after the resignation of President Graham to accept appointment to the United States Senate. Billy Carmichael, as he was widely known, played a leading role in securing financial support for the University from foundations and from private sources. Gordon Gray became president of the Consolidated University in 1950 after having been secretary of the army under President Truman. He was on leave for service with the federal government for several years, and the trustees insisted that he remain on leave, but he resigned his position with the University in 1955 and soon afterwards became director of the Office of Defense Mobilization.

The eleven students gathered here on the steps of South Building were elected to campus office in the spring of 1950. Standing is John Sanders, newly elected president of the student body. The three seated nearest the camera, *left to right*, are: Herb Nachman, Augusta, Georgia, editor of *Tarnation*, campus humor magazine; Graham Jones, Winston-Salem, editor of *The Daily Tar Heel*; and Jim Mills, Charlotte, editor of the 1951 *Yackety Yack*. *Middle row:* Frances Drane, Monroe, president of the YWCA; Dick Murphy, Baltimore, Maryland, attorney general of the student body; Kash Davis, Weldon, speaker of the Co-ed Senate, woman's government legislative body; and Herb Mitchell, Asheville, vice president of the student body and speaker of the student legislature. *Back row:* Banks Talley, Bennettsville, South Carolina, secretary-treasurer of the student body; Ed McLeod, Maxton, president of the YMCA; and Larry Botto, Brandenton, Florida, chairman of the student council.

The Carolina Playmakers preparing to depart on
their forty-first state tour in the early spring of 1950
pose beside one of the army surplus buildings, typical
of many moved to the campus in the late 1940s
and early 1950s to provide emergency classroom and
office space. The bus taken by Playmakers on
their tenth state tour, shown here in Asheville in
1925, was considerably more crowded.

The new addition to the University library was completed in 1951, about the same time that the old gravel walks were giving way to brick pavement. The corner of one of the army surplus buildings is shown at the left.

Officers and guests of the Friends of the Library at the annual dinner meeting at the Carolina Inn, 11 May 1951. *Left to right:* Chancellor Robert B. House; Thomas D. Clark, guest speaker; Professor J. G. de R. Hamilton; former President Harry W. Chase; Mrs. Lyman Cotten; Professor L. R. Wilson, chairman of the Friends of the Library; and John Sprunt Hill, generous benefactor of the library and honorary chairman of the Friends.

An ROTC parade passing Battle Hall on Franklin Street, May 1951. The Air Force ROTC unit was established at the University in 1947; the naval unit was established in 1940 and made notable contributions to national military training programs during World War II.

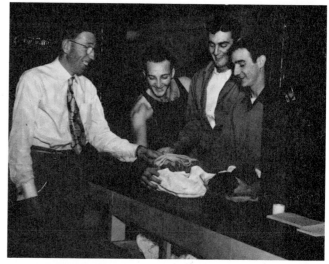

J. J. Keller, Jr., issuing athletic equipment in the men's locker room, Woollen Gymnasium, in 1951.

May Queen Jean Arden Boisseau, center front, and attendants in the arboretum, 1951.

The Dialectic Senate, 1951.
Front row: Heath Carriker, Gerald Parker, Ed Smith, Bob Clampitt (president), Jim Maynard, Bob Smith, Gene Cook; *middle row:* Bill Walker, John Schnorrenberg, Ken Penegar, Fred Coker, Wayne Thompson, Tom Alexander, Sid Thompson; *back row:* John Sullivan, Charlotte Davis, Dave Woodruff, Dick McLean, Toby Selby, Gina Campbell, Tom Sully.

The staff of Graham Memorial, 1951.

The Daily Tar Heel staff, 1951.

Mrs. Jessica Valentine, second from left, presiding over the informal Bull's Head Bookshop, 1951, on the first floor of the University library. The Bull's Head was established in 1928 in Murphey Hall when there was no other bookshop in Chapel Hill and was moved to the new library building when it was opened. The Bull's Head proved to be a popular place for browsing, reading, and buying until it was closed in 1968. The name was retained when an order counter and a corner of the new student stores in Daniels Building was established, but the atmosphere and pleasant surroundings were gone.

Many late winter mornings in Chapel Hill are foggy, but the warm mist in the air brings hints of approaching spring. The bare limbs of the bush at the left bore spikes of purple flowers in the summer which attracted dozens of butterflies, but when ground was broken here for Dey Hall it was crushed and rooted out by a bulldozer.

Professor Guy B. Phillips's table at registration time in Woollen Gymnasium in 1951. Phillips (1890–1968), class of 1913, joined the faculty as professor of education in 1936 and made a host of friends for himself and the University. At different times he also served as an advisor in the General College and as director of the summer school.

For a number of years in the 1950s Robert Frost visited the University campus, sometimes lecturing, sometimes reading his poems, but always chatting with students. He is shown here on his visit in 1952 with Professor Clifford Lyons on his right, flanked by two students who are obviously amused by his comments.

The University through the years has served the people of North Carolina in a variety of ways with institutes, extension work, and correspondence courses. In 1952 the first U.N.C.-High School Radio Institute was held and a number of young people, some of whom are shown here, gained practical experience in writing, producing, announcing, and participating in radio broadcasts.

Before the end of the decade of the 1940s the University Book Exchange had outgrown its old quarters in the YMCA building. By 1952 the basement of Steele Dormitory had been converted into a combined warehouse and sales area for textbooks and other classroom supplies.

Crowded bulletin boards have been a tradition on the campus since some time before World War I. As student election time approaches each spring they become even more crowded as shown here with this array of political flyers in Graham Memorial in 1952.

A group of three buildings similar to and facing Saunders, Murphey, and Manning was completed for the School of Business Administration in 1953. On the left is Gardner Hall, with Carroll Hall in the center, and Hanes Hall on the right. These buildings were named for Governor O. Max Gardner, Dean Dudley D. Carroll, and the Hanes family.

The main entrance to North Carolina
Memorial Hospital in 1953. This teaching
hospital associated with the School of Medicine was opened in 1952.

A popular tradition of long standing in
Chapel Hill for many years was the Bull's
Head Bookshop tea in the library. Usually on
a monthly schedule, but whenever an author
could be cornered long enough, tea and
cookies would be served followed by a talk by
the guest author. Afterwards those present
were free to chat with the author and with
each other. If some books were sold both the
manager and the author were pleased, but
everybody had a good time anyway. On
9 December 1953 University alumnus
William T. Polk talked about his new book,
Southern Accent. He is shown here with
Chancellor House, his friend since their
student days together in Chapel Hill.

The very popular outdoor dramas in the United States had their beginning with Paul Green's *Lost Colony* in 1937 and the Playmakers have had an important role in nearly all of them, even in those produced outside North Carolina. The Institute of Outdoor Drama was founded in January 1963 to serve as a central agency for outdoor drama activities throughout the country, but before that time, on an informal basis, the Department of Dramatic Art provided much of the same service. Shown here is a group on the steps of the Playmaker's Theatre in 1953 during the course of a meeting at which the outdoor drama, *Horn in the West*, was discussed.

In 1953 Mrs. Eleanor Roosevelt was a guest on the campus at the invitation of the Carolina Forum. Shown here at the Carolina Inn with Mrs. Roosevelt are Robert Pace, Joel Fleishman, Kenneth Penegar, and Dean Dampier.

Some members of the faculty of the School of Business Administration on the steps of Bingham Hall in 1953. *Front row*, *left to right*, C. P. Spruill, D. D. Carroll, Earle Peacock; *back row*, Clarence Heer, Gustave Schwenning, Milton S. Heath, John B. Woosley, and Harry Wolf.

An aerial view of a portion of the campus 16 April 1953. The veterans' club near the southwestern corner of Emerson Field may be seen between Lenoir Hall and the Tin Can and a number of the temporary wooden army surplus buildings are shown. A careful examination of the photograph also shows that new brick walks were being laid at several places.

By 1953 a problem had arisen that was not destined to be settled in the foreseeable future.

(*Above, left*) After operating in Memorial Hall at registration time for many years, the Communication Center moved its camera for making identification pictures to the basement of the new addition to Swain Hall in 1954. Students who worked with the contraption fondly called it "Scrogg's Folly," in honor of their supervisor, Ross Scroggs.

(*Above, right*) Four sensitive seniors on the steps of South Building studiously avoid looking at each other's bare feet on Barefoot Day.

(*Center, right*) Hillel Foundation, 1954. Rabbi Rosenzweig, director from 1952 to 1962 and remembered fondly by students of this decade, is seated at the left back corner of the table.

(*Below, right*) The advisory council of the Division of Humanities, 1954. *Left to right*, Lyman Cotten, secretary, Alfred Engstrom, Harry Russell, Walter Allen, Jr., Werner Friederich, W. L. Wiley, John Allcott, Neil Luxon, Everett W. Hall, Sturgis E. Leavitt, Floyd Stovall, Samuel Selden, Earl Wynn, Loren MacKinney, and Glen Haydon, chairman.

During World War II most of the fraternities leased their houses to the University for use by the navy for the duration of the war. Those with members in Chapel Hill during this time found quarters elsewhere—on the upper floors of commercial buildings on Franklin Street, in private houses rented in town, or in cottages on their own property. By 1954 when this picture was made in Fraternity Court off Columbia Street, activity had returned to normal.

University Day, 12 October, is marked each year with a public program. Frequently, as shown here in 1954, there is a reenactment of the laying of the cornerstone of Old East in 1793.

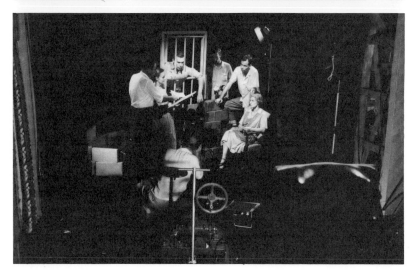

Filming a motion picture, *Domino*, at the Communications Center, 1954.

The Department of Radio had become
a separate department in 1947, and in
1954 it became a part of the Department of Radio, Television, and Motion
Pictures, occupying newly renovated
quarters in Swain Hall. Practical
experience was offered to students
in writing, producing, acting in, and
filming motion pictures.

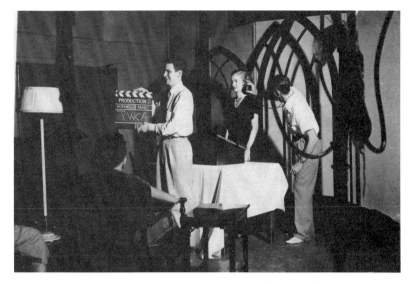

Dr. Hollington K. Tong, Chinese
ambassador to the United States,
meeting with students at a reception
in Graham Memorial following his
address under the sponsorship of the
Carolina Forum in September 1956.
Speaking on "Communist Advance
in Asia," the ambassador labeled as
insincere the Communists' appeals
for peace.

Les Petites Musicales, presented regularly as one of a series of public programs at Graham Memorial, were very
popular. Local talent as well as guest
artists from outside the University
community performed. This performance was photographed in 1955.

Each September found the campus cluttered with small groups of bewildered new students under the watchful eye of an upperclassman. This 1955 orientation class pays rapt attention to the advice of its leader.

Librarian Andrew H. Horn began a popular series of television programs called "Of Books and People" in which he and other members of the library staff discussed and displayed interesting library resources and talked about books with authors and other guests. Shown here, *left to right*, are Lambert Davis, director of The University of North Carolina Press; Dr. Warner Wells, member of the faculty and translator of *Hiroshima Diary*, which the press published in 1955; and Dr. Horn. The program was presented on 4 October 1955 and Dr. Wells, later in the fall, spoke at a Bull's Head Bookshop tea in the library.

The Carolina Symposium, a student-sponsored activity generally held semi-annually, involves students, faculty, and national and international figures in significant dialogue and discussions. A series of public addresses and small group discussions built around a theme for each symposium has contributed greatly to the involvement of many students in a new experience. The 1956 symposium had a three-fold subject: "Old Problems in the New South," "The Emerging World Community—Problems and Prospects," and "The United States in the World Today." In connection with the series this group gathered for dinner in the Pine Room at the Carolina Inn.

Newly paved brick walks, freshly
planted shrubs, and a remodeled Old
Well changed the appearance of a
familiar site in the spring of 1955.

Many mornings in winter and early spring are foggy in Chapel Hill. This scene was recorded in February 1957, looking toward South Building from Bingham Hall.

A student dance in 1956.

Shirley Carpenter, Miss Modern Venus, at the Sigma Chi Derby Day in 1956.

A group of administrators, faculty, old grads, and friends gathered in Emerson Stadium on many pleasant spring afternoons to watch the Tar Heel nine. On this particular occasion those present were James A. Williams, assistant business manager of the University; James L. Godfrey, dean of the faculty; Ray Strong, director of central records; W. B. Aycock, chancellor; George E. Shepard, professor of physical education; Roland McClamroch, retired professor of English; Grady Pritchard, retired Chapel Hill businessman; W. P. Jacocks, class of 1904, retired physician; and Phillips Russell, class of 1904, professor of journalism. It was in this stadium that George Stirnweiss played college ball in the 1930s before going on to join the New York Yankees in their peak performance days.

In his fifth year as head coach, Frank McGuire molded the 1957 U.N.C. basketball team into the best in the nation. Led by All-American Lennie Rosenbluth (number 10 in the picture), the Tar Heels compiled a 32-0 record, defeating the University of Kansas for the national championship. This team effort fulfilled the promise of individual performers in earlier years, such stars as the McCachren brothers, Hook Dillon, and George Glamack, who is the only U.N.C. basketball player to be named to the Helms Hall of Fame.

Rehearsing on the stage of Hill Hall for an orchestral program in the 1957–58 concert series.

William C. Friday received a B.S. degree in textile engineering from State College in 1941 and was assistant dean of men there briefly before becoming a naval officer in World War II. After the war he entered law school in Chapel Hill, and in 1948 he was admitted to the bar. He was assistant dean of men at the University from 1948 until 1951, when he became assistant to President Gordon Gray. In 1956 he was chosen to succeed Gray as president of the Consolidated University of North Carolina; he served in this role until his retirement in 1986. Under Friday's leadership long-range planning was introduced and the use of computers was promoted. He also cooperated in the creation of the Research Triangle Institute, and during his administration the Consolidated University system grew from three to sixteen campuses. Friday supported Proposition 48, a proposal before the National Collegiate Athletic Association (NCAA) that favored guidelines for academic standards for freshmen athletes. In 1961 he ended the highly popular Dixie Classics basketball tournament when it became embroiled in a nationwide gambling scandal. Recognized nationally for his leadership in higher education, he was a member of the Carnegie Commission on Higher Education, the President's Task Force on Education, and the Regional Literacy Commission, among others. In 1985 he received the Distinguished Service Award for Lifetime Achievement from the American Council on Education. Since his retirement he has been actively involved in a statewide attack on poverty and illiteracy. He also served as president of the William R. Kenan, Jr. Fund, established in 1984 to support the University's Institute of Private Enterprise.

William Brantley Aycock, a 1936 graduate of North Carolina State College, received the M.A. degree in history in Chapel Hill in 1937 and, following service as an army lieutenant colonel during World War II, returned to the University for a law degree. He joined the faculty of the School of Law in 1948 and was chosen chancellor to succeed Robert B. House in 1957. During his period in office student enrollment increased from 7,038 in the fall of 1957 to 11,303 in the fall of 1964. A number of important improvements and additions to the physical plant also were made, including an addition in 1960 to Phillips Hall for the Univac Computer System, a new pharmacy building, an addition to Peabody Hall, 208 permanent housing units for married students, and new seats in Memorial Hall. In addition Dey, Coker, and Mitchell halls for romance languages, botany, and geology, respectively, were completed, and two new multi-floor dormitories for men, Craige and Ehringhaus, were opened.

Snowy white dogwood across campus, Virginia
creeper beginning to conceal the walls of buildings,
and lacy young leaves on the trees are all well-
known trademarks in Chapel Hill. These views
made in 1952 were little changed from many years
past and it is hoped they will continue to be timely
for long years in the future.

Norman C. Cordon (1904–64) studied two years at the University before leaving for special voice training and an operatic career that took him to the Metropolitan Opera in New York and back to Chapel Hill where he was associated with the Opera Institute at the University. His WUNC radio program, "Let's Listen to Opera," was enjoyed throughout piedmont North Carolina where the University radio station brought good music, educational programs, and entertainment to thousands. Mr. Cordon is shown here in 1957 in the radio studio with Victor S. Bryant of Durham, an active member of the University Board of Trustees.

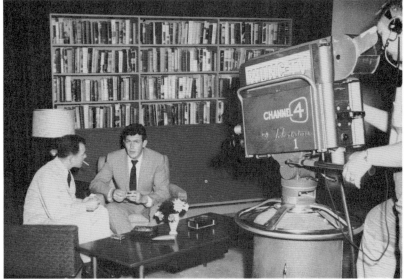

Andy Griffith, class of 1949, who later gained fame in motion pictures and television, is shown here being interviewed in 1957 at the University educational television station in Swain Hall. Griffith first gained national notice through his record, "What It Was Was Football," which he made in Chapel Hill. Television channel 4 went on the air on 8 January 1955. Studios are located on the University campus and transmission is from Terrell Mountain in Chatham County, seven miles southwest of Chapel Hill.

Professor H. D. Crockford, chairman of the department, gets a new chemistry class off to a good start in the big classroom in Venable Hall in the fall semester of 1957.

The William Hayes Ackland Memorial Art Center, facing Columbia Street at the north-western edge of the campus, was named for the Tennessee native whose bequest provided funds for the building and an endowment for the purchase of art objects. The building was opened in the fall of 1958 and houses a gallery as well as the Department of Art. Joseph C. Sloane became director of the Ackland in 1959 and oversaw the acquisition of a distinguished collection until his retirement in 1978.

In 1959 the Department of Radio, Television, and Motion Pictures had four radio studios, including the small one used by WUNC, one classroom, film editing rooms, and, for produc-tion classes, a sound stage. The faculty, shown here, consisted of (*left to right*) Elmer Oettinger, radio production; Ross Scroggs, motion picture production; Earl Wynn, chairman; John Ehle, writing; Mack Preslar, studios and recording; Wesley Wallace, programming, management, and research; and Don Knoepfler, television production.

English Professor Harry K. Russell in his classroom on the first floor of Bingham Hall.

The visiting committee of the Board of Trustees was on campus 2 July 1958 and some of them are pictured here in a botany laboratory with Professor John N. Couch, center in white short-sleeved shirt. Behind Professor Couch is Dean of the Faculty James L. Godfrey and to his right is Dean of the Graduate School Alexander Heard. On the right in a white suit is Chancellor Aycock.

Harvey Miller, class of 1958, at the manual keyboard in the Morehead-Patterson Bell Tower. The bells were electrified in the late summer of 1967 and programmed by a spindle player similar to that of a music box.

Professor H. Roland Totten, class of 1913, on a botany field trip, 8 April 1958. Until his retirement in 1963 Dr. Totten was a very popular teacher of courses in general botany, and almost every student of pharmacy who attended the University took his course in pharmacognosy dealing with the science of drugs made from plants.

Professor Edward A. Cameron, class of 1928, explains a formula to his math class in Phillips Hall, 16 April 1958.

Under the direction of a lab instructor, a group of students examine material arranged in a zoology exhibition in Wilson Hall, 9 May 1958.

Five loyal members of the class of 1904 who were living in Chapel Hill in November 1959. Seated are Dr. William P. Jacocks and Professor Phillips Russell; standing, the Reverend Sidney S. Robins, Dr. Alfred W. Haywood, and Professor Felix Hickerson. The lectern, now in the North Caroliniana Gallery in Wilson Library, was given to the University in June 1904 by the class of 1904.

Davie Poplar and other ancient trees provided cool shade for relaxing and reminiscing by a few students who remained on campus between the end of final examinations and commencement activities in 1958.

Students listening to Portuguese in a language laboratory in Murphey Hall in 1959. Professor Lawrence A. Sharpe, class of 1940, is teaching the class.

A picnic for members of the women's physical education association on the lawn beside the women's gymnasium in September 1959.

Students in classics are taught by Professor Robert J. Getty (1908–63), native of Northern Ireland and a graduate of Cambridge University, who joined the University faculty in 1958 as Paddison Professor of Classics. He made a host of friends among the students and faculty before his death.

As he had done for many years before, and as he continued to do until his retirement in 1972, Kenan Professor Hugh T. Lefler held his students spellbound in this 1959 class in North Carolina history.

Kenan Stadium in the late afternoon of 19 November 1960 when the final score was Carolina 7, Duke 6.

Dey Hall, the foreign language building, was opened during the 1961–62 academic year. Romance, Germanic, Slavic, and various non-Western languages and their literatures are taught here. Language laboratories with recording and listening devices are also in this building.

President John F. Kennedy spoke in Kenan Stadium on University Day, 12 October 1961, and was afterwards awarded an honorary degree. On the president's left is Chancellor William B. Aycock and to his right are President William C. Friday and Governor Terry Sanford.

The editorial staff of *The North Carolina Law Review* in 1961. Seated, *left to right:* Francis Willett and William B. Rector, Jr.; standing, Julius Chambers and Marlin Evans.

Professor Foster Fitz-Simons (1912–91), class of 1934, of the Department of Dramatic Art coaches five dancers in rehearsal in January 1962.

At the annual Law Students' Association awards dinner in Lenoir Hall in 1962, Professor M. T. Van Hecke (1892–1963) delays shaking hands with Marlin Evans long enough to make one final point.

Mrs. Otelia Connor (1892?–1969), self-appointed "good manners arbiter," gently but firmly instructed University students—wherever she found them—in the fine points of mannerly behavior. So effective was her work that she was the subject of articles in several national newsmagazines.

Kippy Carter, Jim Fullwood, Ed Fuller, and Ralph Yates pitch horseshoes in front of Mangum Dormitory in April 1963.

Representatives of the Peace Corps find interested students in
the lobby of the YMCA in July 1963.

The University's trophy-winning debaters of 1963 pose before the stair-
way in Davie Hall. Coach Donald Springen is third from the left in the
front row.

Paul F. Sharp, recently president of
Hiram College in Ohio, became chancellor in September 1964 and announced
his resignation on 29 December 1965
effective 15 February 1966. He became
president of Drake University, Des
Moines, Iowa. His administration was
marked by concern over the Speaker
Ban Law, which he said had nothing to
do with his abrupt departure.

William M. Geer, popular lecturer in
the modern civilization course is shown
with his class near Davie Poplar in May
1964.

The executive committee of the Men's Residence Council, November 1964.

The starting lineup of the 1964 football team poses in Kenan Stadium. Coached by Jim Hickey, this team finished the regular season with an 8–2 record and defeated the Air Force Academy in the Gator Bowl to give Carolina its first postseason victory.

Professor C. Ritchie Bell, class of 1949, member of the Botany Department since 1955, became director of the North Carolina Botanical Garden in 1965 following a five-year period when he was acting director. This 329-acre natural area south of the campus, containing forests and fields laced with streams and public trails, provides a natural setting for the growth of many of North Carolina's 3,000 native plants.

Hitchhiking has always been an acceptable form of transportation out of Chapel Hill and these students on "old firehouse hill" beside the town hall try their luck.

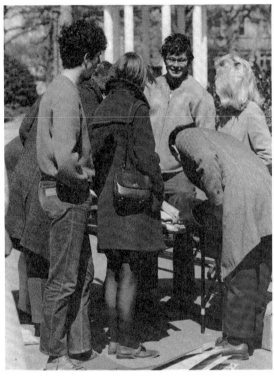

An antiwar petition attracts some willing signers in March 1966.

Baseball in the intramural field in the spring of 1966.

Motorcycles as a means of campus transportation had become so popular by November 1965 when this photograph was made that special lots and parking places for them became a new problem.

A gathering of distinguished leaders in the chancellor's office in South Building on the occasion of the formal installation of J. Carlyle Sitterson as chancellor on 12 October 1966. *Left to right:* Former President Frank P. Graham, Former Chancellor Robert B. House, Chancellor Sitterson, President William C. Friday, Former President Gordon Gray, and Governor Dan K. Moore. The "Sitterson Years" were momentous ones for the University with extensive periods of student unrest over various causes—the Speaker Ban Law, the federal military draft, the war in Vietnam, the drug problem, strikes, and labor unrest. The chancellor met the problem with calm good sense and a spirit of fairness that enabled the University to avoid the serious consequences that plagued a number of other universities throughout the world. During his administration student enrollment rose from 12,419 in the fall semester of 1965 to 19,160 in 1971. The faculty during the period increased from 1,000 to 1,395. Two large dormitories, Morrison and Hinton James, opened on South Campus; a new building for the Law School, an undergraduate library, a student union, and a building for the student stores were also completed. In the fall of 1971 a ten-story addition to Venable Hall, named the William Rand Kenan Laboratories, was opened, and an addition was completed to Carroll Hall to accommodate advanced management and graduate programs. A pass-fail grading system, with certain controlled restrictions, was instituted in 1967, and regular biweekly conferences with the president of the student government, his assistant and administrative officers were begun.

The Men's Glee Club, November 1966, which went on a tour of Europe and the British Isles.

On 11 July 1966 the old wooden shop then occupied by Kemp's record shop burned. An older generation of students knew this as Ab's book shop.

A bicycle for two could easily be expanded to accommodate a third by an ingenious student in the fall of 1966.

Jubilee, an annual presentation of the Student Union, features a long weekend of concerts by various groups. This concert in the spring of 1966 was held on the lawn south of South Building, between the YMCA and Steele Building.

A South Seas party at the Phi Gamma Delta fraternity in the fall of 1966.

The girls of Chi Omega test the tires of a trim sports car in the fall of 1966.

Midnight snacktime in the Phi Mu
house in the fall of 1966.

A party at the Chi Phi house on an
early fall evening in 1966.

Girl-watchers in Y court between
morning classes in the spring of 1967.
In many cases these young men are
doing the same thing their fathers
and grandfathers did at this same
site.

Hinton James residence hall (*upper left*) on South Campus was completed in June 1967.

The front portion of old Davie Hall (*above*), long the home of the Botany Department, was torn down and a new Davie Hall constructed. Completed in August 1967, it is the home of the Psychology Department.

The English Department faculty, October 1967.

William E. Thornton, class of 1952, who also received his M.D. degree from the University in 1963, was interviewed in the Morehead Planetarium by a *Daily Tar Heel* reporter in November 1967 when he returned for two days of intensive training in astronomy there. As a student at the University, Bill Thornton majored in physics, received an Air Force ROTC commission, and earned a letter in football. After serving in the air force and completing his medical training, he began training as an astronaut with the expectation of serving in a space laboratory.

Freshmen waiting on the steps of the library, 11 September 1967, to be taken on a tour of the building.

Signs designed by the orientation committee were erected at various places on campus to direct freshmen during orientation week, 1967.

There has never been any such thing as an unexpected performance in Y court—the unusual is to be expected. Midday folk dancing on 26 May 1968 in the midst of examinations pleased but did not surprise anyone.

A wistful student observing the academic procession on University Day, 12 October 1967.

The high hurdle championship, Atlantic Coast Conference, at Fetzer Field, 9 May 1968.

Theoretical physicists of the Department of Physics faculty, *left to right*, Hendrik Van Dam, Eugen Merzbacher, John P. Hernandez, Bryce S. DeWitt, Cecile DeWitt, and Sang-il Choi in October 1968.

The Richardson Fellows pose at the entrance to Vance Hall, November 1968. *Front row, left to right:* Tom Bello, Judith Hippler, Melinda Lawrence, John Patrick McDowell; *back row*, Thomas Osborne Stair, Michael A. Almond, Bill De-buys, Jerry R. Leonard.

Under the guidance of Coach Dean Smith, the University basketball team of 1968, featuring outstanding players such as Larry Miller and Charlie Scott, finished second in the nation with a 28–4 record. Fighting their way through conference and regional tournaments, the Tar Heels finally fell to U.C.L.A. in the national championship game.

The first black athlete to represent the University of North Carolina was Edwin Okoroma of Oweni, Nigeria, who played and lettered in soccer in the fall of 1963. He was graduated in 1965 with an A.B. in chemistry. He attended medical school and became a physician on the staff of Children's Hospital in Washington, D.C.

The new Law School building (*above*) was completed
in September 1968. Located near the eastern edge of the
campus, it overlooks the playing fields east of Woollen
Gymnasium and adjoining Carmichael Auditorium.

The Robert B. House Undergraduate Library (*below*) on
the east side of the older University library was opened
in 1968.

The Frank Porter Graham Student Union, built on the southern limits of old Emerson Field, was opened in 1968. Replacing Graham Memorial as a center of student activities, it contains a variety of meeting rooms of various sizes, a snack bar, several lounges, offices for student organizations, a number of bowling lanes and pool tables, a barber shop, locker space, and other facilities. Regular programs of entertainment and information are scheduled throughout the year.

Jessie Rehder, a popular member of the English faculty who taught creative writing, was a master practitioner of the subject she taught so well. After her death in 1967 her friends and former students established a scholarship in her memory. To raise funds for the scholarship an annual flea market is held; this one in November 1968 took place in the parking lot behind the Varsity Theatre.

The Music Department's production of "The Marriage of Figaro" in 1969.

The North Carolina String Quartet, composed of Chapel Hillians, presents frequent concerts on campus and elsewhere in the state. *Front row*: Dorothy Alden, violin, and Ann M. Woodward, viola; *back row*: Charles Griffith, violoncello, and Edgar Alden, violin. Griffith, Woodward, and Edgar Alden are members of the music faculty.

Officers of the Glee Club, May 1969.

During the freshman orientation period in September 1969 a number of students voiced their objection to the kind of information being presented by "the Establishment." These students organized a "counter-orientation" at which their own views were presented. This photograph was made at one of their sessions.

The war moratorium march down
Franklin Street in October 1969.

Members of Delta Sigma Pi pose informally before their house at 111 Pickard Lane in January 1970.

Rastus Faucette, who helped keep the campus neat in the late 1960s and early 1970s, was a friendly gentleman with a cordial greeting for all. He was responsible for returning numerous stray notebooks and textbooks left by students on walls and steps.

This large cube on which students are free to paint their own "thing" stands outside the student union. Occasionally the whole surface is given a fresh coat of paint and the process begins again.

An interruption of proceedings on
the temporary platform erected in
Kenan Stadium for the 1970 commencement. *Front row, left to right:*
Chancellor Sitterson, President Friday,
Governor Robert Scott, Charles M.
Ingram (president of the senior class),
and other platform guests enjoy a
break in an otherwise formal occasion.

The nineteenth-century gargoyle on top of Carr Building silently observes a campus that has moved toward the south.

The killing of four students at Kent State University by the Ohio National Guard on 4 May 1970 had a moving effect on students at Chapel Hill and on other American campuses. Already aroused by a strike of food service workers at Carolina, whose cause many of them espoused, and by the United States invasion of Cambodia, a great mass of milling and shouting students gathered on May 6. More than 4,000 people, mostly students, marched along the business streets of Chapel Hill, around campus, and through classroom buildings.

Although South Building remains unchanged in appearance, the two young men in the foreground are clearly of a new generation.

Students in the School of Library Science, objecting to an automobile manufacturer's national advertising that his sports car would be acceptable to those who are young in heart but not to librarians, sent him this photograph in December 1970 to demonstrate that not all librarians are quiet little old ladies.

A corner of the duplication center in the student union from which flows a seemingly endless variety of posters, handbills, and announcements.

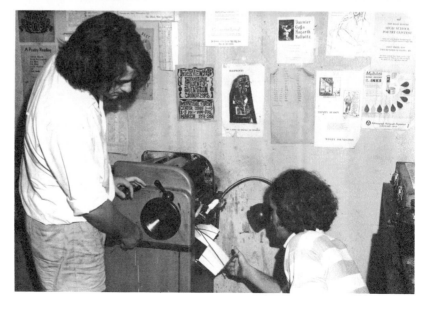

"The Pit," a paved sunken courtyard in the quadrangle formed by the undergraduate library, student stores, student union, and Lenoir Hall, quickly became the Hyde Park Corner of the campus where anyone with a cause might expect to find an audience. Here an ABC television cameraman records the peaceful activity of some members of the Women's Liberation group.

In spite of computers, punch cards, and various other devices, registration in the fall of 1971 in Woollen Gymnasium was just as frustrating as ever.

Greenlaw Hall, home of the English
Department, between Bingham Hall
and Lenoir Hall. This new classroom
building was dedicated in formal
ceremonies on 4 October 1970, and
a portrait of the late Professor Edwin
Greenlaw, which hangs in the building, was presented at that time by
his family.

When Lenoir Hall ceased to be used as
a cafeteria in 1970 it was taken over
by the rapidly growing Art Department, and the large dining room
became several studios. This is a
portion of one studio class being held
there.

A tradition at least twenty-five years
old has endured into 1971. Married
students and their young children
might be seen on campus at almost
any time of the day, and the campus
dogs, of course, are also a tradition.

The 1970 football team under
Coach Bill Dooley recorded
eight victories and only three
losses before losing to Arizona
State in Atlanta's Peach Bowl.
A major reason for the team's
success was the superb play
of Don McCauley, record-
breaking tailback shown running against Duke behind the
blocking of fullback Geoff
Hamlin after taking a hand-off
from quarterback Paul Miller.

Carolina defeated Duke 5 to 0 in the
soccer game played in the fall
of 1970.

All-American tennis player Fred McNair contributed to Carolina's 1971 tennis record of 22–2.

Flying Bill Chamberlain contributed to Carolina's score of 73 to Duke's 67 in the National Invitational Tournament in 1971.

To the delight of Tar Heel supporters, the basketball team of 1971 displayed desire, depth, and teamwork to amass a 26–6 season's record and win the National Invitational Tournament in New York City.

Art students are frequently seen sketching on the campus and on Franklin Street.

A pleasant interval along the walk by Bingham Hall between classes in the early fall of 1970.

Budding chemists at work in Venable Hall.

The ten-story William Rand Kenan chemistry laboratory annex to Venable Hall was opened in the fall of 1971.

An extension to the west side of Carroll Hall, which was completed in January 1971, provides a study in contrast. With expansive glass surfaces at various levels, this side of the building is in stark contrast to the east side with its classic columns that look across formal walks and plant beds toward matching Manning Hall.

The clean, light, and roomy *Daily Tar Heel* office in the Frank Porter Graham student union, October 1971, is strikingly different from the older cramped offices in Graham Memorial. In its eightieth year of publication, this paper has long been recognized as one of the top-ranking college dailies in the country.

Vermont Royster, class of 1935 and long-time editor of *The Wall Street Journal*, returned to Chapel Hill in September 1971 as a member of the journalism faculty. Winner of a Pulitzer Prize and author of several books and numerous periodical articles, Royster is a member of a family associated with the University for more than a century. The University has produced a number of other outstanding journalists, including Jonathan Daniels, Clifton Daniel, Robert Ruark, Tom Wicker, Charles Kuralt, and Louis Harris.

A group of distinguished faculty
members gathered before Alumni
Building in March 1971 to be
photographed near the site of ear-
lier faculty photographs. Some of
them are shown seated in old chairs
that once were in Gerrard Hall (see
page 109). *Front row, left to right*:
Rupert B. Vance, Raymond W.
Adams, Louis R. Wilson, Robert
B. House, Chancellor J. Carlyle
Sitterson, U. T. Holmes, and
Dougald MacMillan; *back row*: H.
D. Crockford, Preston H. Epps, W.
L. Wiley, J. P. Harland, Hugh T.
Lefler, John N. Couch, Fletcher M.
Green, and J. B. Linker.

One of every four of the University's 19,160 students was
riding a bicycle in the fall of
1971. These parked in front
of Hinton James Dormitory
are only a sampling of this
commuting trend in Chapel
Hill.

Morehead scholars in the Carolina Inn where they were entertained at dinner, September 1971. The John Motley Morehead awards and fellowships were established in 1951. Scholars, who are undergraduates, and Fellows, who are in law, medicine, or graduate school, are appointed on the basis of merit without regard to need.

For the fall semester of 1971 the University accepted 3,200 freshmen in a student body of 19,160. Four of the arriving freshmen are shown here, *left to right:* Mike Stephens, Greensboro; Belk Daughtridge, Charleston, South Carolina; Martha Bowles, Greensboro, and Fairfax Reynolds, Wilmington.

The 1971 annual sidewalk sale of student art held just inside the rock wall along East Franklin Street.

An aerial view of North Carolina Memorial Hospital and the Division of Health Affairs, a distinguished educational institution with a heritage of excellence which seeks to correlate its teaching, research, and service functions with health agencies and services throughout the state. The division includes the Schools of Medicine, Dentistry, Public Health, Nursing, and Pharmacy.

The Division of Health Affairs uses air transportation to move personnel about the state where they are needed for conferences or consultation. Pilot Alan Fearing is shown at the controls of the plane kept at the University's Horace Williams Airport with two passengers from the Department of Psychiatry.

The Cary Boshamer Stadium, erected in 1971 east of the Kenan Stadium fieldhouse, gave the baseball team and spectators adequate and handsome quarters.

In many respects Franklin Street, shown here in early November 1971, is little changed from the early years of the century. Sutton's Drug Store and Foister's Camera Store, for example, were establishments undoubtedly familiar to the grandparents of some of the students shown on the sidewalk here.

Franklin Street as seen from the steeple of the Methodist Church on a quiet Saturday afternoon in November 1971 when almost everyone in Chapel Hill was in Kenan Stadium. The changing face of Rosemary Street is evident in the background.

The "flower ladies" have sold their wares on Franklin Street for many years, becoming one of the established and colorful features that attract many visitors to Chapel Hill. In the 1970s when the sidewalks became crowded with people selling assorted crafts, the flowersellers were obliged to move into an alley between Franklin and Rosemary Streets.

In December 1971 the trustees appointed N. Ferebee
Taylor, *right*, to succeed J. Carlyle Sitterson, *left*, as chancellor in February 1972. A native of Oxford and a member
of the class of 1942, Taylor was graduated from Harvard
Law School and was a Rhodes Scholar at Oxford University. After a number of years as an attorney in New York,
he returned to Chapel Hill in 1970 to serve as vice president of administration in the Consolidated University. He
resigned as chancellor in January 1980 and returned to
teaching in the law school.

Wesley H. Wallace, popular professor and sometime chairman of the Department of Radio, Television, and Motion Pictures, also serves as an advisor in the General College.

This candid Y-court scene suggests that marked lanes for bicycle traffic and perhaps some Keep Right signs might be in order.

Trustees of the James M. Johnston Trust on the occasion of the presentation of the first gift of money for Johnston Scholarships to the University. *Left to right:* Norman B. Frost, Bonner D. Sawyer, Barnum L. Colton, and Harvey B. Gram, Jr.; and Webb C. Hayes III, counsel. The scholarships are named for the donor who was a native of the New Hope community north of Chapel Hill. Johnston attended the University from 1913 to 1915 and afterwards was graduated from the University of Illinois. His business affiliations were broad and included membership on the Board of Governors of the Philadelphia-Baltimore-Washington Stock Exchange and extensive banking, investment, and retail-trade connections. In his will he created a trust that provides scholarships for students at Chapel Hill, at the University in Greensboro, and at North Carolina State University in Raleigh. Trustee donations in excess of three million dollars during the period 1970–77 supported almost two thousand scholars on the Chapel Hill campus alone. Around a hundred Johnston scholarships are awarded each year, and about the same number of scholars are graduated each spring. This means that there are some four hundred students on campus at all times who are beneficiaries of the Johnston Trust.

Richard Epps, native of Wilmington, took office in the spring of 1972 as the first black president of the student body. He was a dean's list student, chairman of the men's honor court, a member of the Order of the Grail and the Order of the Old Well, and was tapped by the Golden Fleece. Upon his graduation he was named assistant director of undergraduate admissions.

Terry Sanford, class of 1939, returned to Chapel Hill for a law degree following service in World War II and was governor of North Carolina from 1960 until 1964. In 1969 he became president of Duke University and in 1972 was a candidate for nomination by the Democratic party for the presidency of the United States. His name was again mentioned prominently in the same connection during the 1974–75 campaign until he withdrew as an unannounced candidate. He retired as president of Duke in 1985 and was elected to the United States Senate in 1986.

All play and no work is the motto of few. This scene of serious concentration in Wilson Library is duplicated at all hours of the day and night.

Hamilton Hall, social sciences building, was opened in the fall of 1972. Named for Joseph G. de Roulhac Hamilton, professor of history and founder and director of the Southern Historical Collection, this building is the home of the departments of history, political science, and sociology.

Charles Kuralt, recipient of a Distinguished Alumnus Award in 1972, was editor of the *Daily Tar Heel* and was graduated with an A.B. degree in history in 1955. As a student he was tapped by the Golden Fleece and was also a member of the Order of the Grail and the Order of the Old Well. Immediately upon his graduation he joined the staff of the *Charlotte News* and at the age of twenty-three won the Ernie Pyle Memorial Award for newspaper writing. After two years in Charlotte he joined CBS, and in October 1967 began his popular "On the Road" series, which won both the John Foster Peabody Award and an Emmy from the Academy of Television Arts and Sciences in 1969.

J. Maryon Saunders, class of 1925 and alumni secretary for forty-three years before his retirement in 1970, ponders a question put to him by University President William Friday on the "North Carolina People" program on the University television station in September 1972.

Winston Dormitory in 1973 was a part of the residence college's learning-by-living experiment. Rooms in Winston were occupied alternately by men and women, and separate bathrooms were unmistakably marked for each. Two other dormitories, Connor and Alexander, provided segregated male-female sections under their roofs—the women in one wing and men in the other. In all cases central gathering spots existed, and hall parties and potluck dinners developed easily. Soon afterwards, of 6,900 students in campus dormitories, 52 percent were living in some kind of coed arrangement.

Roy Armstrong, *left*, retired in June 1972 after fourteen years as executive director of the Morehead Foundation. A member of the class of 1926, he had previously been a member of the Extension Division staff, director of pre-college guidance, and director of admissions. Mebane Pritchett, *right*, a member of the class of 1957, succeeded Armstrong as executive director of the Morehead Foundation. Pritchett left in 1986 for Atlanta, where he became president of the Coca-Cola Scholars Foundation, Inc.

Barry B. Bridger, class of 1962, an Air Force ROTC student, was commissioned upon graduation and became a Phantom-jet pilot in Vietnam. Downed by a surface-to-air missile on 23 January 1967, he was presumed dead for almost two years. In 1969, through a newspaper photograph, it was discovered that he was a prisoner of war. After six years as a prisoner he returned home in 1973 to a hero's welcome in his hometown of Bladenboro.

The scene and the season change from semester to semester, year to year, but the inevitable lines always appear. Registration, picking up class tickets, drop-add, and paying bills result in long lines. Moods and tempers vary but the memory of the lines is indelible.

Complaints of crowding and unsatisfactory dormitory conditions lured some University administrators to spend the night in Winston Dormitory on a hot night in early September 1973. Shown here are, at the left in North Carolina Diving shirt, Director of Undergraduate Admissions Richard Cashwell; in the center, Chancellor Taylor, in white shirt; Housing Director James Condie, in plaid shirt and wearing glasses; and Dean of Student Affairs Donald Bolton, in striped shirt.

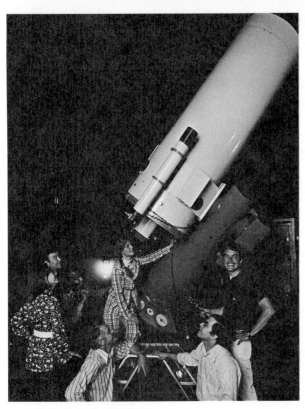

Professor Wayne A. Christiansen, *right*, with students gathered around the twenty-four-inch telescope installed in the Morehead Observatory in 1973. In this Cassegrain reflector light from a celestial field is reflected by a parabolic mirror to a secondary mirror near the "top" of the telescope from which it is reflected once more towards the principal mirror. A hole in the mirror permits the light to be brought to a focus at the "bottom" of the telescope where the image may be examined with an eyepiece or photographed. Its magnifying power is three hundred to twelve hundred times that of the unaided eye, and its light-gathering power is ten thousand times that of the unaided eye.

The ground-floor reception room of the Morehead Foundation in 1973 following the completion of a three-million-dollar addition to the Morehead Planetarium Building. A five-hundred-seat banquet hall was opened on the first floor and overnight guest rooms, a lounge, living room, and board room occupy the second floor. Foundation offices and meeting rooms are also on the ground floor.

A strange new American college fad, in the tradition of tree sitting and goldfish swallowing, apparently had its origin in Chapel Hill in March 1974 before spreading abroad in the land. Attributing their actions to"a bad case of springfever," a group of students in Mangum Dormitory on or about the fifth of March organized the American Streaker Society. Over two hundred males removed their clothes and raced across the lower and upper quadrangles and through the undergraduate library. Twenty women from Joyner Dormitory were said to have "pranced naked" under the windows of Mangum. A short time afterwards three males strolled leisurely down Franklin Street wearing only shoes and socks. On the evening of the seventh, accompanied by the UNC Pep Band, more than nine hundred students in the buff moved single file through a roaring crowd estimated to number six thousand. Campus security guards sealed off the streets and watched along with the others, and afterwards the participants posed for a mass photograph near South Building. There were sporadic outbursts of streaking for a short time afterwards, but it was a short-lived fad.

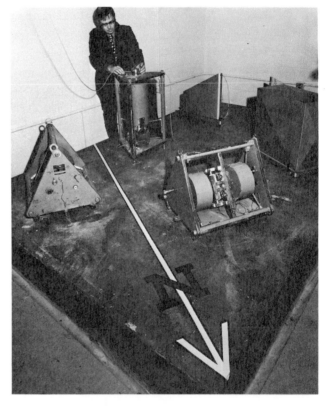

The Gerald R. MacCarthy Geophysics Laboratory was dedicated on 8 November 1973. Dr. David Stewart, laboratory director, here adjusts one of six seismometers in the facility, mounted on a twelve-ton concrete slab and capable of measuring any earthquake in the world with a magnitude of 6.0 or more on the Richter scale.

Beginning in 1974 University buildings were altered for the benefit of the handi- capped. Ramps for easy entrance were installed into more than seventy-five buildings. Revolving doors were removed, many doors widened, doorknobs and elevator buttons lowered, shag rugs re- moved, and sidewalk curbs cut for wheelchairs to move easily. The ramp into Gerrard Hall, shown here, blends well with the design of the older building.

Charles H. Long, an authority on African religions and black folklore in the American South, became a William Rand Kenan, Jr., Professor of Religion at the University and a professor of religion at Duke University in 1974. This was the first joint professorship involving the two universities. At the time of his appointment he was president of the American Academy of Religion and professor of the history of religion at the University of Chicago. Resigning from UNC at the end of 1987, he joined the faculty of Syracuse University.

With the male-female ratio in the student body at approximately 50 percent, women in the seventies began filling more positions of leadership. In 1974 three significant campus publications had women editors. Scottee Cantrell, class of 1974, *left*, was editor of *She*; Susan Miller, class of 1974, *center*, was editor of the *Daily Tar Heel*; and Emma Pullen, class of 1975, *right*, was editor of *Black Ink*.

Tony Waldrop, a Morehead Scholar who was graduated in 1974 with a degree in political science, ran the world record-breaking mile at the San Diego Indoor Games at 3:55 on 17 February 1974. He became the second University alumnus to hold the record, Jim Beatty having first held it in 1962 with 3:58:9, history's first sub-four-minute mile indoors. Between January and April 1974, Waldrop ran nine consecutive sub-four-minute miles, seven of them indoors. He won the Wannamaker Mile at 3:59:7 in the Millrose Games at Madison Square Garden and also received the Patterson Medal at commencement in 1974. He was Atlantic Coast Conference Athlete of the Year at the same time and held the NCAA indoor championship and ACC titles, indoor and outdoor. His 3:53:2 victory at the Pennsylvania Relays was the fastest mile ever run in the eastern United States. In 1977 he was inducted into the North Carolina Sports Hall of Fame.

With justice for all and malice toward none, student parking-lot monitors take their work seriously.

Necessity certainly was the mother of invention in the provision of campus bus service when the University and the town of Chapel Hill joined forces in the summer of 1974. For the previous several academic years buses from Raleigh had been leased to cover campus routes. They were driven to Chapel Hill each morning and returned to Raleigh in the late afternoon, also offering inexpensive transportation between the two cities for commuting students. The campus U-loop bus, as it came to be called, began running frequently between Franklin Street and the Health Affairs area of South Campus. In 1977 the bus service was extended to Carrboro where several thousand University students and large numbers of employees live.

Bernard H. Boyd (1910–75), James A. Gray Professor of Biblical Literature, joined the faculty in 1950. He was an ordained Presbyterian minister and during World War II was a chaplain in the Marine Corps where he received the Purple Heart. Beginning in 1963 he conducted archaeological expeditions to the Holy Land for University students and others, and his "Introduction to New Testament Literature" was a popular course on the University television station. For his excellence in teaching he received both a Tanner Award and Nicholas Salgo Award.

E. Maynard Adams joined the faculty in 1948 as a member of the department of philosophy and afterwards became a Kenan professor and served as departmental chairman during 1960–65. He served as president of both the North Carolina Philosophical Society, 1952–54, and the Southern Society for Philosophy and Psychology, 1968–69. For a time he was secretary of the faculty and in 1975 became chairman of the faculty. In 1971 he was recipient of the Thomas Jefferson Award.

A mock battle staged on McCorkle Place beneath Davie Popular by the North Carolina Continental Brigade and the Royal North Carolina Highlanders, on 16 April 1975, served as a preview for events to come during the observance of the bicentennial of the American Revolution.

Chancellors all. *Left to right*, J. Carlyle Sitterson (1966–72), William B. Aycock (1957–64), Robert B. House (1945–57), and Ferebee Taylor, who assumed office in 1972, the year this picture was made following a luncheon at the Carolina Inn.

A helicopter landing pad directly in front of North Carolina Memorial Hospital was put into use for emergency service in the fall of 1975, resulting in a twenty-minute savings in transportation time over the earlier-used route through midtown Chapel Hill from the Horace Williams Airport. It also is used in conjunction with the Military Assistance to Safety and Traffic helicopter from Fort Bragg in transporting seriously injured victims to the hospital. On landing, patients are transported quickly to the emergency room in a specifically modified transport vehicle that suggests a cross between a golf cart and a minibus.

Of the nearly seven thousand students living in University residence halls, up to 75 percent cook at least one meal a day, either in their rooms or in common kitchens that are now a standard part of all residence halls. Refrigerators were first permitted in rooms in 1970, and soon about 90 percent of all rooms were so equipped. Toasters, broiler ovens, crock pots, electric frying pans, coffee percolators, blenders, fondue sets, and other equipment are widely used, and charcoal grills appear on porches, balconies, and lawns. This 1975 glimpse of the corner of a dormitory room suggests with what style and grace meals can be prepared and served.

Ernest David Duke, national information director for the Knights of the Ku Klux Klan, was invited by the Carolina Forum to speak in Memorial Hall on 16 January 1975. He was shouted down and prevented from speaking by a mob organized by the Black Student Movement when more than two hundred black students lined the periphery of the hall. They were joined by a group that called itself the Coalition to End Racism and other predominantly white protestors who filed into the aisles minutes before Duke came on stage. As the invited guest of the University attempted to speak, he was met with chants of "Power to the people" and "Go to hell Duke." This denial of the exercise of free speech on the campus was condemned by many.

The Southern Historical Collection housed in Wilson Library is a resource widely used in the study and writing of southern and American history, biography, and genealogy. The arrival late in 1975 of the papers of Senator Sam J. Ervin, class of 1917, contributed temporarily to a growing problem of space. Shown here, standing, is Carolyn A. Wallace, Ph.D. 1954, who became director of the collection in 1975, fourth in the series that included the founder, J. G. DeR. Hamilton; James W. Patton; and J. Isaac Copeland. Following Wallace's retirement in 1987, David Moltke-Hansen became curator of the collection.

Men, women, and children took up jogging, and as the 1970s increased so did the number of joggers. The soft, regular rhythm of the joggers' feet could be heard after sunset and before sunrise, in rain and sunshine, and even the snow of winter did not stop them.

Franklin Street reaction when the University of North Carolina defeated the University of Kentucky 77–72 at College Park, Maryland, in the NCAA Eastern Regionals on 19 March 1977. Carolina went on to play Nevada— Las Vegas at the Omni in Atlanta on 26 March.

The increasing number of women students in Chapel Hill resulted in crowded conditions in the women's section of Woollen Gymnasium, as this group of uncomplaining students attempting to reach lockers in February 1976 demonstrates. They ceased to accept their fate good naturedly by the end of 1977, however, and by petition, plea, and demonstrations succeeded in obtaining more space when the faculty section was converted to locker rooms for women.

Taking office in 1976, Grace Rutledge Hamrick (Mrs. Charles Rush Hamrick, Jr.), A.B. in journalism, 1941, became the first woman president of the General Alumni Association. She has served as an at-large elected director of the association, 1971–73, vice president, 1973–74, advance gifts co-chairman for Alumni Annual Giving, and as a member of the Cleveland County Morehead Awards Committee. She is shown here with Clarence Whitefield, general secretary of the Alumni Association.

Joseph Ezekial Pogue (1887–1971), class of 1906, native of Raleigh, and one of the nation's leading geologists and mineralogists, specialized in petroleum research. His bequest of eleven million dollars to the University was received in 1976 and was the largest gift in the history of the institution. This unrestricted gift was added to the University's endowment funds, and income from it is known as the Pogue Fund. It is designated for the acquisition of library books, faculty research and study, fellowships, scholarships, and for the University development program.

International and American students and Chapel Hill families gather at a reception at the home of University President and Mrs. William Friday. Bob Hollister of Chapel Hill, one of the organizers of the foreign-student orientation program, and Daniel Chen of Taiwan receive refreshments from Mrs. Sandy Marks of Chapel Hill. The Chapel Hill Host Family Program, sponsor of this reception, involves approximately sixty local families and a hundred international students at the University.

WUNC, a 50,000-watt noncommercial radio
service, began broadcasting at 91.5 FM in April
1976. With a broadcast schedule of nineteen hours
each day, the station can reach a potential 1,200,000
listeners in its primary coverage area. Licensed to
the University of North Carolina at Chapel Hill,
WUNC functions as a public service extension of
the University and provides educational and cultural programs. It is supported by the University,
by the Corporation for Public Broadcasting, and
by contributions from private and corporate citizens. The station has a full-time staff of nine and
approximately forty-five volunteers. Barbara
Bernhard, radio news and public affairs producer,
is shown in the on-air studio.

The Totten Memorial Center, the first permanent building in the North Carolina Botanical Garden, was dedicated on 11 April 1976, the tenth anniversary of the
opening of the garden's trails to the public. Built by the
North Carolina Botanical Garden Foundation, the building honors Dr. Henry Roland Totten, for fifty years
professor of botany at the University, and his wife, Addie
Williams Totten, both of whom died just three weeks
apart in 1974. The building contains offices, a library of
Mrs. Totten's horticultural books and records, space for
displays, a shop, storage space, and classrooms. Dr. Totten,
a member of the class of 1913, helped develop the arboretum on campus, and Mrs. Totten, class of 1933,
organized the Chapel Hill Garden Club. Portraits of both
hang in the new center.

Dogs and students on campus
create an early spring display of
mutual affection in March 1977.
Chapel Hill town officials employed a dog catcher in the
early seventies, but students
managed to secure an exemption from his raid on campus
dogs.

A day-long Louis Round Wilson Centennial Festival was held in the winter to mark the birth of the oldest living University alumnus on 27 December 1976. Two public symposia sponsored by the University Library and the School of Library Science drew librarians from around the nation. In the evening, at a dinner attended by Dean Wilson (class of 1899), he was accorded many honors and announcement was made of the establishment of an endowed scholarship to bear his name. He was recognized for his work in forming the School of Library Science, the University Extension Division, the University of North Carolina Press, the *Alumni Review*, and the North Carolina Library Association. Shown here toasting Dr. Wilson are Chancellor Taylor, *center*, and President Friday.

Students in an American Military Traditions Survey course taught by Professor James R. Leutze of the Department of History have taken a field trip to visit battle sites each semester since 1972. At one time or another sites have been visited in nine states. This group, in the spring of 1977, is studying the Stone House at Manassas in Virginia.

Person Hall, 180 years old in 1977 and the second oldest state university building in the nation, has been restored. The historic chapel in the east wing of the H-shaped building accommodates about a hundred on movable seats in an intimate recital hall that also serves as a classroom for the Department of Music. Shown here are a tracker-action Schlicker organ and a Steinway grand piano in the east wing. The center section contains offices for the piano faculty, and the west wing contains a choral rehearsal room.

Student owned and operated FM radio station WXYC began broadcasting in March 1977 as the successor to WCAR, the student operated AM station that transmitted its broadcasts through electrical wiring into the dormitories on campus. The new station, located on the lower level of the Frank Porter Graham Student Union, was funded by a student referendum passed in 1973. It provides training experience for students in the broadcast media and related fields. Shown here is Barbara Gordon.

Jimmie W. Phillips, a junior from Lexington, taking the oath of office as president of the student body on 22 March 1977 before Darrell Hancock, a law student from Salisbury, attorney general in student government.

Racing bicyclists on a hot July day in 1977 pass through Carrboro toward Chapel Hill.

The prolonged severe drought of the summer of 1977 made everyone water conscious and stringent conservation measures were implemented. To save valuable trees and shrubs on campus, creek water was hauled in, but to avoid the University's being suspected of using the precious water from University Lake, each load was labeled. This scene on Raleigh Road also shows the former site of the Tin Can being graded for construction of Fetzer Gymnasium.

Students in one of Professor Rudolph J. Kremer's classes in the music department build a harpsichord.

The Burnett-Womack Clinical Sciences Building, a $6.5-million addition to the School of Medicine, provided space in 1977 for the pathology department as well as for the state's chief medical examiner and his laboratories. The building now houses various medical school offices, including the cardiology and hematology divisions and the surgery department. A portion of the covered overpass across Manning Drive between the parking deck and North Carolina Memorial Hospital appears in the lower right corner.

Ever the same yet ever changing, the academic procession forms for University Day in 1977.

During the summer of 1977 Carolina's most historic "temporary" building met its fate. Constructed of corrogated iron siding in 1923 by the Athletic Association at a cost of $54,000, the Tin Can was the home of the Southern Conference Indoor Track Meet. In addition to track, it also provided space for basketball, volley ball, and other indoor sports. Nearly all of the nation's big-name bands played for dances here in the decades of the twenties, thirties, and forties. The Tin Can was also the site of initiations, meetings of all sorts, concerts, picnics, and class demonstrations. After World War II it housed some two hundred students at a time in double-deck bunk beds.

The John M. Reeves All Faiths Chapel at North Carolina Memorial Hospital opened in 1977 to serve the needs of patients, families of patients, students, and the staff and faculty of the hospital. Reeves, class of 1910, gave $125,000 for the chapel, and it was matched by a like amount from the North Carolina Department of the American Legion. The chapel serves as a place of worship, meditation and devotion, conferences, and consultation and is also a teaching area for clergymen learning about hospital chaplaincy.

(page 328)
Katherine Kennedy Carmichael (1912–82) was dean of
women at the University from 1946 until 1972, and during
many of those years she also taught a course in English
literature. From 1972 until her retirement in 1977 she was
dean for supportive services in the Office of Student Affairs,
and during the final two years she was director of research
and planning. At one time she was a Fulbright lecturer in
American literature at the Philippine Normal College in
Manila and, later, a Smith-Mundt Professor at the University
of Saigon. Upon retiring from Chapel Hill she accepted an
appointment to teach English to Turkish students at the
Istanbul Language and Cultural Association.

Samuel R. Williamson joined the faculty in 1972 as the first
director of the Curriculum in Peace, War, and Defense. He
has served as special consultant to the director of the Office
of Emergency Preparedness in the Executive Office of the
President, on the presidential panel that investigated student
unrest, and as a consultant for the office of the secretary of
defense. In 1977 he became dean of the College of Arts and
Sciences and dean of the General College, and in 1984 he
was appointed University provost. In October 1988 he was
installed as vice chancellor and president of the University
of the South, Sewanee, Tennessee.

W. Reece Berryhill (1900–1979), class of 1921, retired in
1973 as Sarah Graham Kenan Professor of Medicine after
having served in various positions since joining the faculty
of the medical school in 1933. He was chief physician at
the infirmary, assistant dean, acting dean, and from 1941
until 1964 dean of the medical school. In 1966 he became
the first director of the Division of Education and Research in Community Medical Care. He received a
Distinguished Service Award in 1955, the O. Max
Gardner Award in 1964, and from the College of
Physicians in 1977 the first Richard and Minda Rosenthal
Foundation Award for his role in laying the groundwork
of the Area Health Education Center program.

Eager to take advantage of the days before serious work
begins, students leave Peabody Hall as the fall 1977
semester gets underway.

David Rushing, a sophomore from
Monroe, rushing the season a bit as he
concentrates on the ball in a game
near Connor Dormitory on 9 November 1977.

The new stacks addition to the
south side of Wilson Library
was opened late in 1977 and
formally dedicated early in the
new year. Designed to accommodate just over 1,000,000
volumes, the addition also
contains 477 individual carrels
and 100 studies for faculty and
graduate students, as well as
study tables, typing rooms, and
comfortable lounges for study
and relaxation.

Despite an enrollment of 13,920 undergraduate students, a number of small classes are taught, and as in years past, when the weather permits, they still gather outdoors. The new ramp for the handicapped leading into Saunders Hall can be seen in the background.

With the approach of examination time in the fall semester of 1977, as always, a frantic search for knowledge began in the undergraduate library. Consultation with a classmate is always reassuring.

The last of the World War II temporary buildings that dotted the campus for so many years was demolished while students were on Christmas vacation, 1977. This building was last used as the scene shop for the Department of Dramatic Art. A corner of Caldwell Hall is visible at the left and Hamilton Hall appears in the background.

The Paul Green Theatre, begun in March 1976 and completed in 1978, stands in the wooded area between Cobb Dormitory and the Old Chapel Hill Cemetery. Its basic design is that of two triangles joined by a hallway and work area. The one-story building is windowless except for a glass area in the lobby. The theatre section will seat five hundred and contains a thrust stage, a three-sided arena with no proscenium or curtain. It also contains dressing rooms, a lobby, and primary storage areas. The second triangle contains the scene shop and other service areas.

The Sigma Phi Epsilon—Phi Mu float in the "Beat Dook" parade, 18 November 1977, pulled by Paul Goldman, Luther Propst, and Gary Joyner.

Just as group pictures from the past suggest early trends in changing styles, so this campus view in the spring of 1978 indicates a return to neater appearance in dress by many students.

Phil Ford, class of 1978, from Rocky Mount, All-American and winner of the John Wooden Award as the best college basketball player in the nation. At the end of his senior year Ford's number 12 was retired. He thus joined Lennie Rosenbluth, class of 1957, as the only two basketball players to be so honored. Five football players' numbers have been retired: George Barclay, Andy Bershak, Cotton Sutherland, Art Weiner, and Charles Justice.

Lap wrap they called it, as these students sat in a large unsupported spiral in Carmichael Auditorium late in January 1978 while waiting for basketball tickets. Each sat in another's lap as these 3,087 Tar Heels tried, but failed, to pass the Air Force Academy record of 3,333 lap sitters. The Chapel Hill feat was certified for the Guinness Book of Records, but it failed to top the existing mark.

Joseph C. Sloane came to Chapel Hill in 1958 to become chairman
of the art department and to serve as director of the Ackland Art
Museum. In 1961 he was elected president of the State Art Society;
in 1963 he was made an Alumni Distinguished Professor; in 1973 he
became chairman of the State Art Commission; and in 1977 the State
of North Carolina recognized his contributions to art in the state by
bestowing upon him a North Carolina Award. Before his retirement
in 1978 he was honored at a public banquet in Chapel Hill attended
by hundreds of people who bore testimony of appreciation for his
contributions to the University and to North Carolina.

With University enrollment approaching twenty thousand and accommodations on campus and in Granville
Towers for some eight thousand, many students must
find housing elsewhere. Approximately four hundred
married students were living in Odom Village during
1977–78, just over eight hundred commuted from Durham, over two thousand lived in Carrboro, and thirteen
hundred came in from other nearby towns. The need for
nearly eight thousand students to find a place to live
spurred the construction of numerous apartments in and
around Chapel Hill. Northampton Plaza, shown here, is
located on North Columbia Street within easy walking
distance of Franklin Street and the campus. Bearing such
names as Camelot, Chateau, Colony, Foxcroft, Kings
Arms, Pinegate, Stratford Hills, and Willow Terrace,
they have brought a new dimension to student life in
Chapel Hill.

From a low point in 1959 when membership
dropped to a mere handful, the Dialectic and Philanthropic Literary Societies have risen to become
a combined organization of considerable activity,
now holding joint meetings as the Di-Phi Society.
In addition to traditional debates and public speaking, the society also sponsors faculty and visiting
speakers and programs appealing to a wide audience. Funds have been raised to restore the large
collection of portraits and to restore both the
Dialectic Society Hall in New West and the Philanthropic Society Hall in New East. Large handsome chandeliers, such as those seen here in New
West, have been installed in both halls. Bronze
busts of distinguished alumni members of the
twentieth century have been commissioned, and a
portrait of Thomas Wolfe, especially painted for
the society, has been acquired.

Walter Spearman (1908–87), class of 1929, served as editor of the *Daily Tar Heel* and was named best college editor in the state; he also was elected to Phi Beta Kappa and acted in Playmaker productions. After five years on the staff of the *Charlotte News*, he began teaching journalism in Chapel Hill in 1935 and remained in that position until his retirement in 1978. In 1967 Professor Spearman received a Tanner Award for excellence in teaching, and in the year of his retirement he received the Thomas Jefferson Award. For many years he produced a weekly book review column that was published in many newspapers in the state.

One of many enduring symbols of campus traditions is Rameses IX.

Bright and comfortable lounges in the stacks newly opened in Wilson Library please this student in the early spring of 1978.

Although the cafeteria upstairs was long ago converted to studios for the art department, the Pine Room in the basement of Lenoir Hall continued to be a gathering place at mealtime as well as for snacks between.

Carolina's cheerleading squad won the national championship in competition in California in April 1978. They were judged on cheers, chants, dances, and spectacle. This practice session in front of Wilson Library suggests something of their skill and strength.

A University employee at the Computer Center in Phillips Hall processes student projects at the end of the spring semester, 1978. The center, with IBM System 370/155 and 360/75 computers, has terminals in Cobb, Connor, Craige, Hinton James, and Morrison residence halls. In 1966 one of the world's largest university computer centers was established by the three Research Triangle universities in the Board of Science and Technology Building in the Research Triangle Park, and since then each campus has been linked by high-speed transmission lines.

The Carolina Quiz Bowl team of 1978 defeated North Carolina State University and the University of North Carolina at Greensboro in preliminary rounds and in the final match defeated Duke to win the state championship. In the national finals at Miami Beach in May the Carolina team reached the final round of sixteen but was then defeated by Oberlin College. *Left to right*, Melania Topp, John Skipper, Sue Lyons, and Margaret Parham.

In November 1979 members of the Communist Workers Party planned an anti-Klan rally at a public housing project in Greensboro only to be met by Ku Klux Klan members and a group of neo-Nazis. Gunfire erupted and five members of the Communist Workers Party were killed. When Klan members were cleared of murder charges, reaction in Chapel Hill was swift: over a thousand students gathered around the steps of South Building, where they were addressed by students, faculty, and administration. Feelings of frustration and anger were vented, tempers cooled, and it was the consensus that further exploration of the case should be undertaken by the courts.

The Indoor Track Facility was approved for construction in 1975 with funds from the Chancellor's Discretionary Fund and completed in 1978. Before long those whose memories stretched back to 1977, when the Tin Can was demolished, were referring to this building as the New Tin Can.

As the decade of the 1980s approached, the subject most often discussed by friends of the University was the continuing standoff between the federal Department of Health, Education and Welfare and the general administration of the University. The threatened "deferral" of up to $20 million in federal aid because of alleged racial discrimination brought a team of inspectors to campus on 22 February 1979. Chancellor Ferebee Taylor guided the director of the Office of Civil Rights on a tour. Some have interpreted this photograph as an indication that the HEW representatives were more interested in the weather than in what the chancellor was telling them.

X
TO THE
BICENTENNIAL

A growing population of retired people in the United States led to the establishment of a network of Elderhostel programs at home and abroad. UNC has been active in this form of adult education and attracts many groups to the campus for brief non-credit courses taught by the regular faculty and conducted between regular sessions. The participants usually live in dormitories and often go from one university to another, taking courses as they travel around the country. This class posed for a farewell photograph on 16 June 1980.

Barbecue has long been a favored fare with Tar Heels, and many True Blue Carolina grads have the real thing packed in dry ice and shipped by air to distant parts of the country. The choice at home, however, is a pig pickin' such as this one at the end of March 1980.

Dr. J. Alan Feduccia, professor of biology at UNC and research associate at the Smithsonian Institution, a specialist on the origin of birds, wrote a popular yet scholarly account of avian evolution and early flight. *The Age of Birds*, published in 1980, was cited as "science writing at its best."

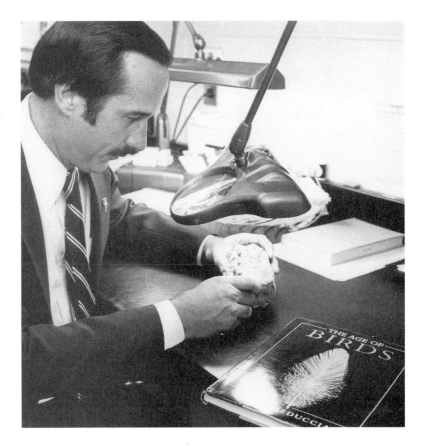

This unfortunate commentary by a graduating senior in 1980 was repeated on other occasions during the decade.

The C. Knox Massey Distinguished Service Awards were presented on 13 April 1981 for the second time since their creation. Established by Massey, class of 1925, to recognize "unusual, meritorious or superior contributions made by an employee, past or present, to the University," they were presented by Chancellor Christopher Fordham, center, to *(left to right)* Anna Brooke Allan for her service to the Southern Historical Collection as manuscript curator, especially in organizing and describing millions of manuscripts; to Elizabeth M. Parker for her service as a secretary and particularly as the leader of a project to assemble a comprehensive General Alumni Directory; to Vivian Cole for her efficient handling of invoices and requisitions for the entire campus, including Memorial Hospital, when she was supervisor of accounts payable in the accounting department; and to Lewis Atwater, Sr., for his 35-year career at the Institute of Government, where he dealt with a wide range of support services, including mail-handling, duplicating and binding facilities, and the supervision of a housekeeping staff.

Doris Betts, Alumni Distinguished Professor of English, joined the faculty in 1966 and quickly became one of the most popular teachers as well as a member of many administrative and advisory committees. In 1980 she was the commencement speaker. She has served as chair of the faculty and received a Tanner Award for superior teaching. In 1988–89 she was chair of the UNC Committee on Athletics and the University. A popular and award-winning author of novels and short stories, she is a member of the American Academy of Arts and Letters and has received the North Carolina Award for Literature. She and her husband, an attorney in Sanford, raise fine horses on their farm in Chatham County.

Georgia Bonesteel, shown here in a photograph made in September 1981, first discussed a quilting show for television on 28 July 1978 with Bill Hannah, producer-director for WUNC-TV, and the first show was filmed in Chapel Hill a month later. Now produced by the UNC Center for Public Television and shown on the University television network, this popular show is credited in large measure with having inspired the growing interest in this art and craft and spurred the rising number of quilt shows held around the country. Colorful quilts have come to be considered creative works of art and are displayed not only in museums and in historic houses but also in prominent places in private offices and public buildings.

James H. Shumaker, noted professor of journalism, would have earned his undergraduate degree at the University in 1947 if he had been willing to take the required freshman hygiene course. Having been recently engaged in World War II combat in Europe, he declined to be subjected to such foolishness and was denied his diploma until some kind of accommodation was reached in 1971. After working on newspapers in Durham, Wilmington, and Chapel Hill, he joined the journalism faculty in 1973. He continued to contribute to state newspapers, and his penetrating editorials and regular columns attracted a broad and faithful band of readers. His insight into human nature, his skill with words, and his good humor endeared him to generations of students, one of whom, Jeff MacNelly, class of 1969, made him the subject of cartoons and the nationally syndicated comic strip "Shoe."

Dorothy M. Talbot of the Curriculum in Public Health Nursing joined the faculty in 1974 and became chair of the department prior to her retirement ten years later. She founded the Association of Graduate Faculty in Community Health/Public Health Nursing, became president of the North Carolina Society for the Prevention of Blindness, and also held positions of leadership on the American Board of Certification of Occupational Nurses and the North Carolina Lung Association. A productive scholar, she contributed to a number of professional journals.

Smith Building, commonly known as Playmakers Theatre, was carefully restored in 1981–82 in keeping with its status as a National Historic Landmark. Thorough research revealed its original colors. The bases and the unique capitals of its columns were repaired and restored, the basement waterproofed, plumbing modernized, and a new roof added.

One of the most highly appreciated programs to originate in the WUNC-TV studios has been "North Carolina People," hosted by William C. Friday, president of the University. Shown here, *left*, on 7 November 1983, is guest Matthew Hodgson, class of 1949 and director of the University of North Carolina Press. In a discussion of the variety of books published by university presses they were considering *Powerhouse for God: Speech, Chant, and Song in an Appalachian Baptist Church*, by Jeff Titon.

Martha Nell Hardy, professor of speech communication, joined the faculty in 1965 and served a term as chair of the department. She previously had been a professional actress and theater manager/producer. In Chapel Hill she has worked with outdoor dramas, conducted workshops, and written and acted for educational television. She is shown here in her one-woman production of "Tamsen Donner," the story of a nineteenth-century Massachusetts woman who taught school in North Carolina, married a native of Rowan County, and moved west with him. Donner Peak in Nevada and Donner Pass between Nevada and California were named for her.

Rugby football players in the Team Sports program, photographed 24 February 1982. A rugby team has been fielded at the University for a number of years, composed to a considerable degree of Morehead Scholars whose early training was in Great Britain.

"WAIT—DON'T TELL ME!... DEAN SMITH'S TAR HEELS WON THE N.C.A.A. CHAMPIONSHIP!"
—Charlotte Observer

Former state archivist H. G. Jones became curator of the North Carolina Collection in Wilson Library in 1974 and soon afterwards was also made an adjunct professor of history, under which title he taught courses in North Carolina history. His wide acquaintance with North Carolinians and with the state's history and his most recent experience as director of the state Department of Archives and History were invaluable as he planned and supervised the growth of the Collection into new quarters in the remodeled Wilson Library. The recipient of numerous awards for research, writing, and administration, he founded the North Caroliniana Society as a support agency for the Collection. In 1990 he received the first University of North Carolina General Alumni Association Faculty Service Award for preserving, writing, and teaching North Carolina history. In the same year he also received the National Historical Publications and Records Commission's Award for Distinguished Service in Documentary Preservation and Publication.

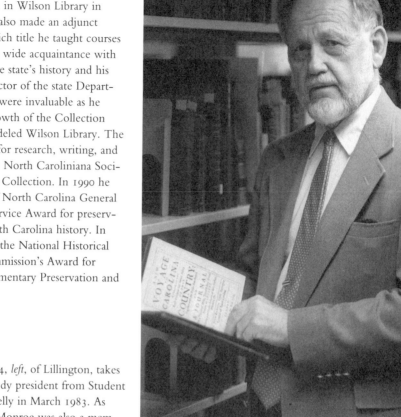

Kevin A. Monroe, class of 1984, *left*, of Lillington, takes the oath of office as student body president from Student Supreme Court Justice J. B. Kelly in March 1983. As president of the student body Monroe was also a member of the Board of Trustees of the University.

Louise McG. Hall, class of 1940, joined the reference staff of the University library in 1947 and became head of the department in 1957. Her understanding of the importance and use of microform publications and her knowledge of the new technology made her a leader in the discussion that led to computerized lists of library holdings. She planned and directed the preparation of a list of theses and dissertations accepted at the University between 1946 and 1959. She retired in 1983.

The process of moving fifty miles of books from Wilson Library to the newly completed Davis Library began in January 1984, when this first library book truck was pushed across a makeshift bridge into a moving van. Helping with the trial run are (*left to right*) Don Glines of the library circulation department and moving crew members Jesse Alston, Luther Brooks, and Nevell Johnson. Although the library was closed for only three days, 3–5 February, seven weeks were set aside to complete the undertaking.

J. Harold Lineberger, class of 1926
(*seated left*), and Joseph W. Lineberger,
class of 1933 (*seated right*), with the gift
agreement for $2 million to establish a
fund at the University to "extend excellence in research, teaching and public
service." Standing are University President William C. Friday and Chancellor
Christopher C. Fordham. Made in
1984, this gift provides both a
Lineberger Library Fund to improve
library user service and an income to
create and support professorships in
cancer research and the humanities.

A generous but extremely modest University benefactor was
Fred W. Morrison, class of 1913, teacher and attorney. For ten
years after his graduation from the University he was superintendent of the Chapel Hill school system, then he taught for a
few years at the North Carolina College for Women in Greensboro. Governor O. Max Gardner relied upon Morrison for a
variety of services on behalf of the state; later they became law
partners. In time Fred Morrison endowed scholarships at both
UNC-Greensboro and UNC-Chapel Hill. The law firm of
which he was a member provided legal service at no cost in
working out the complicated terms by which the University
secured the Ackland art bequest. He was a generous donor
toward the establishment of Educational Television at the University of North Carolina, and he endowed the Southern Studies Fund which came to bear his name and which enabled the
UNC Press to expand its program of publishing books on the
South. Some of his benefactions were revealed only after his
death in 1985.

Daniel W. Patterson, Kenan Professor of English and chairman of
the curriculum in folklore, joined the faculty in 1957. He is a specialist in religious folk songs and southern folklore and has been
largely responsible for a statewide revival of interest in both of these
areas. Frequent Sunday afternoon gatherings for the singing of
shape-note hymns have brought many visitors to campus. He is the
author of articles and books in this field, and his book *The Shaker
Spiritual* won an award from the American Society of Composers,
Authors, and Publishers.

A trio of University alumni writers gathered for a literary panel discussion in the spring of 1984 at the Catawba County Library in Newton under the guidance of retired journalism professor Walter Spearman, himself an alumnus, journalist, and writer. *Left to right*: Loyd H. Little, Jr., class of 1962, of Hickory and Durham, business editor of the *Durham Morning Herald*, author of *Parthian Shot*, winner of the 1975 Hemingway Award for Best First Novel, and teacher of creative writing in the University 1979–82; Gail Godwin, class of 1959, author of many short stories and novels, who grew up in Asheville and whose fifth novel, *A Mother and Two Daughters*, had recently been published; Walter Spearman; and Bland Simpson, class of 1970, of Chapel Hill, musician, teacher of creative writing, and author of *Heart of the Country*, published in 1983. Simpson's *The Great Dismal: A Carolinian's Swamp Memoir* was published in 1990 by the UNC Press.

This photograph of Holly Murray, class of 1987, *left*, and Joan Nesbit, class of 1984, *right*, of the women's track team, appeared in the Fall 1984 *Carolina Alumni Review* illustrating an article by Professor Mary Turner Lane, "The University in Transition: The Female Presence." In 1983, she reported, female students comprised 58.2 percent of all undergraduates.

Increased enrollment in the 1980s resulted in a shortage of dormitory space and a rise in apartment dwelling. This growth in the number of students living off-campus contributed to the transportation problem and resulted in the development of a bus system and the further use of bicycles. Living farther from campus, students could not rush "home" between classes to pick up books, tennis rackets, and snacks, so they began to carry backpacks.

1984 champion women's soccer team. It won its fourth consecutive overall and third consecutive NCAA championship with a 24–0–1 record.

The Walter Royal Davis Library, largest educational building in North Carolina, is the main building in the University library system. It has a book capacity of 1.8 million volumes and a seating capacity of over three thousand people. On a three-acre site, it contains about ten acres of floor space in eight floors above ground and one below. Ten large colorful banners of historic printers' marks hang opposite a gallery that runs the length of the main floor. The library is linked to databases with records representing millions of publications held by thousands of American libraries. In August 1985 a computer catalog linking library collections at Chapel Hill, Duke University, and North Carolina State University was opened for public use. The Triangle Research Library Network, making the libraries of these institutions appear as one with more than eight million volumes, was the first of its kind in the nation.

Brick mason Nick Pennix helped to complete the final phase of the landscaping around the new library as he built a planter along the east side of Lenoir Hall. Cherry trees and low shrubs were planted here and, facing them, in planters on the west side of the library.

After teaching several generations of Chapel Hill youth in the local high school, in 1984 Joyce Day Clayton became a lecturer in the School of Education. From there she became an assistant dean in the General College, where her practical experience has made her an effective adviser as well as a counselor and friend to those fortunate enough to come to her attention.

In 1985 Robyn S. Hadley of Burlington became the University's eighth Rhodes Scholar in ten years and was also named one of *Glamour* magazine's top ten college women for the year. She is shown here with Chancellor Christopher Fordham.

The Story of Student Government at the University of North Carolina at Chapel Hill, by Albert and Gladys Hall Coates, was published in 1985. To mark that significant contribution to a very important aspect of University history, a number of former presidents of student government, joined by a few others, met to honor Mr. and Mrs. Coates. Pictured here are (*left to right*) James Evans Davis (1939–40), Gladys Hall Coates, Albert Coates, Robert Mayne Albright (1930–31), Virgil Stowe Weathers (1933–34); *second row*: Robert Worthington Spearman (1964–65), William Howard Moss (1977–78), Bryan Christopher Hassel (1986–87); *third row*: Craig Burdeen Brown, David James Morrison (1940–41), Scott Frederick Norbert (1981–82), Robert Walter Saunders (1982–83); *fourth row*: Charles Fogle Vance, Jr. (1945–46), John Brendan Kelly (1983–84), Paul Gray Parker (1984–85), Donald Atlas Furtade (1958–59); *fifth row*: John Lassiter Sanders (1949–50), Christopher Columbus Fordham III, Charles Dowd Gray III (1959–60), Henry Bowers (1951–52); *back*: Douglass Hunt.

April Heinrichs, class of 1986, national player of the year in both 1985 and 1986.

The Hanes Art Center was dedicated on 30 March 1985 and was named for Frank Borden and Barbara Lasater Hanes, whose family has supported the arts and sciences at the University for more than fifty years. An award-winning building, the Center contains many classrooms and studios as well as a gallery, an auditorium, a library, and offices.

The Student Activities Center, named in January 1986 for basketball coach Dean E. Smith, seats 21,426 spectators. Smith became head basketball coach in 1961, and his teams have won NCAA championships, the National Invitational Tournament, and an Olympic gold medal. This convenient indoor arena became the scene of concerts and entertainments of various kinds as well as public meetings, including visits from candidates for national office and noted scholars. It also has been decorated in imaginative fashion for receptions and dinners.

C. D. Spangler, Jr., was inaugurated as president of the Consolidated University of North Carolina on 17 October 1986 in Polk Place on the University campus. A native of Charlotte, he was graduated from the University in 1954 and later received the M.B.A. degree from Harvard. A successful businessman, he previously had served on the Mecklenburg County Board of Education and became chairman of the state Board of Education in 1982. Shown here in the conference room in the General Administration building accepting his nomination by the University's Board of Governors, he stands before a portrait of his predecessor, William C. Friday. His wife, Meredith Spangler, sits behind him.

Half a century apart, these two photographs suggest the extent of the University's growth. The smaller group is the faculty of the Department of History and Government in 1932–33. *Front row* (left to right): William S. Jenkins, William W. Pierson, Mitchell B. Garrett, R. D. W. Connor, Wallace E. Caldwell, and J. G. deR. Hamilton; *back row*: Fletcher M. Green, Keener C. Frazer, C. C. Crittenden, Edward J. Woodhouse, Loren C. McKinney, Charles B. Robson, and Henry McG. Wagstaff.

The larger group comprises as many members of the history faculty as could be persuaded to appear on the steps of Manning Hall on the afternoon of 26 March 1986. *Front row*: C. O. Cathey, Monica Green, Carl H. Pegg, J. Isaac Copeland, Samuel H. Baron, Judith M. Bennett, Colin A. Palmer, Donald M. Reid, James R. Caldwell, and Leon R. Fink. *Second row*: William E. Leuchtenburg, Jacquelyn D. Hall, Henry C. Boren, Lawrence D. Kessler, William S. Powell, George B. Tindall, Richard A. Soloway, Robert M. Miller, and John M. Headley. *Third row*: W. James McCoy, William L. Barney, W. Miles Fletcher, Michael H. Hunt, E. Willis Brooks, Josef Anderle, Elisha P. Douglass, Joseph S. Tulchin, and Harry L. Watson. *Fourth row*: Herbert L. Bodman, Jr., David M. Griffiths, Michael R. McVaugh, John K. Nelson, Richard W. Pfaff, Gillian T. Cell, James R. Leutze, Stephen B. Baxter, and Roger W. Lotchin. *Back row*: Frank W. Ryan, Jr., James L. Godfrey, J. Carlyle Sitterson, John Montiere, Samuel R. Williamson, Jr., Peter G. Filene, R. Don Higginbotham, Donald G. Mathews, and John F. Kasson.

In 1986 there were 121 Native Americans among the University's 22,781 students. During the academic year 1974–75, when there were fewer than ten, the Carolina Indian Circle was organized to help them support and encourage each other and to ease the adjustment of others who might follow. As president of the Circle, Alicia Hardin, class of 1987, worked to lessen the feeling of isolation and to provide opportunities for Native Americans to become more active in campus affairs. She was aware of the need for such concern because her father, J. Benford Hardin, M.D., class of 1977, was a charter member of the Circle.

Homecoming Weekend in 1986 was highlighted by an exhibition game between the Chicago Bulls and the Los Angeles Lakers at the Smith Center on Saturday night. With Michael Jordan (shooting), class of 1986, on one team and James Worthy, class of 1986, on the other, it is needless to say that "a good time was had by all."

Neal Cheek, who was director of student services in the School of Nursing between 1979 and 1990, began riding a bicycle to campus when he was in graduate school in 1972 and had still not been concerned by the parking crunch when this photograph was made in 1986.

Students in 1985–86 became concerned over such questions as the handling of the proposed Black Cultural Center, a mandatory meal plan, the administration of the Campus Y, and the use of vending machine revenues from the Student Union. On 23 January 1986 around five hundred students, some of whom cut classes to attend, assembled on the Polk Place side of South Building, where they were addressed by Todd Hart, student government executive assistant. In response, Chancellor Christopher Fordham named a panel of students and faculty to examine the operations of the Division of Student Affairs.

Eleftherios Karkadoulias helps Silent Sam settle once more into his McCorkle Place home. The statue, a fixture since it was unveiled by the United Daughters of the Confederacy in 1913, was taken down in 1987 to be cleaned, restored, and given a protective coating against corrosive automobile exhaust and acid rain.

George Watts Hill, class of 1922, *foreground*, at the groundbreaking ceremony on 13 May 1987 for the George Watts Hill Alumni Center. Also shown are Douglas S. Dibbert, class of 1970, *left*, executive director of the General Alumni Association, and Chancellor Paul Hardin.

Students in the School of Public Health in 1987 using IBM personal computers in the learning lab.

Craig Turner joined the faculty in 1986 as assistant professor of dramatic art. As the movement coach for the PlayMakers Repertory Company, he teaches professional and student actors how to fight safely and dramatically on stage. Here he demonstrates swordplay with third-year graduate student Brian Hotaling. Turner's teaching specialties are movement analysis, movement training, stage combat, mime, and juggling.

Five of the original seven Mercury astronauts were present at Morehead Planetarium when Tony Jenzano (*third from left*) unveiled a plaque commemorating the facility's use as an astronaut training center from 1959 to 1975. Jenzano was the planetarium director when (*left to right*) Wally Schirra, Scott Carpenter, Alan Shepard, Gordon Cooper, and Deke Slayton came to Chapel Hill for celestial navigation training.

The astronauts returned in 1989 to help the planetarium celebrate its 40th anniversary. Shepard, the first American in space, remarked that "the training we had here was very, very helpful to us." The foresight of people like Jenzano and the programs like the one at Morehead Planetarium were critical, he said.

The Kenan Center, which opened in 1987, provides comfortable quarters for the Kenan Institute of Private Enterprise. The Institute is one of several projects through which the University works to develop a closer and more productive relationship with the business community.

Peter S. Bearman, assistant professor of sociology, joined the faculty in 1986. A graduate of Brown University with a doctorate from Harvard, he is representative of generations of scholars from around the nation and from abroad who have found the intellectual climate of Chapel Hill conducive to work in their chosen field as well as in allied areas. While Bearman's specialty is sociology, he also has a deep interest in southern history. He has gathered a number of graduate and undergraduate students to comb the files of North Carolina Confederate soldiers and of post–Civil War census records. The purpose of their project is to understand the role of localism in the life of young men in the waning years of the nineteenth century.

Many Carolina faculty members are renowned both at home and around the country. One leader of this description is John Shelton Reed, Jr., professor of sociology and director of the Institute for Research in Social Science, who came to Chapel Hill in 1969. His books and articles cannot easily be categorized, as he has followers in sociology, history, politics, religion, and good writing. His southern point of view, expressed reasonably and well, makes him a regional favorite. A native of Tennessee and a graduate of the Massachusetts Institute of Technology and of Columbia University, he has been a Fulbright Scholar, a Guggenheim Fellow, a Fellow of the National Humanities Center, and a member of the National Council for the Humanities. He has lectured in England, India, Israel, and throughout the United States. *The Enduring South* and *Southern Folk Plain and Fancy* are two of his many books that have gained national attention.

George A. Kennedy, Paddison Professor of Classics, joined the faculty in 1966 and quickly began to demonstrate his ability as a valuable asset to the University and as an outstanding teacher. He was named Paddison Professor in 1973 and has won a Tanner Distinguished Teaching Award and the Thomas Jefferson Award for research, teaching, and service. He served a three-year term, from 1985 until 1988, as chairman of the faculty council; he has also served as chairman of the Board of Governors of the UNC Press. The American Philological Association presented him with an Award of Merit, and President Carter appointed him to the National Humanities Council.

Lars Schoultz, a professor of political science who received his doctorate at Carolina in 1973 and joined the faculty three years later, became director of the University's Institute of Latin American Studies in 1985. With the aid of a $500,000 Mellon Foundation grant he created a cooperative program with Duke University combining a faculty of thirty-six political scientists, historians, anthropologists, economists, sociologists, geologists, and linguists to implement a new approach to teaching graduates and undergraduates in both institutions.

William F. Little, University Distinguished Professor of Chemistry, joined the faculty in 1956. In addition to outstanding service to the University in various capacities, he was president of the Triangle Universities Center for Advanced Studies, secretary of the University Institutional Development Foundation, and a member of the Board of Governors of the Research Triangle Institute, the Governor's Science Advisory Committee, and the North Carolina Board of Science and Technology.

Chancellor Christopher Fordham and Consolidated University President C. D. Spangler, Jr., prepare to introduce the seven Democratic candidates at Education '88, the first forum of presidential candidates devoted entirely to education. They fielded questions from Edward B. Fike, education editor of the *New York Times*, and Judy Woodruff of public television's "MacNeil/Lehrer NewsHour."

Rob Koll, class of 1989, pins one of his many opponents on his way to capturing the NCAA wrestling championship in the 158-pound class. Koll was the top wrestler in UNC history, with a career record of 151–20–1.

On 8 April 1988 the Board of Governors of the University announced their appointment of Paul Hardin III to succeed the retiring chancellor, Christopher C. Fordham III. Hardin officially took office on 1 July and was formally installed on University Day 1989. A native of Charlotte, he was graduated from Duke University in 1952 and received a law degree in 1954. He practiced in Birmingham, Ala., before joining the Duke law faculty in 1958. He was president of Wofford College from 1968 to 1972; of Southern Methodist University from 1972 to 1974; and of Drew University from 1975 to 1988.

Edward C. Holley joined the faculty as dean of the School of Information and Library Science and served in this position until 1985. He was elected president of the American Library Association for the 1974–75 term. The Association honored him in 1983 with its Melvil Dewey Award for "professional achievement of a high order" and in 1987 with its Joseph W. Lippincott Award for distinguished service to the profession. In 1988 the Association of College and Research Libraries named him the Academic-Research Librarian of the Year, and in 1989 the University named him a William Rand Kenan, Jr., Professor.

New students arriving in the fall of 1989 faced the same problem that had plagued their predecessors since the beginning of the age of the automobile—unloading and getting everything into the dormitory. Now, however, the problem was even greater. Because of crowded conditions and the loss of parking space to new construction, parking was limited to thirty minutes per car. Bicycles, refrigerators, television sets and record players, golf clubs and tennis rackets, and occasionally some books had to be stacked hurriedly by the curb before the car was sent off to a satellite parking lot on the edge of town.

A natural resource long overlooked on campus was the tremendous quantity of leaves that fell every fall. For many years they were hauled away and dumped across the creek beyond Finley Golf Course. In 1989–90, however, the University began composting them for use around the plants and trees on campus.

Ida and William Clyde Friday stand before the Friday Center for Continuing Education, located east of Chapel Hill on Laurel Hill Parkway. Opened on 1 March 1991 and formally dedicated on 12 April, the Center has accommodations for classes and conferences and contains special equipment for scientific demonstrations of many kinds. The University's Division of Continuing Education is housed here and includes the Independent Study Program, the Continuing Studies Program (formerly the Evening College), Off-Campus Credit Programs, the Correctional Education Program, the Office of Conferences and Institutes, and the Elderhostel Program.

Students, faculty, and staff enter the Student Union in September 1990 to protest budget cuts by the General Assembly. Deteriorating economic conditions were blamed for the serious reduction in funds, which cut severely into the University's budget. Library acquisitions were reduced, funds for graduate assistants were cut, and sections were eliminated for many classes.

A University Distinguished Professor of English, Louis Rubin came to Chapel Hill in 1967 and soon proved to be a man of very broad interests. A newspaper reporter and editor in his earlier life, he often chatted, lectured, and wrote about baseball and fishing—on both of which he was an expert—but his scholarly specialty was American, particularly southern, literature. He wrote or edited thirty-five books, mainly in the fields of southern literature and history but also including two novels and a variety of short stories. He founded the *Southern Literary Journal* and encouraged and guided the career of many young writers of distinction who added to the reputation of the South as an important source of American literature. In 1982 he was instrumental in establishing a publishing firm, Algonquin Books of Chapel Hill, that quickly acquired a national reputation for the excellence of its books, many of which have received national acclaim. In 1989 he received the O. Max Gardner Award.

"The Student Body," seven bronze figures by sculptor Julia Balk, was a gift to the University from the class of 1985. When the figures were erected in front of Davis Library on 23 October 1990, they created a furor. Over five hundred students signed a petition to have the work removed, saying that it "perpetuated racial and sexual stereotypes already ingrained in society." Objection was voiced particularly to the figures of a black man balancing a basketball on his finger, a black woman balancing a book on her head, and a white couple with the woman holding an apple and apparently leaning on the man for support. There also were a few references to an Oriental woman carrying a violin. After due consideration by members of the administration, the sculpture was moved to a small enclosed park north of Manning Hall and west of Hamilton Hall.

The William B. Aycock Family Medicine Building was dedicated on 13 September 1990. It provides state-of-the-art facilities for teaching, research, and patient-care facilities along with offices for the Department of Family Medicine. Aycock, who served as chancellor from 1957 to 1964, retired in 1985 from a Kenan professorship in the School of Law.

Richard J. Richardson joined the faculty in 1969 and in the course of events became Burton Craige Professor and chairman of the Department of Political Science. On occasion he has filled a temporary vacancy on the staff of the president of the Consolidated University, and in 1987 he received the Thomas Jefferson Award. At the request of a number of campus administrators he has headed study committees to review troublesome campus issues. In September 1991, when he was named chairman of the bicentennial observance, Chancellor Paul Hardin commented on his "sterling reputation with faculty, staff, students, and alumni."

In 1990 a unique choice faced Dr. Joseph C. Edozien, professor and chairman of the nutrition department in the School of Public Health. With an M.D. and other degrees from the University of Edinburgh and the National University of Ireland, he had been at the University of North Carolina since 1971. A native of Nigeria, Dr. Edozien was the grandson of King Obi Edozien of Asaba, Nigeria, and the nephew of recently deceased King Obi Onyetenu. The 65-year-old Professor Edozien was chosen to succeed to the position, and, recognizing the opportunity to serve his people, he accepted.

The approaching bicentennial of the University's establishment prompted Virginia Redfern Heath of Monroe to give the University this Masonic apron in 1990. Made of white lambskin with gold fringe and tie, it reportedly was worn by William McCauley at the laying of the corner-stone of Old East on 12 October 1793. The Masonic symbols are printed in gold and blue.

Old East—an address of distinction in Chapel Hill
during three centuries.

XI
THE UNIVERSITY
IN MAPS, 1772 to 1992

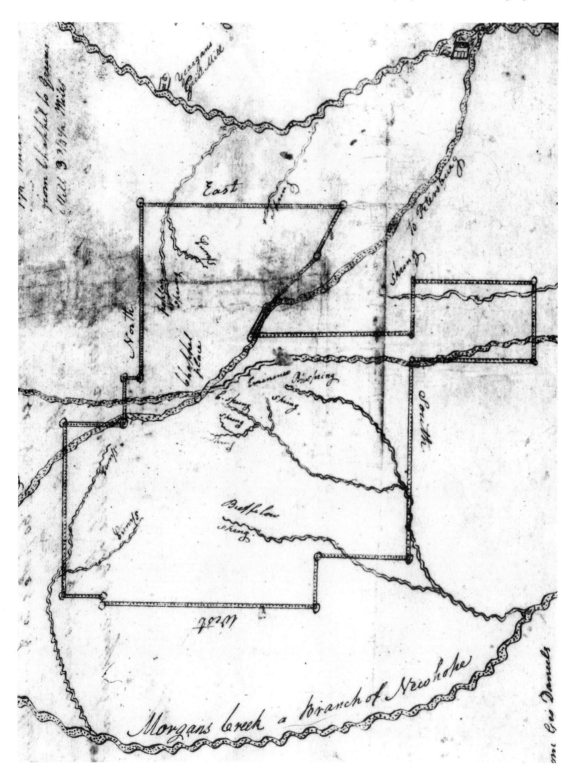

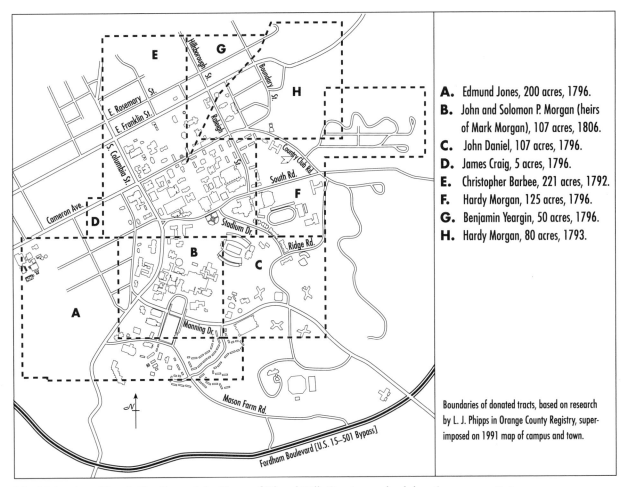

A. Edmund Jones, 200 acres, 1796.
B. John and Solomon P. Morgan (heirs of Mark Morgan), 107 acres, 1806.
C. John Daniel, 107 acres, 1796.
D. James Craig, 5 acres, 1796.
E. Christopher Barbee, 221 acres, 1792.
F. Hardy Morgan, 125 acres, 1796.
G. Benjamin Yeargin, 50 acres, 1796.
H. Hardy Morgan, 80 acres, 1793.

Boundaries of donated tracts, based on research by L. J. Phipps in Orange County Registry, superimposed on 1991 map of campus and town.

The University of North Carolina and the Town of Chapel Hill. Contiguous land donations, 1792–1806.

(preceding page)
The University, ca. 1792. Contiguous land holdings with roads and streams. Detail. *Manuscript map in University Archives, Wilson Library.*

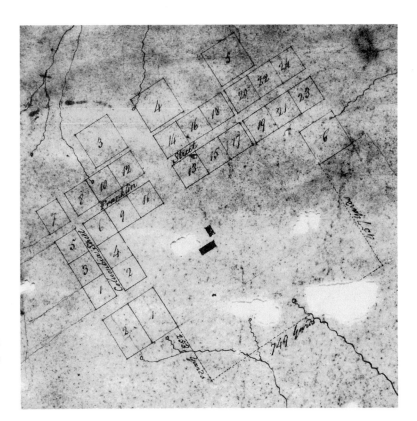

The University and the Town of Chapel Hill, July 1793, showing Old East, South Building, and town plan, with streams. *Manuscript map in University Archives, Wilson Library.*

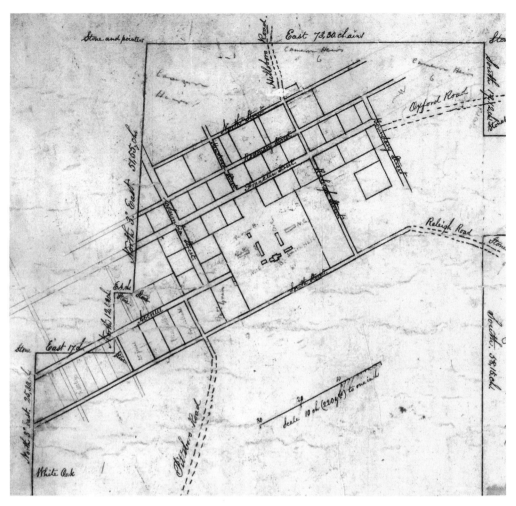

The University and the Town of Chapel Hill, 1852, showing in ink buildings standing in 1852, with pencilled-in additions to 1860. (South Road is shown but was not built until 1920s.) *Manuscript map in North Carolina Collection, Wilson Library.*

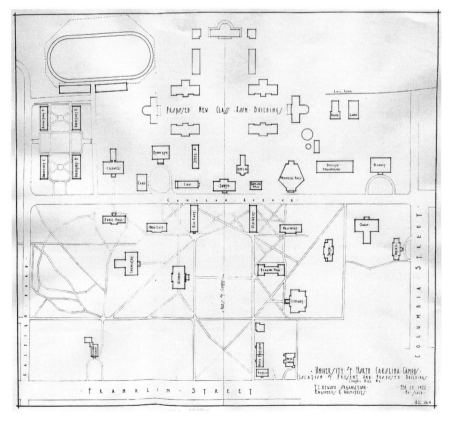

The University, 1922. Existing buildings are named, projected buildings are unnamed. (Note that north is toward bottom of map.) *Map by T. C. Atwood Organization, published in* The Alumni Review, *vol. X, no. 7 (April 1922), 198–99.*

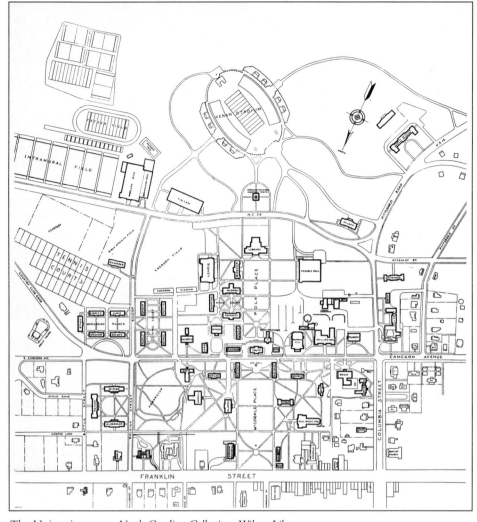

The University, 1940. *North Carolina Collection, Wilson Library.*

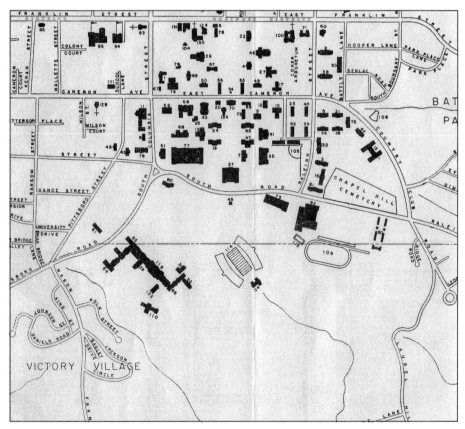

The University, 1954.
Detail. *Map in North
Carolina Collection,
Wilson Library.*

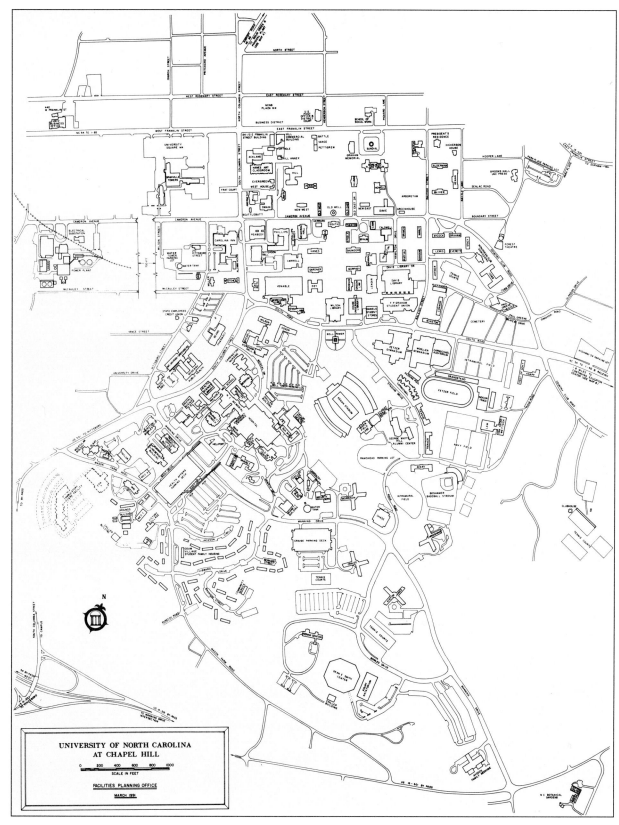

The University, 1991–92.

Credits

ACKLAND ART CENTER, *top p. 265, center p. 297*

STEVE ADAMS, *bottom p. 298, upper left p. 299*

ALUMNI OFFICE, *p. 197, p. 198, bottom p. 311, all p. 312, center p. 316, top p. 319, top p. 320, top and center p. 322, bottom p. 323, top p. 334, top p. 336, bottom p. 338 (Billy Newman), bottom p. 341, bottom p. 342, bottom p. 343, bottom p. 344, bottom p. 347, top p. 350, bottom p. 351, bottom p. 353 (Beth Velliquette), top p. 354, bottom p. 355 (Hugh Morton), top p. 357, center p. 357 (Beth Velliquette), top p. 358 (Dan Charlson), top p. 359 (Will Owens), bottom p. 361, top left p. 362, top p. 363 (Allen Dean Steele), top p. 364*

H. G. BAITY, *top p. 193*

FRED BARBOUR, *center p. 329, bottom p. 332*

GEORGE BARCLAY, *Chapel Hill, lower left p. 192*

KEMP P. BATTLE, *History of the University of North Carolina, top p. 19*

MRS. LEE BAYLEY, *Springfield, Ohio, p. 166, top p. 167*

DR. REECE BERRYHILL, *Chapel Hill, bottom p. 111*

SAM BOONE, *p. 191, upper right p. 192, top p. 194, third from top p. 229, p. 240, bottom p. 247, center p. 256, top p. 258, pp. 262–63*

WILLIAM BRINKHOUS, *p. 293*

BOB BROOKS, *center p. 236*

WALLACE E. CALDWELL PAPERS, *Southern Historical Collection, center left and right p. 204*

CAROLINA INN, *top p. 110*

CATHARINE CARTER, *top p. 324*

HOPE S. CHAMBERLAIN DRAWING, *North Carolina Collection, top p. 17*

CHARLOTTE OBSERVER, *bottom p. 346*

JERRY COTTEN, *top and bottom p. 315, bottom p. 317, top p. 331, center and bottom p. 333, center p. 336*

DAILY TAR HEEL, *center p. 310, center p. 311, bottom p. 316, center p. 320, center p. 321, top p. 326, top and center p. 328, top p. 329, center p. 331, top p. 333*

DAVIDSON COLLEGE, *bottom p. 36*

DIALECTIC PAPERS, *University of North Carolina Archives, bottom left and right p. 24, center p. 45*

DIALECTIC SOCIETY, *p. 6, top p. 25, top p. 32, bottom p. 34, bottom p. 39, center p. 41, lower left p. 50, lower right p. 53, p. 56*

JOHN O. DUNN, *Wilmington, bottom p. 138, top p. 139, top p. 140*

DURHAM HERALD-SUN, *bottom p. 320*

MAURY FAGGART, *p. vi, p. 165, p. 271, upper left p. 282, bottom p. 285, bottom p. 286,* bottom p. 287, bottom p. 290, p. 291, bottom p. 294, top p. 295, top p. 296, top and bottom p. 297, top p. 298, upper and lower right p. 300, top p. 301, top p. 302, bottom p. 304, bottom p. 305, pp. 306–7

GARY FREEZE, *bottom p. 310, bottom p. 329, top p. 330, p. 335*

JOHN GELLMAN, *upper right p. 299*

GLEN LENNOX, *top p. 238*

E. K. GRAHAM SCRAPBOOK, *Southern Historical Collection, center p. 157, top p. 158*

FRANK P. GRAHAM PAPERS, *Southern Historical Collection, bottom p. 212, center p. 215, top p. 220*

MRS. LOUIS GRAVES, *Chapel Hill, top p. 16*

J. G. DE R. HAMILTON SCRAPBOOK, *Southern Historical Collection, center and bottom p. 154*

MARK HANDLER, *top p. 321*

MRS. WILLIAM T. HANNAH, *Waynesville, upper left and right p. 132*

ERNEST HAYWOOD COLLECTION, *Southern Historical Collection, bottom p. 104*

HELLENIAN (1898), *center p. 130*

ARCHIBALD HENDERSON PICTURES, *North Carolina Collection, lower left p. 7, bottom p. 14, top p. 18, bottom p. 41, center p. 47, upper and lower left p. 48, left p. 55, top p. 57, top and center p. 63, bottom p. 64, center p. 65, center and bottom p. 74, p. 89, p. 97, bottom left p. 122, top p. 159*

J. E. HERSHEY, *center p. 217*

MRS. ALICE STRINGFIELD HILL, *Morristown, Tennessee, upper left and right p. 133*

FRANK HOLYFIELD, *p. 30, bottom p. 38, bottom p. 126, top p. 127, bottom p. 257, bottom p. 267, top p. 287, top p. 290, bottom p. 296, center p. 307*

ROBERT B. HOUSE UNDERGRADUATE LIBRARY, *p. 207*

L. VICTOR HUGGINS, *Chapel Hill, bottom p. 176, bottom p. 343*

ALLEN JERNIGAN, *upper left p. 317, top p. 327*

PETER KACHERGIS, *p. 52*

THOMAS L. KESLER, *Rome, Georgia, bottom p. 179*

MARVIN KONER, *bottom p. 302*

TED KYLE, *center p. 330, bottom p. 331, top p. 332, bottom p. 334*

KAY KYSER, *Chapel Hill, center p. 180*

MRS. CHARLES L. LAMBETH, *Charlotte, top p. 36*

JOCK LAUTERER, *lower right p. 274, all except lower right p. 277, bottom p. 279, top p. 280, bottom p. 281, lower left p. 282, p. 283, top p. 288*

BRIGADIER GENERAL W. C. LEMLY, *Coronado, California, lower right p. 132*

JAMES LEUTZE, *center p. 324*

MCDANIEL LEWIS, *Greensboro, bottom p. 115, top and bottom p. 152, top p. 156*

WILLIE JONES LONG, *Garysburg, bottom p. 25*

JERRY MARKATOS, *p. 1, p. 6, p. 31, upper left p. 68, pp. 106–7, top p. 294, p. 369*

MRS. ROBERT C. MASTERTON, *Chapel Hill, top p. 37*

METROPOLITAN MUSEUM OF ART, *New York, bottom p. 69*

MOREHEAD FOUNDATION, *top p. 304*

MOREHEAD PLANETARIUM, *p. 46, top p. 115*

HUGH MORTON, *p. 211*

NATIONAL ARCHIVES, *Washington, top p. 186*

BILLY NEWMAN, *upper right p. 317*

NORTH CAROLINA COLLECTION, *p. 4, top p. 5, upper and lower right p. 7, bottom left and right p. 8, p. 9, top p. 10, upper and lower left p. 11, p. 12, lower left and right p. 13, top p. 14, upper left and right p. 15, bottom p. 17, p. 21, p. 23, top p. 24, bottom p. 26, bottom p. 29, center p. 32, top p. 33, top p. 34, p. 35, center and bottom p. 37, top and center p. 38, top and center p. 39, upper right p. 40, pp. 42–44, bottom p. 45, top and bottom p. 47, right p. 48, right p. 50, p. 51, p. 54, bottom p. 57, center and bottom p. 58, left and lower right p. 59, p. 60, lower left p. 61, upper and lower left p. 62, lower right p. 63, top p. 64, top and bottom p. 65, p. 66, lower right p. 67, lower left and right p. 68, top and center p. 69, pp. 70–71, p. 73, upper left and right p. 74, top p. 75, p. 76, top and center p. 77, pp. 78–79, center p. 81, pp. 82–85, upper and lower left p. 86, upper and center and lower left p. 87, bottom p. 88, pp. 90–93, pp. 95–96, pp. 98–99, center and bottom p. 100, pp. 101–3, top p. 104, center and bottom p. 108, top and bottom p. 109, bottom p. 110, top and center p. 111, pp. 112–14, pp. 116–23, top and bottom p. 124, p. 125, top p. 126, center and bottom p. 127, pp. 128–29, top and bottom p. 130, p. 131, lower left p. 132, bottom p. 133, pp. 134–37, top and center p. 138, center p. 139, all except top p. 140, all except lower right p. 141, pp. 142–49, center and bottom p. 150, p. 151, center p. 152, bottom p. 153, top p. 154, top p. 155, top p. 160, top p. 162, top and bottom p. 163, p. 164, bottom p. 167, p. 168, top and bottom p. 169, pp. 170–75, top and center p. 176, p. 177, center and bottom p. 178, top and center p. 179, bottom p. 180, pp. 181–82, pp. 184–85, p. 187, bottom p. 188, pp. 189–90, center and bottom p. 193, bottom p. 194, pp. 195–96, pp. 199–200, top p. 201, bottom p. 202, lower left p. 204, top p. 205, top*

Index

Russell, Phillips, 141, 259, 268
Ryan, Frank W., Jr., 356

Sadie Hawkins Day, 239
Salaries, 89, 92
Salisbury, 4, 11, 15, 94
Sanders, John L., 242, 353
San Diego Indoor Games, 316
Sanford, Terry, 273, 310
Saunders, J. Maryon, 311
Saunders, Robert W., 353
Saunders, Romulus M., 50
Saunders, William Lawrence, 87
Saunders Hall, 173, 249, 330
Sawyer, Bonner D., 309
Sawyer, Samuel, 5
Schinhan, Philip, 228
Schirra, Wally, 360
Schnorrenberg, John, 246
Scholarship program, 115, 309, 322, 324.
    See also Grants-in-aid
School of Applied Science, 164, 188
School of Business Administration, 190,
    249, 251
School of Commerce, 190
School of Dentistry, 305
School of Engineering, 187, 200
School of Journalism, 228
School of Library Science, 189, 198, 295, 324
School of Medicine, 100, 111, 126, 137,
    149, 203, 209, 250, 305, 326, 328. See also
    North Carolina Memorial Hospital
School of Nursing, 305
School of Pharmacy, 188, 305
School of Public Health, 305
School of Public Welfare, 210
Schoultz, Lars, 362
Schwenning, Gustave, 251
Scott, Charlie, 285
Scott, Robert, 293
Scroggs, Ross, 253, 265
Sea-Gift, 98
Seal, University, 8, 11, 94
Seawell, Henry, 35
Secession Convention, 57, 168. See also
    Ordinance of Secession
Security guards, 315
Seismometers, 315
Selby, Toby, 246
Selden, Sam, 253
Senate (state), 25, 36, 58
Senior Week, 212
Severin, Paul, 214
Shaker Spiritual (Patterson), 349
Shakspere Club, 103
Sharp, Paul F., 275
Sharpe, Lawrence A., 269
Sharpe, William, 5
Shaw, George Bernard, 208
Shaw, John Duncan, 79
She, 316
Shepard, Alan, 360
Shepard, George E., 259
Sherman, W. T., 89
Shoes, high-top, 110, 128, 138

Showers, 69
Shull, S. F., 130
Shumaker, James H., 343
Sickles, Daniel E., 90
Sigma Alpha Epsilon, 132, 188
Sigma Chi Derby Day, 258
Sigma Nu, 122, 197
Sigma Phi Epsilon, 331
Silent Sam. See Confederate monument
Silin, Charles I., 172
Simpson, Bland, 350
Sims, Richard, 20
Singing, 117, 212. See also Chorus; Glee
    Club
Site of the University, 8, 9, 10, 11
Sitgreaves, John, 10
Sitterson, J. Carlyle, 278, 293, 303, 308,
    319, 356
Skinner, Joshua J., 140
Skipper, John, 336
Slade, James J., 69
Slade, Thomas T., 61
Slavery, abolition advocated, 33
Slayton, Deke, 360
Sloan, Samuel, 104, 108
Sloane, Joseph C., 265, 333
Slover, George, 91
Smith, Benjamin, 5, 7, 69
Smith, Betty, 220
Smith, Bob, 246
Smith, Dean E., 285, 355
Smith, Ed, 246
Smith, Fred, 145
Smith, Richard, 138
Smith Building, 57, 63, 69, 74, 108, 124,
    127, 136, 139, 146, 177, 344. See also
    Playmakers Theatre
Smith Center, 355, 357
Smokehouse, 16
Snow, 127, 129, 159, 170, 196, 313
Soccer, 285, 298
Soccer team, women's, 351
Social Forces, 210
Societies, literary, 24, 38, 157; libraries, 114.
    See also Dialectic Society; Philanthropic
    Society
Society of Mayflower Descendants, 204. See
    also Mayflower Award
Society of the Alumni of the University,
    61. See also Alumni Association
Soloway, Richard A., 356
Sororities. See names of sororities
South Building, 16, 18, 19, 23, 25, 27, 33,
    35, 36, 38, 43, 44, 75, 76, 80, 85, 89, 91,
    95, 113, 126, 143, 152, 160, 181, 182,
    186, 195, 242, 253, 258, 278, 280, 295,
    315, 337, 339, 358; portico added, 178
South Campus, 282, 317
South Carolina, 43
Southern Accent, 250
Southern Conference Indoor Track Meet,
    327
Southern Folk Plain and Fancy (Reed), 361
Southern Historical Collection, 181, 206,
    311, 320

Southern Intercollegiate Athletic Associa-
    tion, 188
Southern Literary Journal founded, 366
Southern Regional Council, 210
Southern Regions of the United States, 210
Southern Studies Fund, 349
Southern University Conference, 234
South Quadrangle, 168
South Road, 227
Spaight, Richard Dobbs, 17, 18, 23, 36
Spangler, C. D., Jr., 355, 362
Spangler, Meredith, 355
Spanish-American War, 132, 133
Speaker Ban Law, 275, 278
Spearman, Robert W., 353
Spearman, Walter, 228, 334, 350
Spencer, Cornelia Phillips, 26, 94, 95, 175
Spencer, James Monroe, 95
Spencer Hall, 77, 175
Springen, Donald, 275
Springs, Adam, 28, 29
Springs, 10, 11, 19
Spruill, C. P., 251
Stacy, Inez Koonce, 169
Stacy, Marvin Hendrix, 169, 183, 184, 201
Stacy Dormitory, 201
Stair, Thomas Osborne, 284
State Bank of North Carolina, 51
State Board of Conservation and Develop-
    ment, 190
State Board of Education, 94
State Historical Commission, 209
Steele, John, 37
Steele, Walter Leak, 168
Steele Building (formerly Steele Dormi-
    tory), 280
Steele Dormitory, 168, 173, 249
Stephens, Mike, 304
Stevens, Harry P., 140
Steward's Hall, 15, 16, 19, 27
Stewart, David, 315
Stewart, Roach, 141
Stirnweiss, George, 259
Stockard, Sallie Walker, 140
Stone, David, 10
Stone House, Manassas, Va., 324
Stovall, Floyd, 253
Strayhorn, Isaac R., 91
Streaking, 315
Street, N. H., 99
Stringfield, Thomas, 133
Strong, Ray, 259
Student Activities Center, 355
Student Affairs, Office of, 328
Student body: earliest picture of, 81
"Student Body" (sculpture), 366
Student government, 194, 198, 278, 309,
    325
Students: list of (1819), 42; foreign, 133,
    160, 235, 322; handicapped, 315, 330
Student stores, 278, 296. See also Daniels
    Building
Student union, 193, 278, 280, 292, 295,
    296. See also Frank Porter Graham Stu-
    dent Union; Graham Memorial